Religion and Political Change in the Modern World

The purpose of this book is to ascertain whether there is a generic impact that 'religion' brings to bear on recent political changes in the modern world. Over the last two decades or so, there have been increasing numbers of political issues with which various manifestations of religion engage. This impact is not restricted exclusively to countries in the 'developed' or 'developing' world. Instead, we seem to be seeing a widespread impact of religion on politics which defies earlier assumptions about secularisation. This presumed that the more 'modern' a country is then the less likely it is that religion will play a significant political role. Recent evidence is, however, firmly to the contrary: the degree of 'modernity' in a country does not correspond well with the amount of 'religiosity' in a country, nor with the role that religion can play in politics.

The book focuses on the recent return of religion to politics. It assesses how religion is involved in recent examples of political change in various countries, including the impact of religion on democratization. The book features both theoretical chapters and case studies. The case studies examine different countries (Israel, Egypt, Morocco, and Iran) and regions (sub-Saharan Africa), with a focus on Islam, Judaism and Protestantism and Catholicism. The overall aim is to get a sense of what is happening when religion and politics interact.

The chapters in this book were originally published in *Democratization*.

Jeffrey Haynes is the co-editor of *Democratization*. He is the director of the Centre for the Study of Religion, Conflict and Cooperation and Professor of Politics at London Metropolitan University, UK.

Democratization Special Issues

Series editors:
Jeffrey Haynes, London Metropolitan University, UK
Aurel Croissant, University of Heidelberg, Germany

The journal, *Democratization,* emerged in 1994, during 'the third wave of democracy', a period which saw democratic transformation of dozens of regimes around the world. Over the last decade or so, the journal has published a number of special issues as books, each of which has focused upon cutting edge issues linked to democratization. Collectively, they underline the capacity of democratization to induce debate, uncertainty, and perhaps progress towards better forms of politics, focused on the achievement of the democratic aspirations of men and women everywhere.

Religion and Political Change in the Modern World
Edited by Jeffrey Haynes

Comparing Autocracies in the Early Twenty-first Century
Two-volume set:
1. Unpacking Autocracies – Explaining Similarity and Difference
2. The Performance and Persistence of Autocracies
Edited by Aurel Croissant, Steffen Kailitz, Patrick Koellner and Stefan Wurster

Twenty Years of Studying Democratization
Three-volume set:
1. Democratic Transition and Consolidation
2. Democratization, Democracy and Authoritarian Continuity
3. Building Blocks of Democracy
Edited by Aurel Croissant and Jeffrey Haynes

Political Opposition in Sub-Saharan Africa
Edited by Elliott Green, Johanna Söderström and Emil Uddhammar

Conflicting Objectives in Democracy Promotion
Do All Good Things Go Together?
Edited by Julia Leininger, Sonja Grimm and Tina Freyburg

PREVIOUSLY PUBLISHED BOOKS FROM DEMOCRATIZATION

Coloured Revolutions and Authoritarian Reactions
Edited by Evgeny Finkel and Yitzhak M. Brudny

Ethnic Party Bans in Africa
Edited by Matthijs Bogaards, Matthias Basedau and Christof Hartmann

Religion and Political Change in the Modern World

Edited by
Jeffrey Haynes

Routledge
Taylor & Francis Group

LONDON AND NEW YORK

First published 2014
by Routledge
2 Park Square, Milton Park, Abingdon, Oxon, OX14 4RN, UK

and by Routledge
711 Third Avenue, New York, NY 10017, USA

Routledge is an imprint of the Taylor & Francis Group, an informa business

© 2014 Taylor & Francis

British Library Cataloguing in Publication Data
A catalogue record for this book is available from the British Library

ISBN13: 978-0-415-74496-6

Typeset in Times New Roman
by Taylor & Francis Books

Publisher's Note
The publisher accepts responsibility for any inconsistencies that may have arisen during the conversion of this book from journal articles to book chapters, namely the possible inclusion of journal terminology.

Disclaimer
Every effort has been made to contact copyright holders for their permission to reprint material in this book. The publishers would be grateful to hear from any copyright holder who is not here acknowledged and will undertake to rectify any errors or omissions in future editions of this book.

Contents

CONTENTS

Citation Information

The following chapters were originally published in various issues of *Democratization*. When citing this material, please use the original page numbering for each article, as follows:

Chapter 2
Did Protestantism Create Democracy?
Steve Bruce
Democratization, volume 11, issue 4 (August 2004), pp. 3-20

Chapter 3
Unfinished business: the Catholic Church, communism, and democratization
Lan T. Chu
Democratization, volume 18, issue 3 (June 2011) pp. 631-654

Chapter 4
Does faith limit immorality? The politics of religion and corruption
Udi Sommer, Pazit Ben-Nun Bloom and Gizem Arikan
Democratization, volume 20, issue 2 (March 2013) pp. 287-309

Chapter 5
Political Islam in the Mediterranean: the view from democratization studies
Frédéric Volpi
Democratization, volume 16, issue 1 (February 2009) pp. 20-38

Chapter 6
Religion and Democratization in Africa
Jeff Haynes
Democratization, volume 11, issue 4 (August 2004), pp. 66-89

Chapter 7
Bullets over ballots: Islamist groups, the state and electoral violence in Egypt and Morocco
Hendrik Kraetzschmar and Francesco Cavatorta
Democratization, volume 17, issue 2 (April 2010), pp. 326-349

Chapter 8

Islamic reformation discourses: popular sovereignty and religious secularisation in Iran
Naser Ghobadzadeh and Lily Zubaidah Rahim
Democratization, volume 19, issue 2 (April 2012) pp. 334-351

Chapter 9

The religious experience as affecting ambivalence: the case of democratic performance evaluation in Israel
Pazit Ben-Nun-Bloom, Mina Zemach and Asher Arian
Democratization, volume 18, issue 1 (February 2011) pp. 25-51

Please direct any queries you may have about the citations to
clsuk.permissions@cengage.com

Introduction: Religion and Political Change in the Modern World

Jeffrey Haynes

The aim of this book is to examine the extent to which religion impacts upon political changes, including democratisation and democracy, in today's world. The starting point is to note that, over the last two decades or so, religion has engaged with a number of political issues in many countries, including successful and failed transitions to democracy. This impact is not restricted exclusively to countries in the 'developed' or in the 'developing' world. Instead, we can note a widespread impact of religion on politics which defies earlier assumptions about secularisation: that is, that as a country gets increasingly 'modern' it will necessarily lose its religion; that modernisation leads to a systematic withdrawal or ousting of 'religion' from the public realm, implying a sustained and overt diminution of political significance. Put another way, this presumes erroneously that the more 'modern' a country is then the less likely it is that religion will continue to play a significant political role. Recent evidence is, however, firmly to the contrary: the degree of 'modernity' in a country does not correspond well with the amount of 'religiosity' in a country, nor with the nature or extent of political roles that religion plays.

The 'return' of religion to politics is a recent phenomenon, which defies conventional social scientific wisdom. Until recently secularisation theory was hegemonic in exhibiting a key social scientific assumption: as societies modernise they secularise and when they secularise religion loses its public, including political, salience. Whereas in the historical past it would be difficult to deny the political importance of various religious entities, during the late nineteenth and twentieth centuries it became conventional wisdom, linked to then-dominant theories of modernisation and political development, that the future of the integrated nation-state lay in secular participatory politics. In order successfully to build nation-states, political leaders needed to remain as neutral as possible from entanglements of particularistic – especially religious and ethnic – claims. Politics had to be separated from such claims in order to avoid dogmatism and to encourage citizens' tolerance. As decades of apparently unstoppable movement towards increasingly secular societies in western and other 'modernised' parts of the world suggested, religion and piety became ever more private matters. Religion was relegated to the category of a (minor) problem that should not intrude into the search for national unity and political stability.

Religion's renewed political significance, involving both state and non-state actors, is notable among many cultures and religious faiths in countries at differing levels of economic development and political system. Domestically, the return of religion to the public realm implies a renewed political voice in various countries and regions, including, for example, Iran, Israel and Poland, as well as North and sub-Saharan Africa. Internationally, the 'return' of religion has major – and continuing – implications for international security and order, clearly illustrated by the notorious September 11, 2001, ('9/11') attacks on the USA, the American government's response (invasions of Afghanistan and Iraq), and the continued impact of expressions of transnational religious extremism recently manifested in, inter alia, Nigeria (Boko Haram attacks on Christian schools) and Kenya (al-Shabaab attack on Westfield Shopping Mall in Nairobi). Such challenges to international security and order often emanate from Islamic 'extremists', people often said to be 'excluded' from the benefits of globalisation for reasons of culture, history and geography.

More generally, post-Cold War globalisation is a key factor which encourages the political 'return' of religion. This is because globalisation facilitates increased links between many kinds of state and non-state actors, both religious and secular, not least because neither geographical distance nor international borders are insuperable barriers to communication. The consequence is that today we live in a 'globalised' social and political environment, where previously significant obstacles to communication have ceased to be of much relevance. In addition, globalisation theoretically increases the ability of cross-border networks, both secular and religious, to disseminate their messages and to link up with like-minded groups across international borders. Finally, over the past two decades or so, global migration patterns have also helped spawn more active religious transnational communities. The overall result is that cross-border links involving religious entities have multiplied, and, in many cases, so have their social and political concerns. In short, globalisation leads to more active religious transnational communities, creating a powerful force in international relations which, added to the myriad manifestations of religion's political significance in today's world, lead to the conclusion that many examples of contemporary and current political change feature religious actors of various kinds.

The book seeks to assess how and in what ways religion is involved in recent examples of political change in various countries and regions, including the impact of religion on democratisation. It is divided into two sections: (1) theoretical and conceptual issues, and (2) case studies. The theoretical and conceptual chapters examine the relationships involving Protestantism and the Catholic Church in relation to democratisation and democracy, the political impact (if any) of religion on 'immorality' and corruption in politics, and the association between democratisation and political Islam in the southern Mediterranean region. The case studies examine different countries (Israel,

Egypt, Morocco, and Iran) and regions (sub-Saharan Africa), with a focus on Islam, Judaism and Protestantism and Catholicism. The overall aim is to get a sense of what is happening when religion and politics interact.

In the first article in the theoretical and conceptual section, Bruce seeks to assess the contribution of Protestantism to the rise of liberal democracy and, more generally, illustrates the possibility of treating religion as a cause of such political phenomena. The account draws attention to some complexities of causation that are often overlooked in the arguments over the role of religion in politics. Chu then shifts focus to the Catholic Church and its recent role in democratisation, with a focus on Poland's liberation from Soviet rule in the late 1980s. In focusing upon the Polish Church's historic role in the collapse of communism, Chu contends that we have overestimated the Church's effects on political liberalisation. Drawing from the Polish case, Chu concludes that the church's moral, self-limiting, and transnational character needs to be recognised and incorporated into a general theory of democratisation.

Sommer, Ben-Nun-Bloom and Arikan are interested in the relationship between religiosity and ethical behaviour. In their chapter, they argue that religion is systematically related to levels of corruption, and that the nature of this relationship is contingent on the presence of democratic institutions. In democracies, they contend, where political institutions are designed to inhibit corrupt conduct, the morality provided by religion is related to attenuated corruption. Conversely, in systems lacking democratic institutions, moral behaviour is not tantamount to staying away from corrupt ways; thus in non-democratic contexts religion would not be associated with decreased corruption. In other words, the authors argue that the correlation of religion with reduced corruption is conditional on the extent to which political institutions are democratic. Volpi's chapter then examines political Islam in the southern Mediterranean, explaining that contemporary perceptions of, and responses to, the growth of political Islam on the southern shores of the Mediterranean are heavily influenced by traditional orientalist views of 'Islam' and by realist notions of regional security. This contributes to the formation of pre-dominantly state-centric responses to what is perceived as a monolithic Islamist threat. Consequently, issues of democratisation and democracy promotion are downplayed because of security concerns. When addressed, liberal-inspired views of democracy and civil society are nonetheless pro-blematically deployed in a social and political context that does not duplicate well the conditions met in previous 'waves' of successful democratisation. Volpi argues that democratisation prospects in the southern Mediterranean are linked to a situation where moderate Islamist movements are expected to endorse liberal-democratic values – albeit reluctantly and by default – while too little attention is paid to alternative forms of participation devised locally by Islamists.

The second section of the book encompasses four case studies. Haynes examines the relationship between religion and democratisation in sub-Saharan Africa (SSA). He is concerned with the relationship of senior religious figures to the state in SSA and the role of the former in the region's attempts at democratisation in the 1990s and early 2000s. The second is the regional political importance of 'popular' religions. The overall aim is to: (1) establish the nature of the links between senior religious figures and state elites in SSA, (2) make some preliminary observations about the political nature of popular religions in the region, and (3) comment on the overall impact of religious actors on the region's democratisation attempts in the 1990s and early 2000s.

Kraetzschmar and Cavatorta are concerned with the political relationship between Islam and democratisation in Egypt and Morocco. They are interested in state-sponsored electoral violence in these countries, which they label 'liberalized autocracies'. The first section of their contribution identifies a number of variables that can help explain the decision calculus of authoritarian incumbents to deploy force against strong electoral challengers. The second section then examines these propositions with reference to Egypt and Morocco. Drawing on recent parliamentary elections in both countries the article questions why, despite facing the challenge of political Islam, the two regimes differed so markedly in their willingness to manipulate the polls by recourse to violence. Whilst the Egyptian authorities decided to abrogate all pretence of peaceful elections in favour of violent repression against the Muslim Brotherhood candidates and sympathisers, no such tactics were deployed by the ruling elite in Morocco. Cavatorta and Kraetzschmar contend that three principal factors influenced the regimes' response to this electoral challenge: (1) the centrality of the elected institution to authoritarian survival, (2) the availability of alternative electioneering tools, and (3) the anticipated response of the international community. The article concludes by suggesting that in order to understand better when and how states deploy violence in elections, we need to focus on a more complex set of factors rather than simply on the electoral potency of key opposition challengers or the authoritarian nature of the state.

Ghobadzadeh and Rahim turn attention to an anomaly: an 'actually existing' – albeit flawed – Islamic democracy: Iran. There, disputes over the outcome of the June 2009 presidential election rapidly developed into a contest about the overall legitimacy of the Islamic state. Far from being a dispute between religious and non-religious forces, the main protagonists in the conflict represented divergent articulations of state–religion relations within an Islamic context. In contrast to the authoritarian legitimisation of an Islamic state, the Islamic reformation discourse is based on secular-democratic articulations of state–religion relations. The contribution of Ghobadzadeh and Rahim article focuses on the ideas of four leading Iranian religious scholars who advocate a secular-democratic conceptualisation of state authority. Disputing the religious validity of divine sovereignty, they promote the principle of popular sovereignty based on Islamic sources and methods. This reformist conceptualisation is rooted in the notion that Islam and the secular-democratic state are complementary.

The final chapter in the collection is by Ben-Nun-Bloom, Zemach and Arian, who examine the role of religion in democratisation and democracy in Israel. They contend that religiosity increases both criticism and instability in democratic performance evaluations, and accordingly decreases reliance on these assessments in the construction of political self-efficacy, trust in institutions, and patriotism. They argue that this is due to the conflicting experiences through which religious citizens of democracies live. That is, while their personal religious environment often exhibits many less-than-democratic characteristics, their experience as citizens in Israel reflects the polity's long-standing democratic attributes and credentials. Overall, the chapter augments the focus of the literature on religion and democratic attitudes by emphasising the strength of attitudes, and shift attention from policy attitudes to other evaluative judgements in Israel.

Did Protestantism Create Democracy?

STEVE BRUCE

This essay assesses the contribution of the reformed strand of Christianity to the rise of liberal democracy. Insofar as it is persuasive, it illustrates the possibility of treating religion as a cause of political phenomena. The account draws attention to some complexities of causation that are often overlooked in the arguments over the role of religion in politics.

Introduction

This essay has a number of purposes. It assesses the contribution of the reformed strand of Christianity to the rise of liberal democracy. Insofar as it is persuasive, it illustrates the possibility of treating religion as a cause of political phenomena. And as far as space constraints allow, it draws attention to some complexities of causation that are often overlooked in the rather ritualistic arguments over the role of religion in politics.

It is common for contemporary scholars to suppose religions so flexible, malleable and variegated as to be capable of producing and justifying any form of social organization, any social action and any set of social mores. Fred Halliday quotes favourably a scholar saying of Islam that it is so broad that

> it is possible to catch almost any fish one wants. It is, like all the great religions, a reservoir of values, symbols and ideas from which it is possible to derive a contemporary politics and social code: the answer as to why this or that interpretation was put upon Islam resides therefore, not in the religion and its texts itself, but in the contemporary needs of those articulating Islamic politics.[1]

Bruce Lawrence takes a similar line when he writes that religion's 'pervasiveness as a general condition was matched only by its malleability as a contextual variant open to limitless interpretation'.[2]

Steve Bruce is Professor of Sociology, School of Social Sciences, University of Aberdeen, Aberdeen AB24 3QY, UK.

Both writers make a valid point. The great religions do indeed contain such a variety of ideas that many different outcomes can be justified as the will of God or Allah. Lawrence is right that context matters a great deal. Even so, there are certain 'socio-logics'. There is an orderliness to the world. Although there are a wide variety of possible combinations of cultures, economies and polities, some are rare and certain combinations are not found because they are impossible. It is not an accident that there are no feudal democracies; the principles of feudal economy and of democratic polity are incompatible. To return to the fish and sea analogy, it may well be the case that similar fish can be found in many seas and many seas support a variety of fish. Nonetheless, there are systematic variations in the kind of fish found in warm and in cold waters, in salt and in fresh waters, in shallow and in deep waters.

A number of preliminary asides may clarify the approach adopted here. First, the writer is not an 'orientalist' deserving of Edward Said's censure for making invidious comparisons between Christianity and Islam.[3] As has been made clear at greater length elsewhere,[4] some of the features of religions that have notable political consequences cut across the civilizations which some hold to 'clash'.[5] Second, the crucial differences tend either to be abstract and or to form part of the deep, rather than surface, structure of each faith. For example, whether a religion mandates in detail a particular way of public life seems of much greater importance than many specific doctrines. Third, as Max Weber argued in his classic essay on the 'Protestant Ethic' (1904–1905), the major consequences of religious innovations are unintended and inadvertent.[6] The approach taken here, like Weber's, cannot be dismissed as unsociological idealism, because its causal connections are generally ironic. They result from socio-psychological and socio-structural imperatives causing ideas to be developed in ways quite other than those intended by the people who promoted the innovations. Fourth, nothing in the approach here requires that major religions be utterly unalike. To point to the many similarities in the major religions as an objection against citing differences as causes of subsequent major political differences is a red herring: there is no reason why small differences cannot cause big differences. Fifth, nothing in the approach requires that major religions be unchanging. Brevity requires us to use terms such as 'Protestantism' with few qualifying adjectives; this does not mean we are unaware of differences within reformed Christianity. To talk of a 'Protestant ethic', as Weber does, is not to suggest that all Protestants, throughout Christendom and over four centuries, were the same. It only requires that he has correctly identified the beliefs and values of certain Protestants and that he is basically correct in supposing those beliefs and values to differ from those of adherents to other religions in comparable circumstances. Far more could be said on these points but their significance should be clearer once the specific argument of this essay is elaborated.

Spokesmen for the Loyal Orange Institution and other Protestant organizations believe that their forefathers were responsible for a variety of social
virtues and social institutions that either constitute or promote liberal democracy: personal autonomy, freedom of choice, literacy, diligence, temperance,
loyalty, democratic accountability, egalitarianism and the overlapping ties of
voluntary association we now call 'civil society'. Hence Popery is not just the
wrong religion; it is a social evil. As a former Presbyterian clergyman and
Ulster Unionist MP explained,

> The seeds of democracy were sown in the Reformation. The liberties of
> Europe began with the growth of new nations. William of Orange stood
> with his family motto, 'Je maintendrai' appended to the slogan 'The
> Protestant Religion and Liberties of England'.[7]

There is enough in the historical record to make such a claim worth
considering.

British political history was shaped by conflicts between despotic Catholic
monarchs and a Protestant parliament. Protestant nations were generally in the
vanguard of the rise of parliamentary democracy. And there is much in the
twentieth-century history of Europe to suggest some non-accidental connection between religion and democracy. There are four major Christian traditions in Europe. There are the two communal religions of Orthodoxy and
Catholicism, the individualist religion of thoroughly Reformed Protestantism
and, somewhere between them, Lutheranism, which promoted most of the
theological principles of the Reformation but constrained them within the
ecclesiastical frame of the pre-Reformation church and moderated political
radicalism by encouraging a quiescent attitude to the state. With varying
degrees of willingness, most of the countries of twentieth-century Europe
have enjoyed a dictatorship of either the right or the left. Looking at the
fascist regimes first, almost all were Catholic: Italy, Spain, Portugal, Slovakia,
Croatia, Austria and Lithuania. Germany was two-thirds Catholic. And there
were three Lutheran examples: the Quisling regime in Norway and the rather
moderately right-wing dictatorships in Estonia and Latvia. The communist
regimes were mostly Orthodox (the Soviet Union, Bulgaria), Catholic
(Poland, Lithuania, Czechoslovakia), Lutheran (Latvia, Estonia and East
Germany) or, as in the case of Yugoslavia, a mixture of Orthodox, Catholic
and Muslim. Given the very large numbers of countries that have had totalitarian or authoritarian regimes in the twentieth century, it might be easier to
compile the list the other way round and ask what religion were those societies
that avoided dictatorship. Holland, the United Kingdom and some of its
former colonies, Switzerland and the USA were predominantly Reformed
Protestant. Sweden and Finland were Lutheran.

Additional examples could be drawn from a very different setting: Latin America. In the twentieth century oppressive regimes of the right were Catholic and there is an apparent connection between the spread of evangelicalism and Pentecostalism and democratization.[8] The matching is nowhere near perfect but there is enough of an apparent pattern for us to understand how many Protestants can believe that their religion confers some sort of resistance to authoritarianism.

The impartial observer could retort that, even in the twentieth century, militant Protestantism has produced its own authoritarian movements. In 1930s Scotland, the Scottish Protestant League in Glasgow and Protestant Action in Edinburgh won local council seats on an anti-Irish and anti-Catholic platform. In the USA, the Ku Klux Klan and various other nativist movements presented a similarly curtailed notion of freedoms and rights: democracy was to be restricted to white Anglo-Saxon Protestant males. And the two contemporary examples of Protestants in power – Northern Ireland from 1921 to 1972 and apartheid South Africa – hardly offer models of liberal democracy. The failure of these movements and regimes actually strengthens the claim for a causal connection between reformed religion and democracy in that all were partly undermined by their own democratic rhetoric. But we can acknowledge them here simply as evidence that social reality is vastly more complex than the partisans would wish.

To state the writer's conclusion before elaborating the grounds for arriving at it, then, the general response to the Orange claim is to accept that there is a strong and non-accidental relationship between the rise of Protestantism and the rise of democracy. But to this must be added the rider that the strongest links between reformed Christianity and democracy are *unintended consequences*. The shift from feudal monarchy to egalitarian democracy was not a result of actions intended to produce that effect. Instead it was the ironic (and often deeply regretted) by-product of actions promoted for quite different reasons. The Reformation contributed to the evolution of democracy but its supporters can hardly take the credit.

The following sections work through a number of possible causal connections between Protestantism and what might commonly be regarded as necessary conditions for, or features of, liberal democracy.

Individualism and Lay Activism

The Reformation did not invent the autonomous individual; it was itself a response in the religious realm to changes in social relations that had seen many organic communities undermined. But it did give a powerful boost to two notions fundamental to liberal democracy: that people are more than their social roles and that, despite their social roles, people are much-of-a-muchness.

The Reformation raised up the individual by ending the possibility of the transfer of religious merit from the more to the less Godly. If the good could not pass on merit to the less good by performing religious acts on their behalf then each individual had to stand on his or her own feet before God. This assertion of the free-standing individual gave very little place to rights. It was an individualism primarily of responsibilities. But by ending the system in which religious officials could placate God on behalf of the community and by making every one of us severally (rather than jointly) responsible for our salvational fate, the Reformers created a powerful cat that would eventually escape the theocratic bag.

At the same time, by removing the special role of the clergy as intermediaries between God and his creation, the Reformers laid the foundations for egalitarianism. Initially this assertion of equality was confined to that small part of life concerned with entry to the next kingdom but it did mean that an important potential was created, which subsequent economic and political changes would allow to be fulfilled. They also gave a new impetus to lay activism. Medieval Christianity tended to mirror the feudal structure in expecting and allowing little of the common people; the Reformers demanded an active laity, mindful and diligent. Lay participation without the mediation of the clergy created a model in the sphere of religion for what later became the ethos of modern democracy.

Factionalism and Schism

One of the most significant inadvertent consequences of the Reformation was cultural diversity. In insisting that everyone could discern the will of God through the reading of his Holy Word, the Reformers shifted the basis of religion from an authoritarian and hierarchical epistemology (in which the truth was available only to a very small number of people) to an essentially democratic one. They did not, of course, endorse the ultimately liberal and relativistic view that what everyone believed was equally true. The long-term consequence of that was not anticipated by the Reformers because, being theists who believed in one God, one Holy Spirit and one Holy Word, they assumed that the false and dangerous cohesion previously maintained by the hierarchical church would be replaced by a true and liberating cohesion that came naturally from responding to the Creator. They were wrong. The human default position is not consensus. Removing the theologically justified coercion of the hierarchical church and permitting open access to the salvational truth allowed many competing visions to arise as different social groups developed the dominant religious tradition in ways that better suited their material and cultural interests.

Although many of the Reformers were highly authoritarian and attempted to impose their particular vision on others (Calvin's Geneva and Knox's

Edinburgh were not after all tolerant democracies) such impositions lacked core theological justification, were short lived, and did little to retard the proliferation of competing convictions. Furthermore, the theocracy version of Calvinism was only one (and the least popular) strand of Reformed thinking about the role of social order. There were at least two powerful alternatives that militated against theocracy. Christianity began by asserting the separation of church and state: Christ said that we should render 'unto Caesar the things which are Caesar's and unto God the things that are God's'.[9] That sentiment was reinforced by Christianity's three centuries in the political wilderness before it moved into the seat of Roman imperial power. That combination of belief and history is quite different to the experience of Islam, which did not at its foundation preach a division between the spiritual and material world and which achieved political power immediately. Of course, when they could, many Christian church leaders attempted to impose their faith upon the world, but the older tradition of pietistic retreat to the catacombs remained a powerful resource which could be called upon when necessary. It returned with the Reformation which 'postulating two "kingdoms" insisted upon the total difference between the spiritual order and the temporal or secular world of physical beings and object'.[10] The Lutheran strand easily accepted the two kingdoms and permitted the secular to dominate. The Calvinists tried to maintain a compact of mutual support between the civil magistrate (or the state, as we would now call it) and the church. For brief periods the preachers ruled their burghs. On the other side, a strong pietist tradition argued that undue entanglement with the temporal world contaminated the righteous.

That position is common in third-world Pentecostalism, where pietistic retreat is seen as an effective way of avoiding the corruption of tribal and 'big man' politics. It remains influential in American fundamentalism. When television evangelists such as Jerry Falwell and Pat Robertson led the New Christian Right (NCR) in the 1980s and 1990s, a section of fundamentalism associated with Bob Jones University argued that the NCR was positively dangerous. This was because it could mislead the unregenerate into thinking that social reform was an alternative to personal conversion. Indeed the pietist case can be taken to the extreme of arguing that a bad society might actually be a better environment for preaching the need for personal redemption than a good one because dire circumstances are more likely to bring the soul under 'conviction of sin'.

One cause of Protestantism's increased factionalism was deliberate, though again, the consequences were not at the time foreseen: the insistence on lay activism. The replacement of a largely passive liturgical mode of religion by one which required that every individual become personally committed to propagating the new faith inevitably increased the tendency to schism by increasing the number of people who felt they had a responsibility to decide what was the true religion.

Factionalism led inadvertently to toleration and eventually to religious liberty. It is important for the argument here to appreciate how reluctant the early Protestant sects were to accept the implications of their voluntarism. The reason for believing there is a genuine causal connection is precisely that people were led by the logic of their own arguments and by the consequences of their actions to do things *they did not want to do*. Only after they recognized the inevitable did they rummage around in their ideology to provide a new interpretation that legitimated the initially undesired outcome. The point can be illustrated by the example of the fragmentation of the Christian Church in Scotland. The first two major schisms were thoroughly committed to theocratic rule. The Covenanters (later called the Reformed Presbyterians) refused to accept the seventeenth-century settlement of the relationship between church and state, not because they were opposed to the idea of the state coercing conformity, but because they had not been given sufficient weight in determining just what was to be imposed.

The second major wave of splits, which gave rise to the Seceders, was also theocratic. The Erskines and their followers broke away from the Church of Scotland in 1733 because they objected to the heritors (the Scottish equivalent of patrons) imposing insufficiently Godly ministers on congregations. They had no problem at all with the imposition of ministers of whom they approved. It was only with the third split (that of Thomas Gillespie in 1751, whose followers styled themselves the Relief Presbytery) that we find a movement opposed on principle to the state support for the church. Gillespie had trained with the English Congregationalists before entering the ministry of the Church of Scotland and had acquired something of their liberal spirit.

It is a mark of the times that this third split was the least popular of the three and grew markedly more slowly than the Secession. The fourth and largest split – the 1843 Disruption that led to the formation of the Free Church of Scotland – was, like the first two, rooted in the intolerant idea that the state should support the true religion. However it is significant that there had, by then, been an important change in what it was thought proper for the state to do to ensure the correct religion. In the seventeenth century it was acceptable for the state to use dragoons: the Covenanters objected not to war but to losing. By the middle of the nineteenth century, social pressure, public taxation and preferential access to such means of socialization as the national school system marked the extent of what the theocrats thought it was proper to do to support the correct religion; contrast that with the current constitution of the Islamic Republic of Pakistan that mandates the death penalty for apostasy! For all that softening, there was little recognition that people had a right to choose their religion and considerable opposition to the idea of secular provision of social services.

The irony of Protestantism is that it was its own impossible combination of an open epistemology and an insistence that there was only one truth that created pluralism. By reducing theological support for human coercion while at the same time insisting that there could be only one way to God, the Reformers encouraged a proliferation of competing groups. The result we can see in the changing attitudes to toleration displayed by the various Scottish sects. Gradually each sect came to appreciate that it had failed in its mission and that it would remain a minority. Not surprisingly, it then began to appreciate the virtues of toleration. Simultaneously the state was also coming to accept that, in a context of increasing religious diversity, social harmony required the state to become increasingly tolerant and finally neutral in matters of religion. And each sect gradually reduced the claims that it made for its unique access to the saving truth and came to see itself as one denomination among others.

This is, of course, a simplifying summary. Nevertheless a good case can be made for saying that one of the greatest impacts of the Reformation on the relationship between church and state was the line that ran from factionalism and schism to increasing diversity to increasing toleration to a finally neutral state. In different countries the accommodation developed in different ways. In Britain, there was a gradual fudge in which the state churches were allowed to retain nominal privileges but were gradually stripped of their real powers. In the early twentieth century, their funding base in public taxation was commuted to a lump sum. Thereafter, they were on their own. In the American colonies the need to devise a new political structure from scratch hastened the process and made it explicit. Although nine of the 13 founding colonies had state churches, many of those were challenged by internal diversity and taken together there could be no state church because the colonies had different religions established. In order to make one out of many, that one had to be religiously neutral (or at least very ill-defined) and that requirement was made explicit in the founding documents of the United States. In Australia, the British began by establishing the Church of England and then responded to the reality of sectarian diversity by briefly supporting a number of churches. The 1836 New South Wales Church Act added the Catholic, Presbyterian and Methodist churches to those financially supported by the state but in 1862 the state shifted to the US position of supporting none.

Metaphor and Privatization

It is worth noting one feature of Christianity that marks it off from Islam, Judaism, Hinduism and Buddhism: its stress on doctrine as distinct from ritual or way of life. Christianity (especially in its Protestant version) is a religion of orthodoxy rather than orthopraxy and this has profound social consequences. A religion that mandates a particular way of life (and in Islam that is quite specific because its founding text contains detailed instructions for the good life) tends to be theocratic. If there is only one God and God requires that we fast during Ramadan, it is difficult for adherents to suppose that they must observe Ramadan while their neighbours do not. Muslims, when they can, impose their faith on the entire society.

All faiths have what we might call a 'bolstering interest' in imposing themselves on others; acquiring social power for our ideas is useful in reassuring us that we are right. But Christians do not have a strong theological imperative to impose on others because there is very little that their faith mandates as a way of life. To understand why that is the case we need to go back to the foundation of Christianity. As we can see in the construction of its sacred text, Christianity begins by taking the religion of the Jews and treating it *metaphorically*. The promises that the Old Testament has God making to the Jews were taken as a metaphor for the real promises that God made to the Christians. Similarly the specific requirements set on the Jews (circumcision, dietary laws and the rest) are re-interpreted as either meaning something else or as belonging only to a particular historical dispensation. Although the Catholic Church reintroduced ways of life in its mode of treating faith as a communal and organic matter, the Protestant reformation swept much of that away and reduced the Christian faith to a series of beliefs and attitudes. Holding the right beliefs did not require much of the surrounding world. The point can be seen clearly if we consider the visibility of the consequences of piety. A pious Hindu, Jew or Muslim is highly visible; an evangelical Christian can be almost invisible.

To repeat, then, Christianity (and especially its Protestant strand) has less of a need than other major religions to govern the social and political worlds. More easily than most religions, Protestantism can become privatized. This is not to deny that Christians in certain times and places have been tempted to introduce theocratic rule.

Economic Development and Egalitarianism

If we accept that the seed of egalitarianism was inherent in the Reformation, what delayed its germination for 300 years? In this regard, Gellner's explanation, which concentrates on the functional prerequisites of economic development, seems plausible.[11]

Economic modernization brought with it an increased division of labour, increased social mobility and an increase in the extent to which life became divided into distinct spheres, each with its own values. The simple hierarchies of the feudal world, with their relatively few opportunities for social mobility, were replaced by a larger (and ever-increasing) number of task-specific hierarchies. The feudal lord could not recognize that his serf and his lieutenant were similar beings because to have granted that degree of likeness would have threatened the feudal order. But with the proliferation of task-specific hierarchies, it became possible to see people in terms of a variety of roles, judged on a number of specific status scales. Thus the mill owner could dominate his workers during the day and yet sit alongside them and even listen to one of them preach in a Methodist chapel. Of course power based in one world could be deployed in another. In the Vale of Leven, an industrial area north of Glasgow, in the early twentieth century, it was still common to find the factory owner who was also the major landlord, the local Member of Parliament, the senior elder of the Church of Scotland congregation, a leading Freemason, a magistrate, a major figure in the Orange Order and patron of almost every voluntary association. But unlike the medieval serf, the worker who resented his employer's power could change churches, change jobs, move house or leave the county. Although the local magnate could hope that his standing in one sphere would entitle him to high status in another, he could not impose himself. And that degree of concentration of power was already rare and died out shortly after the First World War.

In the circumstances of economic modernization it becomes possible to distinguish between the roles people play and their essential selves. It thus becomes possible, at least in theory, to accord to all humanity a common worth while maintaining specific status differences in specific fields. It took a long time and much social conflict before that basic egalitarianism was translated into a language of civil liberties and human rights, but gradually the privileges of the rich were extended to all men and then to rich women and to all women and then to children. If it is the case that economic modernization and increased prosperity were crucial to the rise of democracy in the West, then it is also likely, if we accept Max Weber's argument for a causal but unintended connection between the Protestant ethic (a psychology created by a combination of popularized Reformation innovations) and the spirit of capitalism, that Protestantism played a part in that particular equation.

If we now return to the point about diversity we can see why egalitarianism is central to the story. In most societies, the response to diversity is to crush it. Enduring supra-national units as the German Holy Roman empire, the extended Hapsburg kingdoms or the Ottoman empire usually found ways of incorporating religions and nations relatively peacefully. But by and large, when two competing religions came into contact, one attempted to impose itself upon the other. Egalitarianism is an important part of the equation because it explains why Western societies gave up trying to impose conformity. The egalitarian impulse of modernization meant that, at the political level, the costs of coercing religious conformity were no longer acceptable: the state was no longer willing to pay the price of social conflict. Instead it became neutral on the competing claims of various religious bodies. In the seventeenth-century Treaty of Westphalia states accepted the need to tolerate neighbours of different religious hue. Two centuries later they came to the same recognition with regard to variations among their own citizens. So in addition to the minority *loser's* route to toleration sketched above with the example of the Scottish sects, we have a majority route. Gradually the modern state reduces its support for the dominant religion and the state church has to come to see itself as one denomination among others.

One of the difficulties in trying to evaluate possible causal connections is that social practices that originated in one place for one reason can become attractive for quite different reasons and hence relatively autonomous. Thus it may be that the Puritans had a particular Protestant ethic that made them unusually susceptible to attitudes conducive to capitalism, but once their work practices were patently paying off, it was quite possible for those practices to become divorced from their original attitudinal base and be adopted by Catholics. The same can be said for toleration. By the second half of the nineteenth century the different routes to toleration found in France (with its cataclysmic revolution), Britain (with its peaceful evolution) and the United States (able to construct a constitution from scratch) were coalescing to form the general idea that modern democracies did not prescribe or proscribe religion. Take the example of Norway in the second half of the nineteenth century: some pressure for increased religious liberty came from dissenters, but the schisms from the Lutheran church (and even the reforming movements within the church) were far less powerful than they had been in Britain. But dissenting self-interest was powerfully augmented by political reformers who on philosophical grounds argued that religious liberty should be a fundamental plank of democratization.

The Catholic Church was extremely reluctant to accept this idea and as late as the 1960s Vatican officials could be found arguing that error should not be tolerated but in most European countries the fatal flirtation with fascism was enough to persuade Catholics to endorse democracy. After 1945, European Christian Democrat parties, although officered and voted for by pious Catholics, allowed the 'Democrat' part of their identity to constrain the 'Christian' part.

Social Democracy

The above mention of the French Revolution reminds us that Protestantism was not the only source of progressive and radical political ideas. However, there is a crucial religious difference in the environment for the playing out of such ideas. There is a very clear contrast in the development of working-class politics in reformed countries and Catholic countries (with the Lutheran states of northern Europe lying somewhere in between) that can be traced back to the eighteenth century. Because Protestantism allowed the creation of religious diversity, movements of political dissent *did not have to be anti-clerical*. The close ties of the Catholic Church to the *ancien régime* meant that the radical forces in France, in rejecting the feudal order, also rejected the Church. But because the culture was Catholic, it did not readily allow new classes to develop their own form of the dominant religion. In contrast, the Protestantism of Britain allowed political rebels to shape their own dissenting religion. External force could be used to suppress the dissenters but there was nothing in the core ideology of Protestantism that prevented them making the psychological break from any particular form of Protestant church. Thus in France political dissent became anti-clerical while in Britain it often led to religious innovation.

This difference carried through to the nineteenth and early twentieth centuries. In Britain, the Labour movement did not oppose religion per se (but only particular privileges of its particular forms). In Catholic countries there was a clear division with a rural, conservative and clerical bloc and an equally powerful organic anti-clerical bloc. Hence it is in those European countries that remained Catholic (Spain, Portugal, France and Italy) that we also find the most powerful communist parties. In the Scandinavian countries, there was initially a split along the Catholic lines with the left-wing parties being anti-clerical and the state churches profoundly opposed to labour movements. In 1917 the Finnish parliament took advantage of Russia's weakness to declare independence. But the Finns then split. In January 1918 the left, or Reds, staged a coup, the Whites retaliated and in the ensuing civil war some 30,000 people died. The Lutheran Church by and large supported the Whites and lost considerable support among the working class. However, over the inter-war years and during the struggles of the Second World War, the Finns gradually developed a strong shared sense of national identity and the Lutheran Church came to occupy an important role as the carrier of a culture and a history that marked Finland off from its ever-threatening Russian neighbour. In all the Nordic countries, the Lutheran churches were able to switch from a strong association with the political right to back the cause of social democracy so successfully that, despite the thorough secularization of beliefs, there remains widespread popular support for the Churches as carriers and symbols of national identity. In contrast, the Catholic Church in Spain and Portugal has found it very hard to shed its historical associations with right-wing dictatorships.

To summarize, the inherently fissiparous nature of Protestantism prevents it becoming intractably associated with any particular ideological position. There is thus a case for saying that it permitted emergent class conflict to be less polarized than was the case in Catholic countries.[12]

Civil Society and Social Inclusion

There is a further sense in which Protestantism has contributed to modern democracy and that is in pioneering a particularly effective combination of individualism and community spirit. The Protestant sects constructed themselves as egalitarian self-supporting voluntary associations.[13] Although every individual was responsible for his or her own fate, the Saints had an obligation to support each other through this vale of tears. In some sects and at times, that support could be thoroughly oppressive and even unforgiving (the English Quakers of the eighteenth century would expel a bankrupt from fellowship even if he was not the author of his misfortunes) but more often there were strong injunctions to mutual support and charity that did a great deal to blunt the harshness of modern industrial life. As Martin has argued in his explanation of the popularity of Pentecostalism in Latin America, evangelical Protestantism offered a functionally adaptive combination of new persona suited to urban industrial capitalism (the self-reliant striving autonomous individual) and a supportive community of like-minded peers.[14]

To the extent that Protestantism thrived, the old organic feudal community of subservience, descent and fate was displaced by a series of overlapping voluntary democratic associations: the sect's business meeting, the conventicle, the self-organizing prayer group.[15] Protestant sects and denominations themselves formed an important part of the network of civil society but more than that they provided the organizational template for savings banks, workers' educational societies, friendly societies, trade unions and pressure groups. They also provided millions of ordinary people with training in public speaking, in committee management and in small-group leadership. And they provided the persona – the autonomous and self-reliant but caring individual – that could operate the new lay institutions. This was recognized by a mid-nineteenth-century historian of the Secession Churches;

> They insisted on the right of popular election in its full and scriptural extent – that every member of the congregation, of whatever sex or social status, should enjoy the right of choice. Called upon in this way to perform a most important duty, the people have been trained to interest themselves in their own affairs, and in attending to their own interest have acquired that habit of exercising individual judgement, which stands closely connected with the continuance of ecclesiastical and civil liberty.[16]

An important part of interesting themselves in their own affairs was learning to read and write. There is a short connection and long links between Protestantism and literacy. The short one concerns the religious need. If people were to be individually responsible for their own salvation, and if that depended more on correct belief than on correct ritual performance, then they had to have access to the means of saving grace. Hearing sermons was useful, as was learning the catechism, but reading the Bible was essential and 'the stress on scripturalism is conducive to high levels of literacy'.[17] Protestants translated the scriptures into the vernacular languages and taught people reading and writing. In many Protestant lands, the state positively encouraged the people at least to read. There was some reluctance to teach writing (Hannah More, in her Mendip schools, refused to do so). If the common people could read, they could be fed a diet of conservative and improving tracts. If they could write, they might write their own not-so-conservative pamphlets. But even with that reservation, Protestantism encouraged literacy. Post-Reformation Sweden required it. In the seventeenth century full membership of the Church was open only to those who could read.

A longer route concerns the more general connection between literacy and economic development. As part of his larger project of explaining the rise and role of nationalism, Gellner makes the case that a shared literate culture was a functional pre-requisite for economic modernization. Any country serious about lifting itself out of feudally organized agriculture had to have an effective communication across the economy, between people of all stations and not just the nobility and their clerks.

We need to be cautious of claiming literacy as an especially Protestant characteristic. Religion had been associated with language long before the Reformation. In the tenth century two Greek priests, brothers Cyril and Methodius, were sent to Moravia to teach Christianity to the common people in the vernacular. They translated the liturgy and some of the Bible into Slavonic and invented a new alphabet with which to write their translations. We might also note that as a response to the Reformation the Catholic Church authorities in a number of countries promoted reading as a new means to instruct the common people against the heresies of the Huguenots and other Protestants.

Nonetheless, with those two qualifications, we can accept the causal connection between the Reformation and the spread of literacy. Cyril and Methodius had the rather limited interest of providing the material for the Church to operate. What distinguished the Protestant interest was its intensity (it was *very* important for people to learn to read) and its democratic reach (it was very important for *all* the people to learn to read). The contrast with Islam is strong. The Muslims of the Ottoman Empire opposed printing because they saw the mechanical reproduction of the sacred text as a threat to traditional methods of teaching Islam. Foreigners in Istanbul had printing presses but the only one used by Muslims was forced to close in 1730 when pietists wrecked the presses. Muslims in India embraced printing only in the nineteenth century and then only because they feared the threat of Christian missionaries. The Koran was translated into Urdu to make it available to the masses but even then there was a Catholic Church-like fear of democratic interpretation. Those who advocated printing also insisted 'do not read any book without consulting a scholar'.[18]

Petards

The sense in which new ideas, when embodied in actual social changes, can then constrain actors, is perhaps made clearer by adding a few more illustrations of people being subverted by the consequences of their own actions or ideas. Various Scottish anti-Catholic movements of the 1930s foundered for reasons that can be similarly traced back to their own nature. Both the Scottish Protestant League and Protestant Action found their ability to act as political parties undermined by their members' inability to agree or to accept direction. Their activists were so committed to the idea of freedom of conscience that they constantly squabbled and voted against each other. They also found that the voting public expected ideological consistency. They built their attack on the state support for Catholic schools on the principle of equity: it was unfair for Catholic teachers to have equal access to jobs in state schools and yet have protected access to jobs in Catholic schools. To the extent that this argument from equity was accepted, it made their other platforms (such as the repatriation of immigrants from Ireland and preferential hiring of Protestants) difficult to promote.[19]

Activists of the new Christian right in the United States has similarly found themselves constrained by the secular embodiment of principles that their forebears promoted. Using the same term 'fundamentalist' to describe US organizations such as the Moral Majority and Christian Coalition and Muslim groups such as Islamic Jihad and Hezbollah disguises the important difference that the first two have confined their campaigns to essentially democratic means.[20] Even if they really sought to impose a theocracy on the American people, Falwell and Robertson have had to promote that goal with secular language. To their 'home boys', they can denounce divorce and homosexuality as contrary to the will of God, but to the electorate they have had to argue that such practices are socially harmful. To their church audiences they can argue against evolution on the grounds that the Bible says God made the Earth in seven days, but in their campaigns to influence school biology classes and textbooks they have had to show that 'creation science' is as plausible an explanation of the facts as is evolution. In so doing, they accept rules of engagement that ensure they will lose. And because they are by and large democrats, they accept the fact that they have lost their campaign to turn America back to God, and instead campaign for conservative Christians to be treated as a legitimate cultural minority.[21]

The fate of Ulster Unionists can be mentioned in this context. For 50 years they defended their domination of Northern Ireland on the grounds that they represented a majority of its citizens. As the population balance shifted and Catholics became an ever-larger part of the electorate, some unionists openly espoused a different argument: that Ulster Protestants were an ethnic grouping that had a right to self-determination irrespective of electoral arithmetic. But even the supporters of Ian Paisley have (albeit grudgingly) accepted that they must confine their politics to democratic means.[22] A narrow majority of Ulster Unionists have endorsed the new power-sharing politics. Most of the rest do not like it but are unwilling to break the law to oppose the new arrangements.

The cynic could easily say that in all these cases theocrats have simply accepted the reality of their impotence. The reason the Scottish Protestant League, the Moral Majority, or Ian Paisley's Democratic Unionist party have largely confined themselves to democratic politics is that, in a secular culture, they lacked the power to do otherwise. It is *realpolitik* that prevents them acting like Hezbollah. The writer's response is the case made above: the reality to which these groups have had to accommodate is in large part an unintended consequence of the very principles that inspire them.

Secularization

The most obvious connection between Protestantism and the rise of liberal democracy has been left until last. Supporters of various Islamist political movements often point out that those movements are considerably more democratic than the regimes which they aim to displace. It is certainly true that the government in Iran is elected by an almost universal franchise. However, Islamic democracies differ from the western European model in allowing Islam to act as a trump card. Only those candidates approved by religious leaders may stand in Iranian elections; laws passed by the parliament have to be approved by the ayatollahs. The laws privilege Muslims over non-Muslims. The core principle of liberal democracy is that each citizen's vote counts the same; for that to be the case rights must be distributed irrespective of religion. Put bluntly, religion taken seriously is incompatible with democracy. Either the will of God or the will of the people is sovereign.

Essential to the liberal democratic character of western European polities is the fact that they are secular. Either few people are seriously religious or the seriously religious (and their churches, sects and denominations) accept that religious imperatives be confined to the home, the family and the voluntary sector. Religion is confined to the realm of personal preference.

Many of the strands of this argument have been mentioned above and are elaborated at great length elsewhere.[23] Simply put, Protestantism, by encouraging individualism and creating religious diversity, undermined the organic and communal basis for religion. As Martin says, 'the logic of Protestantism is clearly in favour of voluntary principle, to a degree that eventually makes it sociologically unrealistic'.[24]

Conclusion

This rather condensed discussion has considered various claims for the proposition that Protestantism was responsible for democracy. The conclusion is that Protestantism has been causally implicated in the development of democratic polities and civil liberties and that in many particulars the causal connection is the unintended consequence.

To return to the point raised in the introduction: what does this tell us about religious belief systems as *causes*? My conclusion is rather banal. It is worth asserting only because a decade of postmodernism has rather confused the nature of sociological explanation (when it has not denied outright the possibility). The model pursued here might be called the Robert Burns theory of social change (after his line: 'the best-laid plans of mice and men gang aft aglay'). Beliefs and values shape motives. Motives produce actions. Because people do not have perfect knowledge and complete control the consequences are often not what was intended. The new circumstances are interpreted in the light of shared beliefs and may cause them to be modified. That produces new motives and new actions and so it goes on. The scope and ambiguity of religious belief systems always permit a range of interpretations of God's will and social circumstances obviously play a large part in explaining why some people prefer one interpretation to another. But this is not the same as saying that religious beliefs are either without consequences or that their consequences are limited to making those who use God as rhetorical justification for base actions feel better about themselves. Religion makes a difference and this essay has given one example of the profound difference it can make.

NOTES

1. Fred Halliday, 'The Politics of Islamic Fundamentalism: Iran, Tunisia and the Challenge to the Secular State', in A.S. Ahmed and H. Donnan (eds), *Islam, Globalization and Postmodernity* (London: Routledge, 1994), p.96.
2. Bruce Lawrence, *Defenders of God: the Fundamentalist Revolt Against the Modern Age* (London: I.B. Tauris, 1990), p.46.
3. Edward Said, *Orientalism* (London: Routledge, 1978).
4. Steve Bruce, *Politics and Religion* (Oxford: Polity, 2003).
5. Samuel P. Huntington, *The Clash of Civilizations and the Remaking of the World Order* (London: Simon and Schuster, 1996).

6. Max Weber, *The Protestant Ethic and the Spirit of Capitalism* (London: George Allen and Unwin, 1930).
7. Martin Smyth, *Stand Fast* (Belfast: Orange Publications, 1974), p.4.
8. David Martin, *Tongues of Fire: the Explosion of Protestantism in Latin America* (Oxford: Basil Blackwell, 1990).
9. Matthew 22: 21.
10. Graham Maddox, *Religion and the Rise of Democracy* (London: Routledge, 1966), p.4.
11. Ernest Gellner, *Thought and Change* (London: Weidenfeld and Nicholson, 1965); idem, *Nations and Nationalism* (Oxford: Basil Blackwell, 1983); idem, *Nationalism* (London: Weidenfeld and Nicholson, 1997).
12. For the record, this is a modified version of the Halévy thesis (Elie Halévy, *A History of the English People in 1815* (London: Penguin, 1937)). Instead of claiming that Methodism prevented an English revolution, I am making the weaker and more general point that Catholicism's resilience to democratic innovation ensured much greater polarization.
13. Ernest Gellner, *Plough, Sword and Book: The Structure of Human History* (London: Collins Harvell, 1988) p.107.
14. Martin, *Tongues of Fire* (note 8).
15. Maddox (note 10) p.18.
16. A. Thompson, *Historical Sketch of the Origins of the Secession Church* (Edinburgh, A. Fullerton and Co., 1848), p.164.
17. Gellner, *Sword, Plough and Book*, (note 13) p.107.
18. R. Robinson, *Islam and Muslim History in South Asia* (New Delhi: Oxford University Press, 2000), p.77.
19. Steve Bruce, *Conservative Protestant Politics* (Oxford: Oxford University Press, 1998), pp.98–142.
20. Steve Bruce, *Fundamentalism* (Oxford: Polity, 2000).
21. Steve Bruce, *Politics and Religion* (note 4) pp.209–13.
22. Steve Bruce, 'Fundamentalism and Political Violence: the Case of Paisley and Ulster Evangelicals', *Religion*, Vol.31 (2001), pp.387–405.
23. Steve Bruce, *A House Divided: Protestantism, Schism and Secularization* (London: Routledge, 1990); idem, *Religion in the Modern World: From Cathedrals to Cults* (Oxford: Oxford University Press, 1996); idem., *God is Dead: Secularization in the West* (Oxford: Blackwell, 2002).
24. David Martin, *The Dilemmas of Contemporary Religion* (Oxford: Basil Blackwell, 1978), p.1.

Unfinished business: the Catholic Church, communism, and democratization

Lan T. Chu

Diplomacy and World Affairs, Occidental College, Los Angeles, USA

Although history has shown us that the church plays a role in the political liberalization of non-democratic countries, the nature of the church's role and *how* it participates in politics has yet to be fully revealed. By revisiting the Polish Church's historic role in the collapse of communism, I argue that we have overestimated the church's effect on political liberalization in that case, which has led us to neglect or be prematurely disappointed in its role in the remaining communist countries such as in Cuba. Drawing from the Polish case, I conclude that the church's *moral*, *self-limiting*, and *transnational* character needs to be recognized and incorporated into a general theory of democratization. It is this aspect of the church that has helped it to remain active within remaining communist societies, and provide the moral support that is an integral part of political liberalization processes.

Religion and liberation have gone hand in hand at different times and for different reasons.[1] In the final quarter of the twentieth century, it was one of the catalysts for the various Latin American liberation movements as well as the collapse of Soviet communism.[2] Scholars generally have agreed that religion – and particularly the Roman Catholic Church ('church') – played a significant role in these processes. Yet, it has been approximately 10 years since we have said farewell to godless communism and little attention or credit has been given to the church's role in those non-democratic countries that refuse to acknowledge the 'end of history'.[3] These analytical gaps or oversights suggest that our studies of the church and democratization are perhaps incomplete. If the church is to be part of a generalizable theory of democratization, scholars should *not* be selective in their analyses, that is, focusing on the church in some countries and not others. Although history has shown us that the church plays a role in the political liberalization of non-democratic countries, the nature of the church's role and *how* it participates in politics has yet to be fully revealed.[4]

To this end, I will examine the validity of the scholarly consensus on the Catholic Church's role in relation to political liberalization and democratization studies. When studying the Catholic Church's affect on the politics of any one country, it would make sense to mainly focus on cases where Catholicism is the majority. After all, there is strength in numbers. Yet, the focus of this article will be on the Catholic Church in communist Poland as well as in Cuba, where it has had an overwhelming reception and following in the former, and only a lukewarm one in the latter. The Polish case offers a near ideal situation for observing the full potential of the church's strength in a political liberalization process.[5] Its strength is reflected in the fact that both *before* and *after* the rise of communism, the percentage of Polish Catholics remained extraordinarily high: 97% in 1946 and 96% Catholic in 1983.[6] Generally, such figures serve as an indicator of the church's strength because they positively correlate with the spiritual (clerical) and material (financial and structural) resources of the church. Yet, this success story may have skewed our understanding of the church's general role in politics. By revisiting the Polish Church's historic role in the collapse of communism, I argue that we have overestimated the church's effect on political liberalization in that case, which has led us to neglect or be prematurely disappointed in its role in the remaining communist countries. By reassessing and recognizing the church's practical political limits, we will have a better sense of how the Church can contribute to democratization.

To better grasp the church's political potential and limits, the insights garnered from this theoretical reassessment will then be applied to the Cuban case. Unlike communist Poland, the church along with other civil society actors in Cuba experience more challenging limits on religious and political freedoms.[7] Also unlike Poland, where the church is historically linked with the Polish national identity, the Cuban Church's relationship to Cuban society was strained because of its relationship with colonial Spain. This relationship partially explains why the Cuban Church is comparatively weaker than in Poland (1953: 93%, 2000: 40–45% Catholic).[8] Finally, while communism in Poland was considered illegitimate because it was installed by a foreign power (that is, the Soviet Union), in Cuba, communism draws its legitimacy from the victory of Fidel Castro with the 1959 Cuban Revolution.

There are nevertheless some similarities between the two cases, specifically with respect to the church's relationship to its transnational base (that is, Vatican/Holy See).[9] Although the Vatican has maintained diplomatic relations with Poland and Cuba's communist regimes, the combination of the religio-national symbiosis that had already existed in Poland and the election of Polish Cardinal Karol Wojtyla as Pope John Paul II allowed the Polish Church to gain a prominent place for itself in the democratization literature. An arguably simple yet tremendously significant outcome of this national connection was Pope John Paul II's three visits to communist Poland (1979, 1983, 1987) as opposed to his single visit to Cuba (1998). Nonetheless, his visits to both countries were well-received by the Catholic community, evidenced by the massive gatherings and displays of religiosity in the public realm.

Overall, interest in Catholicism in Cuba has waned both in religious and scholarly practice with a growing role and interest instead in evangelical churches. Examining the Cuban Church, however, allows us to test the validity of the revised conclusions from the Polish Church's experience with democratization. If there is significant evidence of the church's unique role and contributions to democratization, scholarly analyses should not shy away from including the church because of its dogmatic doctrines or unpopularity. By taking it seriously in this capacity, we can learn the nuances of this social institution, and clarify how it participates in politics without necessarily being political. The Catholic Church in Poland and Cuba, therefore, are two cases having distinct experiences with communism. By critically revisiting the Polish case and applying a reassessed understanding of that church's experience to Cuba, we are reminded that the correlation between the Catholic Church and democratization is neither causal nor spurious.

Why the Catholic Church?

In his book *The Third Wave* (1991), Samuel Huntington named the post-Vatican II church as one of five significant variables responsible for bringing about the third-wave of democratization.[10] The Second Vatican Council (Vatican II) was an important turning point in the church's history. Convened by Pope John XXIII with meetings held between 1962 and 1965, the goal of Vatican II was to redefine the church's position in the modern world. This is so it could more effectively engage in politics through civil society by moving itself away from its traditional stance, which sought privileges only for itself, its members, and a confessional state.[11]

With a special emphasis on the freedom of religion, the Council discussed the value of human dignity, the relationship between reason and responsibility, the role of the church in a modern, plural society, the significance of dialogue, and the duty of civility. The Council called for the moral obligation of governments and peoples to respect human dignity and human rights. It warned that repression of religion is 'a violation of the will of God and of the sacred rights of the person and the family of nations'.[12] By linking freedom from coercion with the inviolability of man, the church made the concept of human dignity and religious freedom at once political and moral for both believers and non-believers. The dichotomy between the moral and political, therefore, was blurred; when it came to the issue of human rights, the church could not be limited to the private sphere and could instead act politically. It is important to note, however, that while acting politically, the post-Vatican II church would not become a political institution, that is, one that seeks formal political power.

In addition to the changes instituted by Vatican II, democratization scholars have recognized how the church's distinct characteristics make it an important component of civil society, especially in non-democratic countries. They find its transnational character, its autonomy and differentiation from the state, its organizational structure and resources, its moral character, and its ability to convene and organize diverse interests particularly important when there is a deliberate effort by the regime to enforce secularization and authoritarian control.[13] According to political scientist Alfred Stepan, the church's transnational character allows local dioceses to receive external spiritual and material support. With ties to the external world, in a totalitarian country the transnational church is also considered a latent source of pluralism.[14] Transnational churches are also more likely to support a robust, oppositional, and *autonomous* civil society because they do not rely on the state for their legitimacy. On the other hand, churches with a national base, such as Eastern Orthodox Churches, are not 'really a relatively autonomous part of civil society, because in Weber's words, there is a high degree of "subordination of priestly to secular power".'[15] As long as the church can operate administratively and financially independent from the state, its ability to support civil society increases. Furthermore, transnational religions 'remind individuals that "the common good" can increasingly be defined only in global, universal, human terms and that, consequently, the public sphere of modern civil societies cannot have national or state boundaries'.[16]

Advantages to the church's uniformity and organization are outlined by Christian Smith in his study of religion and social movements.[17] Smith refers to the established leaders and members, pre-existing communication channels, and 'enterprise tools' (for example, general office equipment and facilities), all of which add to the efficiency and speed in the dissemination of the teachings and methods of the Holy See.[18] According to Smith, an established hierarchy within each church allows for quick mobilization and helps in the growth and maintenance of a dissident movement. When church leaders decide to support a cause, this decision is passed down from Pope to priest to church member in an organized and efficient manner via the church's pre-existing communication channels: weekly newsletters and bulletins, pulpit announcements, monthly magazines, synods, and councils. In non-democratic societies, therefore, popular support for the opposition can increase exponentially. When teamed up with the church, oppositional groups within civil society are also not burdened with 'creating [their] own structure *ex nihilo*' and can dedicate themselves to direct political activism.[19]

This uniformity in the church's organization helps to structure behaviour across borders as well. Thus, despite its presence in different cultural contexts, both the doctrinal and institutional aspects of the church allow it to regard itself as a universal institution. It is universal because

> [I]n the Church no-one is a stranger: each member of the faithful...is in his or her Church, in the Church of Christ, regardless of whether or not he or she belongs, according to canon law, to the diocese, parish or other particular community where the celebration takes place. In this sense...whoever belongs to one particular

Church belongs to all the Churches; since belonging to the Communion, like belonging to the Church, is never simply particular, but by its very nature is always universal.[20]

This dialectical relationship between the universal and national[21] is a reminder that the presence of a church in a particular country has immediate ties to the international community. Such ties allow it to quickly and easily affect domestic political behaviour as well as foreign policy.

Yet, despite the uniformity of its constitution, the Holy See does recognize that each national church will face different, contextually-specific structural constraints and opportunities to effect political liberalization. While the universal church guides its units in larger issues such as moral dictum and ecclesiastical appointments, to be more effective, resource allocation (physical, financial, and spiritual) is left to the discretion of the hierarchy in each country. The lower clergy (non-bishopric positions) and the laity anchor the church to the country with political activism reserved for the latter. Lay Catholics, Pope John Paul II stated,

...have the duty and the right to participate in public debate on the basis of equality and in an attitude of dialogue and reconciliation...*The Church*, immersed in civil society, *does not seek any type of political power in order to carry out her mission*...[H]er first concern is the human person and the community in which the individual lives...All that she claims for herself she places at the service of people and society (emphasis in original).[22]

In comparison to the national bishops, these groups are more active, localized agents of the church, infusing deeper, cultural meanings to the church's universal laws. The laity, furthermore, stands at the cross-section of the political and civil society spheres. Whether they are official or unofficial agents of the church, they are directly involved in the daily life of the people by providing the social services, which fit within the church's pastoral plan.

Thus, the Roman Catholic Church is more than just the Holy See and is better viewed as a complex, multidimensional institution. As noted by Ian Linden in *Global Catholicism*, aside from being viewed as a hierarchical or ideological institution, the church may be regarded as having a split personality represented either by its hierarchy or the community of the faithful it serves. It is what he calls 'a "two-speed" Church, at best complementary in a fruitful internal dialectic, at worst divided'.[23] With regard to this analysis, I highlight the complementary dialectic between the Vatican, church hierarchy within each country, and lay people, since they share a common political condition of religious repression. Turning now to the cases of Poland and Cuba, we will see that the church's role in promoting political liberalization remains unchanged even when its popularity and strength differ. Although the current political situation in Cuba suggests otherwise, the Catholic Church nonetheless has the potential to help effect political change in that country.

Poland: reassessing self-limits and possibilities

Communism in Poland has always been considered to be somewhat of a paradox. Even Stalin once remarked that communism fit Poland the way a saddle fit a cow. The analogy of the beet and the radish, however, perhaps more aptly describes communism in Poland. Rather than being fully communist 'red', like a beet, Poland prior to 1989 was considered an exclusively non-communist country ruled by a handful of communists.[24] As a radish – red on the outside, white within – communism was only a superficial part of a mainly Catholic country (white being one of the colours of the papal flag). It was well understood that Poland's high religio-national symbiosis would hinder any efforts to totalize the country. Going as far back as the late eighteenth century, when Poland was divided among the empires of Russia, Germany, and Austria-Hungary, church activities were what helped society maintain a Polish national identity. This was possible because the church was the only public institution where Polish was freely spoken.[25] Throughout Poland's history, to be Polish was to be Roman Catholic and the church was consistently recognized as the defender of the nation's identity.[26]

The prominence of the Polish Church in the democratization literature, however, does not imply that it spearheaded Poland's democratization movement.[27] Instead, it served as the moral foundation from which the worker's movement drew its strength. As the communists consolidated their power from the mid-1940s onwards, clashes between workers and the regime peaked in the 1970s. In December 1970, the raising of food and fuel prices without a parallel raise in wages enraged shipyard workers throughout Poland. Thousands of workers from the Lenin (Gdańsk) shipyard took to the streets in protest, many leaving in their wake burning cars and shops. While the workers engaged in political protest, the church limited its action to issuing moral statements regarding the situation. Immediately following the protests, the Catholic bishops issued a pastoral letter defending the rights of Polish citizens to make demands for social justice, to be treated with dignity, and the state's responsibility to abide by a moral standard when dealing with their demands. This articulation by the church was important because, using its own moral language, was the church able to speak with impunity what the workers were demanding. To restore order, a new leader was appointed to the Polish United Workers' Party (PUWP) and the old food prices were reinstated but 45 were dead, nearly 1200 were seriously wounded, and 3000 were arrested.[28] The December 1970 strike showed the significance of the Polish workers as a collective force because it was the workers, and not the church, who forced the change in both the party's policies, and the party itself.

The political action of the workers, nevertheless, was complemented by the moral support of the church. Throughout the strike period, the church spoke on behalf of the workers and pointed out the contradiction of the communist regime. In its support for workers' rights, the church demanded from both the regime and civil society a commitment to moral standards. By not officially or formally allying with either side, the church distanced itself from crossing into the realm of the political and it was also prudent in its own actions by refraining from criticism during times of national crises.[29] In a 1977 sermon, referring to human and not just workers' rights, Wyszyński stated:

> A man should not be thought irritating when he speaks out about his rights as a human person. [...] How can a nation live when basic human rights are not being observed? [...] It would then be not a nation but a mass of dummies without a soul, and with soulless beings neither the nation nor the state would be able to achieve their tasks.[30]

This exemplifies the core of the church's most lasting and consistent contribution to a political liberalization process. Rather than being the lead organizer of political protest, the church, via pastoral letters and sermons, offered words of encouragement, moral support, and spoke for those who could not. In an environment where communist ideology reigned supreme, but lacked legitimacy, words had lost their meaning. When the regime was called on its empty rhetoric and promises, its only substantive answer was force, which was meant to silence popular outcry.

With the signing of the 1975 Final Act of the Conference on Security and Cooperation in Europe (CSCE) by the Soviet Union and the Warsaw Pact countries in Helsinki, the church's concern with human dignity and human rights became a part of the political discourse and was incorporated into the political agenda. As political scientist Daniel C. Thomas notes,

> [T]he 'natural rights' of humanity had long been part of Church teachings – but the new, post-Helsinki salience of 'human rights' within public discourse enabled the Church to engage in contemporary political issues more directly without appearing to depart from its traditional role. Over the next couple of years, a tacit but crucial Church-opposition alliance solidified in Poland under the human rights banner.[31]

The Helsinki Accords was the symbolic banner under which both the opposition and the church rallied together.

In 1976, to further strengthen and unify civil society, Polish dissident Adam Michnik promoted the idea of a 'new evolutionism', a gradual programme aimed at giving 'directives to the people on how to behave, not to the powers on how to reform themselves. Nothing instructs the authorities better than pressure from below'.[32] According to Michnik, a united civil society with the church as an advocate could hold the regime responsible for its promises of political and social justice. Michnik included the church in his framework of a new evolutionism because of the attitude of the Polish episcopate. The church no longer addressed solely the atheist element of communism, but broadened its critique to the totalizing nature of the regime. Although Michnik saw the church as a key source of encouragement, he added:

> [W]e do not expect the Church to become the nation's political representative, to formulate political programs and to sign political pacts. Whoever wants such a Church,

whoever expects these things from Catholic priests, is – whether he likes it or not – asking for the political reduction of the Christian religion. [W]e do not need a Church that is locked up, that is hidden behind the walls of a particular ideology. We need an open Church [...].[33]

With these words, Michnik was pointing out the political limitations and the institutional character of the church. In the church's view, only when the faith is directly attacked will it take action that might make martyrs of its followers. Until that point, however, it is the church's task to act prudently when the lives of believers and non-believers may be at stake.

The role of the national churches changed with the election of Poland's Karol Wojtyła as Pope John Paul II in October 1978. He instituted a policy that blurred the line between the universal and national church, with the Vatican and the national churches working together to negotiate church-state relations. By blurring the line between the universal and national church when dealing with a particular regime, the Pope's intention was to emphasize the universality of the church, and to demonstrate that both the Vatican representative and bishop are 'members of a hierarchical order [who] speak with one voice and one will'.[34] The indivisibility of the universal church's normative principles in the face of varying cultural and historical contexts, and its uncompromising attitude towards the violation of human dignity and human rights, require all national churches to act accordingly regardless of their particular institutional strength.

In August 1980, the historic Gdańsk Accords were signed, ending the strikes in Poland. As a result, approximately 35 separate unions, all representing Poland's major industrial centres, agreed to legally register as a single national, independent trade union under the name of Solidarność, that is, Solidarity.[35] Former Gdansk shipyard electrician (and devout Catholic) Lech Wałęsa was chosen as Solidarity's leader.[36] Prior to this point, Poland's civil society was asymmetrical, more or less dominated by the single institution of the church because it alone had the resources to interact with the regime. The civil society that democratization theorists credit with effecting political change, however, is a balanced collaborative by all of its members. Thus, by the end of the 1980 strikes, the church was not, for the first time,

the sole representative of the interests of the whole nation in dealings with the Party...In contrast with the workers' upheavals of 1970 and 1976, the Church was now faced with formidable competition in the form of a cohesive, well-organized, disciplined and mature work-force.[37]

To conclude, civil society may have found its moral strength in the church, but its force of action was found in Solidarity. The church's promotion of human rights (and not specifically those of workers, students, or intellectuals) reminded secular civil society actors of their common goal of greater political liberalization. A common ground for dialogue between members of civil society quantitatively and qualitatively strengthened civil society. Political scientist Juan Linz states, the church 'is not apolitical, it can never be, but is as nonpartisan as possible, and that is what most of the faithful and those who are nonpractising and religious indifference expect from it'.[38] Even in Poland, Polish priest and philosopher Jozef Tischner defined the church's role in the political realm 'as that of "witness", not that of political institution'. In his analysis of the Polish Church, historian Lawrence Goodwyn explained,

> As an agency of emotional self-preservation the Church played a political role of a very high order...The Church could console and thus help maintain morale for the struggle ahead; it could provide a bedrock of ethical belief; but it could not provide the explicit strategic or tactical ideas that might move Poland to a freer social life. Those ideas had to come from elsewhere. In short, the Church in Poland was reactively relevant. But it was not a source of causation.[39]

What remained was for the members of civil society to carry out their goals responsibly with respect to the common good.

Through self-limitation, the church – free of political allegiances – was able to equally challenge civil society actors and the state to be responsible to the people. The value of the church in this connection is that it contributed to the gradualism and moral character of the political liberalization process. Thus, the worth of its contributions is not dependent on formal policy changes per se, but on its ability to foster the development and well-being of civil society where it is suppressed. As concluded by religion scholar David Herbert, '[T]he Church may be able to contribute to human solidarity in a way in which few institutions in advanced capitalist societies are able to do.'[40] The church's *moral*, *self-limiting*, and *transnational* character coupled with the *concerted* efforts of both secular and non-secular aspects of Poland's civil society are what transformed the process of political liberalization into the democratization of Poland.

Post-totalitarian Cuba

In comparison to Poland, the church's historical development in Cuba placed it at a disadvantage. From the introduction of Catholicism to the island in the fifteenth century by Spain until Cuba's independence in 1899, the institutional church maintained close ties with the Spanish crown via the *patronato real* (that is, 'the king's patronage').[41] Corruption within the church, its support for slavery, and its association mainly with the urban middle class to the neglect of Cuba's rural population, contributed to feelings of anticlericalism.[42]

Although the church at first welcomed the overthrow of Fulgencio Batista's regime, it did not appreciate the socialist leanings of the new revolutionary leaders. The position of the Cuban Church in the early years of Castro's Cuba was 'profoundly marked by conservatism and anti-Communism'.[43] In 1960, the Cuban bishops issued a pastoral letter condemning communism. In the letter, the bishops stated: 'Today the church stands on the side of the humble and will always stand there, but it does not, nor will it ever, stand on the side of communism...'.[44] During this time, however, the church was becoming increasingly isolated from the Cuban community. As political scientist Margaret Crahan explains, 'When the revolution occurred, the Catholic Church was frozen in a pre-Vatican II mold which was reinforced by an exodus of clergy, religious and laity.'[45] In the early years of the regime, furthermore, there was a period of church repression. Many of the priests, seminarians, and lay Catholic and other religious leaders were denounced by the regime as 'social scum' and sent to 'forced labor camps euphemistically called *Unidades Militares de Ayuda a la Producción* (UMAP) [Military Units to Aid Production] in Camagüey province'.[46]

While the situation in communist Poland has brought great attention to the church's role in processes of democratization, the church in Cuba does not appear to be utilizing its resources. For example, political scientist Juan Lopez has stated that because the Cuban Church has 'refused to help strengthen civil society, [. . . and] has not engaged in political opposition [. . .] its behavior is different from that of the Catholic Church in Poland'.[47] If, however, the Cuban Church is viewed as a moral, self-limiting, and transnational institution, we see that it closely parallels the Polish Church. Contrast Lopez's statement with that of a Cuban Church leader, who is more cognizant of the church's limits and abilities. According to Cuba's now retired Archbishop Pedro Meurice Estiú, if any comparison of Cuba was to be made, 'it would be appropriate to do so with countries that used to belong to the Soviet bloc, who also possessed more practicing Catholics than we do. If we compare the Cuban Church with those countries, in my opinion the Cuban Church stands up very well'.[48]

In 1991, the collapse of the Soviet Union had serious negative effects on Cuba's economic and social situation due to the loss of Soviet aid that amounted up to 6.7 billion USD a year.[49] Although fear of Castro's security forces discouraged organized dissent during this time, Castro did not use massive violence and arbitrary repression as a means of deterrence. Instead, he instituted liberal political reforms, removed potential political rivals, and appeared more open to Cuba's social diversity; in doing so, the Communist Party attracted new members, growing faster in the 1990s than it did in the 1980s.[50]

In addition to Castro's ability to pre-empt the mobilization of civil society, Cuba's civil society is in some, but important ways different from Poland's. With Michnik's idea of the 'new evolutionism', the actors in Poland's civil society were encouraged to cooperate with one another so that a greater good could be achieved. In Cuba, however, differences in the way each civil society group believes how political change is to be achieved have kept them divided. For example, in 2003, a group of dissidents issued a statement acknowledging the divisions within Cuba's civil society. They stated, 'No person is entitled to speak on behalf of the whole of the dissidence. . .Any pronouncements made by anyone must be formulated only in the name of the organization or group itself.'[51] The cooperation that was seen in Poland, therefore, is clearly absent here.

In response to the social and economic distress, and the regime's handling of the situation, the Cuban Church issued a pastoral letter in 1993 titled 'Love Hopes All Things'. In the letter, the Cuban bishops denounced the US embargo, reiterated their solidarity with the Cuban people, and articulated the church's duty to remain within the self-limiting bounds of civil society. The bishops stated,

> We, shepherds of the Church, are not political and we know well that this limits us [...] The Church cannot have a political program, because its sphere is of the other, but the Church can and it should give its moral opinion over all that is humane or inhumane, with respect always to the autonomy proper to each sphere.[52]

The church, therefore, is aware of its political limitations as a religious institution. Yet, according to Cuban sociologist Aurelio Alonso Tejado, the bishops are nonetheless seeking to 'mobilize secular society and give it another perspective, different from that offered by the political system'.[53] Thus in their letter, the Cuban bishops also identified the need to eradicate 'irritating politics'.[54] These 'irritating politics' included the limitations on freedom, the intrusion of state security agents into private life, prisoners of conscience, religious discrimination, and the ubiquity of the official ideology that has only added to the country's demoralization. This ideology uses interchangeably terms that are not necessarily synonymous, such as 'Homeland and socialism, State and Government, authority and power, legality and morality, Cuban and revolutionary.'[55]

Statements issued by the Cuban Church may still appear to some as a weak form of dissent. In reaction to the 1993 pastoral letter, the regime issued statements in its official publications and called the letter 'a deliberate provocation, [...] a stab in the back, [...] a crude political pamphlet dressed up as a pastoral letter'.[56] Throughout the communist period, however, the Polish Church had followed a similar path. To dismiss the church as being weak or withdrawn from Cuba's civil society would be an oversight of an institution that has proven to be extremely valuable.

In 1998, Pope John Paul II's visit provided the Cuban Church with an additional opportunity to publicly articulate its concerns for the Cuban nation. As noted by a Vatican official, 'The pontiff came not just to preach to Cubans, but to allow Cuban church leaders a platform for their own thoughts [...] On something this essential [...] it was best that Cubans hear it from a Cuban.'[57] The papal visit to Cuba, however, did not have the same effect that it did in Poland, that is, the strengthening of civil society actors. The existing divisions within Cuba's civil society may explain this difference; a new evolutionism in Cuba has yet to occur.

Although Cubans did experience greater religious freedom during the Pope's visit, Castro made it clear that little would change in Cuba.[58] By meeting with the Pope, Castro hoped to demonstrate that he himself had no fear in 'receiving the religious leader to whom some people have attributed the responsibility of having destroyed socialism in Europe'.[59] As if to preempt Cuba's emulation of Poland's dissident movement, *Granma*, the Communist Party's official newspaper, dismissed any parallels between the two countries in their May 2000 issue. Following a visit by Polish Senator Zbigniew Romaszewski, the newspaper published an article entitled the 'Counter-Revolutionary Adventure of the Polish Government in Cuba'. The article described in detail the senator's visit, which included viewing an exhibit that recounted the rise of the trade union Solidarity, the democratization of Poland, and the church's role in that process.[60] The newspaper also reported that the senator presided over talks that compared the civil societies and political processes of Poland and Cuba. The report referred to such comparisons as 'ludicrous...between truth and parody, between heroism and ridicule'.[61]

To further distance Cuba from Poland, in 2001, the Cuban Communist Party circulated an internal document that indicated the need to 'de-papalize' Cuba and encouraged the 'forgetting' of the papal visit. The regime criticized the church for providing social assistance to the community and considered such actions as meddling in the affairs of the state; theoretically, providing social assistance is the responsibility of the communist state.[62] The Vatican and the Cuban Church regarded the document as an attack on the church writ large. Both believed it was the state's attempt to curb the church's assistance to the people, thereby reflecting a failure of the revolution. An attempted *depapaficación* of Cuba, however, was not enough to discourage the church as it continues to release statements promoting civic responsibility.

One way in which the church promotes civic responsibility is via *Palabra Nueva*, a major publication of the Archdiocese of Havana.[63] These magazines are distributed to parishioners (at least) on a monthly basis after being hand copied, collated, and stapled by a team of five or six people.[64] According to Cuban Cardinal Jaime Ortega y Alamino, submissions to these publications are open to all as long as they contributed to the construction of a better world based on human values.[65] With a circulation of approximately 10,000 copies, *Palabra Nueva* often publishes messages from the Cuban Cardinal, the teachings of the universal church, and commentary on social, political, and economic issues. Such commentary, however, is made on the side of caution and therefore does not appear as explicit criticism of the regime or its policies. Yet, as noted by its editor Orlando Márquez, 'caution doesn't mean silence or complicity'.[66] Thus, upon political dissident Oswaldo Payá Sardiñas' receipt of the 2002 European Parliament's Sakharov Prize for Freedom of Thought for his work on the Varela Project, *Palabra Nueva* congratulated him for following his Christian conscience and assuming 'a political obligation knowing that this new mission was distinct and independent of the mission of the Church'.[67]

In this description of Payá, the magazine re-asserted the difference between the church and a religious layman's reaction to socio-economic and political problems. While the church believes it cannot and should not act as a political institution, lay Catholics do have the moral right to act politically. Their only obligation as a Catholic is to ensure their actions in political life correspond with the values of the church. Ortega's letter of congratulations to Payá was written precisely in this vein

As Pastor of this Archdiocese, I express my appreciation to you for [...] carrying ahead with a steady fight the obligation, that in your conscience, you reckon is necessary for the good of the country. In your position as a Christian layman, you have always known to act following your Catholic conscience, without depending on the church in your laical action, but assuming your responsibilities as a layman and a Christian.[68]

Clearly, these congratulatory messages are words of encouragement for the opposition while keeping in line with the church's formal policies and remaining within the bounds of civil society. The church is reiterating its explicit non-political nature while indicating that political activism may be undertaken by the faithful to speak out against all forms of injustices.

In the summer of 2003, Márquez published in *Palabra Nueva* an editorial titled 'Will the Church be Heard?' In it, he elaborated on the church's call for dialogue with the regime, and the church's distinct way of acting in the political realm. According to Márquez, the manner in which the church acts, which 'at times confuses some and irritates others, reflects precisely the *critical distance* that the Church must maintain in respect to active and partisan politics'.[69] He asserted that it is this critical distance that allows the church to uphold the principle of universality – by not solely championing one specific cause, it can remain free to support all movements consistent with its programme.[70] By maintaining a certain degree of critical distance, the church does not overplay its hand in any one particular instance and becomes overtly political. Rather, it can keep far enough back from the political fray to maintain its 'non-political' character, while continuing to fight for freedom and human dignity by other means.

Furthermore, the church's self-limiting character allows it to continue to remain active on behalf of the Cuban people. In response to Castro's 2003 arrest of nearly 80 political dissidents, the United States Government imposed greater restrictions on travel and aid to Cuba in the summer of 2004. Rather than supporting this censure to the Castro regime, the Cuban Church protested the United States' decision to implement such a policy. The Cuban bishops argued that Cuba's future must be decided by Cubans and efforts, especially by foreign powers, which result in the suffering of the Cuban nation, are unacceptable.[71] As noted by Ortega, governments can be different from one another but the church is part of a larger, united family.[72] Thus, the Cuban bishops found solidarity with the United States' Catholic Bishops' Conference, who also have spoken against the economic embargo instituted by their own government. It is a reminder that the Cuban Church cannot be the political pawn of any regime and that its potential resources are not limited to what is present in Cuba but outside of it as well.

Ortega's description of the church being 'between two fires', aptly summarizes the situation of the Cuban Church today. That is, the church is caught between those who want it to critically oppose the government and those in government who want it to be a passive church. In response to this, the Cardinal stated:

Some within government are beginning to understand it is necessary that the Church behaves as those in other countries of the world, speaking of man, of his problems of liberty, dignity, of rights, that are not only related with nourishment, health, education, but also with freedom of expression.[73]

Thus, in pursuing these tasks, the Cuban Church stands a good chance of getting burned. To critically oppose the government in the form of an opposition movement would be to close the critical distance that is required of the church; such a distance is imperative for the church to properly carry out its moral and normative mission within the bounds of civil society.

There is evidence that the Cuban Church will continue on its course of critiquing the regime from a critical distance. Referring to Pope John Paul II, Ortega stated, 'The Holy Father has with Cuba the same attitude that he had with the countries of the East before the fall of the Berlin Wall. We intend to do our part.'[74] According to Ortega, however, it is often the unfortunate case that the messages of the Cuban Church are better known outside of the country than within.[75] The regime's ability to control the spread of ideas in Cuba poses a great challenge to the church. Yet, Ortega expressed his belief that change will come to Cuba, while being cautious not to articulate how those changes may come about. Rather than believing in the Marxist-Leninist teleological laws of history that have been used to explain Cuba's 1959 Revolution, Ortega historicized the regime's ideology by stating that even the laws of history change.

The situation in Cuba during the last few years, furthermore, has not gone unnoticed by East European dissidents.[76] In his August 2003 letter to the Cuban dissidents, Michnik wrote that he recognized an 'enormous similarity' between the current state of civil society in Cuba and that of Solidarity in Poland.[77] It would be fair to say that Michnik's understanding of the church's role in Poland's civil society would apply to Cuba as well. While the former East European dissidents are optimistic, the Cuban Church has expressed frustration with the current situation. In his somewhat dire reflections on the Pope's visit to Cuba, Meurice stated in 2002, 'Nothing has changed in Cuba. Perhaps the Church has not risen to the heights that were expected of her' and added that there continues to be a misunderstanding regarding the church's mission, 'which has to do with politics but is not in itself political'.[78] The Pope's visit in 1998, followed by the events of 2003, however, may yet serve as a catalyst for the church's ascension towards fulfilling the people's expectations. Although it is a slow and cautious rise, the events in Poland and throughout the former Eastern Bloc, demonstrate that it is nonetheless possible.[79]

The communist state's adaptability to changing political and economic contexts and its control over a divided civil society have stymied Cuba's democratization process. Nonetheless, aside from the nationalism aspect, Cuba scholar Eusebio Mujal-León recognizes relevancy of the Central and East European cases, which suggest a 'tipping point' that may lead to a transition in Cuba.[80] With regard to the church, however, while referring to it as 'probably the best-organized civic organization on the island', Mujal-León indicates its political neutrality has led it to be in 'negotiation, if not accommodation, with the regime'.[81] Statements such as these prematurely discount the church's role in Cuba. As the church as well as the Polish and Cuban dissidents close to it have noted, political neutrality and accommodation are not synonymous and that the Catholic Church has and does utilize a similar self-limiting approach towards Poland and Cuba's communist state and civil society,

Conclusion

When looking at the cases of Poland and Cuba, democratization scholars, focusing mainly on the structural and institutional resources of the church were correct to point out the church's abilities in relation to civil society. This includes providing an institutional space for freedom in an otherwise regimented society, serving as a symbolic resource to counter communist ideologies, providing a connection to the international community and the nation's past (typically co-opted by the party), and helping to constitute intellectual thought.[82] What is often given insufficient attention, however, is exactly *how* the church utilized its resources to strengthen civil society. The moral and self-limiting character of the church, whose principles were standardized in the 1960s by the Second Vatican Council, provides us with answers to this question. This aspect of the church has helped it to remain active within remaining communist societies, and provide the moral support that is an integral part of political liberalization processes.

Along the lines of Vatican II's themes of dialogue, dignity, and difference, the Cuban Church assumes the 'preeminence of the human person' as the standard by which all ideologies are to be judged and does not take political sides. As noted by Márquez,

> [t]he *disappointment* of John Paul II. . .is not motivated by the existence in Cuba of a government that declares itself socialist, but by the decision made by this government to impose hard penalties on persons that expressed or express 'their own personal opinion' and asserted it as a 'manner leading to the common good'.[83]

Also in the spirit of Vatican II, the Cuban Church has reminded lay Catholics of their specific role in the polity. According to the bishops, lay Catholics are to express themselves in order to ensure political power is just, and that the rule of law corresponds to moral law and the general good. In a Church bulletin released in September 2003, one Church spokesman reminded the faithful once again that 'The political participation of the Christian is not only a right. Above all it is a duty. Your voice, united and at times dissenting must not be silenced: society, any society, needs it. Cuba needs it.'[84]

Overall, there are many valuable lessons that can still be learned from the experience of the Polish Church and civil society under communism. Rather than measuring the church's effectiveness by looking for a direct causal link between the church's efforts and liberalization of a communist state's policy, we can appreciate how the church focuses its resources (spiritual and material) on the promotion of broadly human and political liberal values. Thus, prior to the collapse of the Soviet Union, in his description of Solidarity and of the dissident movements in Eastern Europe, Hungarian dissident George Konrád stated,

> We languish in the depths of defeat. Is it possible that the monolith can never be moved off of us? [...] I believe not in victory but in the stubbornness of a few. Oppression is bearable but unacceptable. Anyone who has tried to take action against it has made no mistake. Three attempts have failed; the seventh will succeed.[85]

In Poland, the church proved to be a reliable partner in these repeated attempts at political change. With a strong secular civil society that was organized, united, and drew on the moral foundation provided by a supportive church, Poland's transition to democracy in 1990 reflected the full extent of how the church's resources could contribute to a political liberalization movement. More importantly, the Polish case illustrates how the church provided the moral and material resources that helped small disorganized pockets of dissent grow into a real, pro-democratic social opposition movement.

From the Polish case, we also can learn that the church's ability and willingness (or unwillingness) to contribute to civil society's efforts may have had little to do with whether the collapse of communism was ultimately on the horizon. In Eastern Europe, dissidents pursued political liberalization simply to have a life that more closely resembled the promises of communism. At the time, civil society was simply looking for a way to live within, rather than remove, the communist regime. The value of the church in this connection is that it contributed to the gradualism and moral character of the political liberalization process. Thus, the worth of its contributions is not dependent on formal policy changes per se, but on its ability to foster the development and well-being of civil society where it is suppressed. As concluded by sociologist David Herbert, '[T]he Church may be able to contribute to human solidarity in a way in which few institutions in advanced capitalist societies are able to do.'[86]

In Cuba, the church has shown that it will continue to support civil society actors regardless of whether or not success is on the horizon. As such, it offers symbolic and real evidence to others that the Polish case continues to be a valuable model to follow. Similar to Payá, Cuba's dissident group 'Ladies in White' ('Damas de Blanco') was awarded the Sakharov Prize in 2005. These women, dressed in white, are the wives of the dissidents who were summarily arrested in March 2003. Together, they gather on Sundays at St Rita's Catholic Church in Havana to attend mass and then meet to offer one another support as well as discuss their shared experiences. By walking to church together in a noticeable stream of white, their walks and subsequent gatherings at the church have become a form of peaceful protest.[87] Once again, similar to Poland, the church provides the physical and moral support for dissent.

The church's relationship to the communist regime in Cuba has been consistent with the universal church's stance towards communism. In Cuba, however, the church's efforts have been overshadowed by factors not found in the Polish case: the flexibility of the communist regimes to pre-empt civil unrest, the unorganized and discrete nature of the secular actors of civil society, and the regimes' use of the nation's revolutionary history to legitimate their policies. As the efforts of secular civil society actors in Cuba, such as the Varela Project, have yet to see substantive changes in state policy, the mere fact that efforts for greater political liberalization exist signifies something very important. It is a sign that democratization is not outside the realm of possibility. The church's encouragement of a democratic political culture in Cuba may not be the quickest route to political liberalization, but it is a proven and remarkably peaceful route by which an emerging civil society in Cuba can strive toward their goal. The conclusions drawn from this article are meant to highlight such possibilities; this reassessment seeks to enhance our understanding of the church as a variable in the process of political liberalization, and serve as a starting point from which more extensive research regarding civil society and democratization in the remaining communist countries, such as Cuba, can be conducted.

Notes

1. John Anderson's edited volume *Religion, Democracy, and Democratization* examines the affect of different religions on democratization efforts.
2. For analyses of the Catholic Church in Latin America, see Gill, *Rendering Unto Caesar*; Burdick and Hewitt, *The Church at the Grassroots in Latin America*.
3. What Francis Fukuyama refers to as 'the end point of mankind's ideological evolution and the universalization of Western liberal democracy as the final form of human government'. See Fukuyama, 'The End of History', 3.
4. In this article, political liberalization is defined by comparative politics scholars studying nondemocratic regimes as 'making effective rights that protect individuals and groups from arbitrary, repressive, or illegal acts committed by a communist or authoritarian state'. See O'Donnell and Schmitter, *Transitions from Authoritarian Rule*, 6. Although political liberalization and democratization do not necessarily go hand in hand, the former does open up the possibility but not inevitability of the latter and, therefore, falls into the realm of democratization studies.
5. For example, see Casanova, *Public Religions in the Modern World*.
6. Casanova, *Public Religions in the Modern World*, 6, 260; Kennedy and Simon, 'Church and Nation in Socialist Poland'.
7. Generally, civil society is understood to be independent non-governmental institutions, associations, and groups. I also incorporate Hungarian political theorist Maria Markus' definition, who emphasizes civility and decency within civil society. She notes 'a decent society is one whose institutional arrangements are oriented by principles, norms, and rules directed at creating and maintaining conditions of dignified, humanly meaningful life for all its members and that is able to extend its civility and decency to nonmembers as well' (p. 1022). Markus' description of a 'decent' civil society echoes Vatican II's outline of the church's role in civil society. See Markus, 'Decent Society and/or Civil Society?'.
8. US Department of State's Bureau of Democracy, Human Rights and Labor, '2005 Annual Report on International Religious Freedom'.
9. Briefly stated, the Holy See refers to the central governance of the Roman Catholic Church (the Pope, the Roman Curia) whereas the Vatican 'was created as a mini-state

to safeguard the absolute freedom and independence of the Holy See. ....In practice, we see that Vatican City State will never act as such, but always through the Holy See. States have diplomatic relations with the Holy See, not with Vatican City State' (Martens, 'The Position of the Holy See and the Vatican City-State', 755). As noted by Kurt Martens, the Holy See and Vatican have been used as mutually interchangeable, although it is incorrect to do so. In this article, I will follow the common usage of referring to the Vatican to avoid confusion. For a detailed analysis, see Martens, 'The Position of the Holy See and the Vatican City-State'.

10. 'Overall, roughly three-quarters of the countries that transitioned to democracy between 1974 and 1989 were Catholic countries.' See Huntington, *The Third Wave*, 76. Daniel Philpott also referred to the third wave as 'overwhelmingly a Catholic wave'. See Philpott, 'The Catholic Wave'.

11. Prior to Vatican II, the church had a double standard of 'freedom for the Church when Catholics are a minority, privilege for the Church and intolerance for others when Catholics are a majority'. See Abbott, *The Documents of Vatican II*, 673.

12. Abbott, *The Documents of Vatican II*, 685.

13. Diamond, *Developing Democracy*, 224; Linz and Stepan, *Problems of Democratic Transition*, 245; Differentiation refers to the extent to which a religion is institutionally separate from the state. See Philpott, 'Explaining the Political Ambivalence of Religion'.

14. Linz and Stepan, *Problems of Democratic Transition*, 260.

15. Stepan, 'Religion, Democracy, and the "Twin Tolerations"', 53. It is important, however, to note that scholars do not believe Eastern Orthodox Churches are inherently anti-democratic (Linz and Stepan, *Problems of Democratic Transition*, 453).

16. Casanova, *Public Religions in the Modern World*, 229.

17. See Smith, 'Correcting a Curious Neglect, or Bringing Religion Back In'.

18. Ibid.

19. Ibid., 15.

20. Ratzinger, *Letter to the Bishops*.

21. Reference to the national church in this work (for example, the 'Polish Church', the 'Cuban Church') reflects the 'particular characteristic and the diversity' of the universal church in different countries (See Ratzinger, *Letter to the Bishops*). The use of the term national church must not be confused with a 'patriotic' Catholic Church, which may be Catholic in nature, following all of the Catholic rituals, but recognize the political regime, and not necessarily the Holy See, as its main authority.

22. Pope John Paul II, 'Homily in Santiago De Cuba'.

23. Linden, *Global Catholicism*, 1–2.

24. Blazynski, *Flashpoint Poland*, 377.

25. Kennedy and Simon, 'Church and Nation in Socialist Poland', 131; Morawska, 'Civil Religion Versus State Power in Poland', 223.

26. Kubik, *The Power of Symbols against the Symbols of Power*; Nielson, *Revolutions in Eastern Europe*, 66.

27. That can be attributed to the independent trade union Solidarity. See for example Ost, *Solidarity and the Politics of Anti-Politics*; Michnik, *Letters from Freedom*; Garton Ash, *The Polish Revolution*.

28. Blazynski, *Flashpoint Poland*, 22.

29. Szajkowski, *Next to God*, 47. National crisis included events such as martial law in 1981 and a possible Soviet invasion.

30. Blazynski, *Flashpoint Poland*, 325–6.

31. Thomas, *The Helsinki Effect*, 105.

32. Michnik, *Letters from Prison*, 144.

33. Ibid., 327.

34. Szajkowski, *Next to God*, 71–2.
35. Garton Ash, *The Polish Revolution*, 80.
36. Wałęsa would later become post-communist Poland's first democratically-elected president in 1990.
37. Szajkowski, *Next to God*, 100.
38. Quoted in Eberts, 'The Roman Catholic Church and Democracy in Poland', 838.
39. Goodwyn, *Breaking the Barrier*, 319.
40. Herbert, 'Christianity, Democratisation, and Secularisation in Central and Eastern Europe', 288.
41. In exchange for financial support and assistance in evangelization, the church provided the crown with the privilege of making ecclesiastical appointments. See Crahan, 'Cuba', 88; Smith, *Religion and Political Development*, 78.
42. Crahan, 'Cuba: Religion and Revolutionary Institutionalization'.
43. Crahan, 'Cuba', 93.
44. Treto, *The Church and Socialism in Cuba*, 32.
45. Crahan, 'Cuba: Religion and Revolutionary Institutionalization', 319.
46. Clark, *Religious Repression in Cuba*, 15.
47. López, *Democracy Delayed*, 88.
48. Llano, 'Entrevista al Arzobispo de Santiago de Cuba'.
49. Werlau, 'Foreign Investment in Cuba', 54.
50. Geyer, 'As Fidel Fades'.
51. Herald Wire Services, 'Cuban Group Urges Dissident Unity in Apparent Swipe at Payá'.
52. La Conferencia de Obispos Católicos de Cuba, 'El Amor Todo Lo Espera' ['Love Hopes All Things'], 404.
53. Quoted in Linard, 'Guarded Rapprochement between Rome and Havana'.
54. La Conferencia de Obispos Católicos de Cuba, 'El Amor Todo Lo Espera' ['Love Hopes All Things'], 410.
55. Ibid.
56. Malone, 'Conflict, Coexistence, and Cooperation: Church-State Relations in Cuba', 8.
57. Tamayo, 'Pope Likens Cuba Trip to Fateful Poland Visit', 1A.
58. Scholars such as Douglas Johnston maintain that the Pope's visit had 'enormous political and religious ramifications', which includes speculation by observers that 'a personal catharsis for this "godless" communist ruler in relation to his religious roots' may have occurred. See Johnson, *Faith-Based Diplomacy*, 22–3.
59. Castro, 'Speech Given by President Fidel Castro Ruz, First Secretary of The Central Committee of The Communist Party of Cuba, at The Farewell Ceremony for His Holiness Pope John Paul II'.
60. El Partido Comunista de Cuba, 'The Counterrevolutionary Adventure of the Government of Poland in Cuba', 2.
61. Ibid., 4.
62. The internal document was titled, 'Political Analysis of the Religious Phenomenon in the Capital'. See Alfonso, 'Ofensiva Contra El Auge Religioso' [An Offensive against the Religious Peak]', 1A; Alfonso, 'Se Prepara El Gobierno Para Dar Una Batida Antirreligiosa En La Habana' ['The Government Prepares to Conduct an Antireligious Search in Havana'], 2A.
63. In 1986, Poland had 33 Catholic newspapers or magazines; See Chrypinski, 'The Catholic Church in Poland, 1944–1989', 112. Compare this to Cuba, which has only 12, see Valdés, 'The Varela Project and the Clash within the Catholic Church in Cuba'.
64. Lionet, 'Cuba: The Exception of the Church', 1.
65. Ortega y Alamino, 'Misión De Una Publicación Católica' ['The Mission of a Catholic Publication'], 23.

66. Lionet, 'Cuba: The Exception of the Church', 3.
67. La Redacción de *Palabra Nueva*, 'Sobre El Premio Sajarov 2002 a Oswaldo Payá Sardiñas' ['Regarding the 2002 Sakharov Prize to Oswaldo Payá Sardiñas'], 16. The Varela Project, named after Catholic priest Félix Varela, is a petition for a 'national referendum to guarantee freedom of expression and association, amnesty for political prisoners, free elections and the right to private enterprise', See Sullivan. 'Cuba: Anti-Castro Forces Mount Petition Drive', A24. The project is spearheaded by Payá's Christian Liberation Movement (CLM) – a non-confessional group organized in 1987 by lay Catholics seeking to reform Cuba through constitutional means.
68. Ortega y Alamino, 'Texto De La Carta Enviada Por El Cardenal Jaime Ortega, Arzobispo De La Habana, a Oswaldo Payá Sardiñas' ['Text of the Letter Sent by Cardinal Jaime Ortega, Archbishop of Havana, to Oswaldo Payá Sardiñas'], 16.
69. Márquez, '¿Será Escuchada La Iglesia?' ['Will the Church Be Heard?'], 6.
70. Interest-based approaches have been utilized to explain why the church entered into alliances with communist or authoritarian regimes. Influenced by economic models, these scholars view the church as a corporation, adjusting its policies to attract and provide security to investors (Iannacconne, 'Religious Participation') or choosing institutional preservation over its theological mission (Gill, *Rendering Unto Caesar*). Interest-based approaches, however, are unable to explain the church's choice to publicly support civil society, even when such actions would jeopardize its institutional existence within the polity. Smith, 'Religion and Politics'.
71. La Conferencia de Obispos Católicos de Cuba, 'Nota Del Comité Permanente De La Conferencia De Obispos Católicos De Cuba' ['Note of Permanent Committee of the Cuban Catholic Bishops' Conference'].
72. Ortega y Alamino, 'Carta Pastoral "Un Solo Dios Padre De Todos"' ['Pastoral Letter "One God the Father for All"'], 13.
73. Ortega y Alamino, 'Entre Dos Fuegos' ['Between Two Fires'].
74. Ibid.
75. Ibid. Such is the case with secular Cuban dissidents as well, specifically the case of Cuban blogger Yoani Sánchez who lives in Havana, Cuba. Sánchez was named one of *Time* magazine's 100 most influential people yet she and her work are unknown to fellow Cuban islanders. See Steinberg and Wilkinson, 'The Heroes of Cuba'.
76. Palous, 'I Add My Voice to Support Cuban Dissidents'.
77. Michnik, 'To the Cuban Dissidents', 4.
78. Llano, 'Entrevista Al Arzobispo' ['Interview with the Archbishop'].
79. It was 10 years between the formation of Solidarity in 1980 and the democratic election of Lech Wałęsa.
80. This tipping point is a combination of economic development, civic organization, and the availability of a political alternative. See Mujal-León, 'Tensions in the Regime', 24.
81. Mujal-León, 'Tensions in the Regime', 30.
82. Herbert, 'Christianity, Democratisation, and Secularisation in Central and Eastern Europe'.
83. Márquez, '¿Será Escuchada La Iglesia?' ['Will the Church Be Heard?'], 6.
84. Almagro Domínguez, 'Católicos Políticos/Políticos Católicos' ['Political Catholics/Catholic Politics'], 4.
85. Konrád, *Antipolitics: An Essay*, 147.
86. Herbert, 'Christianity, Democratisation, and Secularisation in Central and Eastern Europe', 288.
87. Robles, 'Cuba's "Ladies in White" Wins Prestigious Prize'.

Notes on contributor

Lan T. Chu is an Assistant Professor in the department of Diplomacy and World Affairs at Occidental College. Her research and teaching interests focus on the political role of religious institutions, the political liberalization processes of existing communist countries, dissent, and revolution. She has published articles, book reviews, and political commentary relating to politics and religion in the *Journal of Vietnamese Studies, Politics and Religion, BBC Vietnam*, and *East European Politics and Societies*. Her chapter on the Vietnamese Catholic church appears in the edited book *Local Organizations and Urban Governance in East and Southeast Asia* (Routledge, 2009).

Bibliography

Abbott, S.J., Walter M. *The Documents of Vatican II*. New Brunswick, NJ: America Press/ New Century Publishers, 1966.

Alfonso, Pablo. 'Ofensiva contra el auge religioso' ['An Offensive against the Religious Peak']. *El Nuevo Herald*, June 17, 2001, 1A.

Alfonso, Pablo. 'Se prepara el gobierno para dar una batida antirreligiosa en La Habana' ['The Government is Prepared to Conduct an Antireligious Search in Havana']. *El Nuevo Herald*, June 17, 2001, 2A.

Almagro Domínguez, Francisco. 'Católicos Políticos/Políticos Católicos' ['Political Catholics/Catholic Politics']. *Ecclesia in Habana: Boletín de la Oficina del Cardenal Arzobispo de La Habana* Año 1, no. 4 (2003): 4.

Anderson, John, ed., *Religion, Democracy, and Democratization*. New York: Routledge Press, 2006.

Blazynski, George. *Flashpoint Poland*. New York: Pergamon Press, 1979.

Burdick, John, and W.E. Hewitt. *The Church at the Grassroots in Latin America: Perspectives on Thirty Years of Activism*. Westport: Praeger, 2000.

Casanova, José. *Public Religions in the Modern World*. Chicago, IL: The University of Chicago Press, 1994.

Castro, Fidel. 'Speech Given By President Fidel Castro Ruz, First Secretary Of The Central Committee Of The Communist Party Of Cuba, At The Farewell Ceremony For His Holiness Pope John Paul II'. *Granma*, January 25, 1998, http://www.granma.cu/juanpablo/ingles/010-i.html (accessed May 20, 2004).

Chrypinski, Vincent C. 'The Catholic Church in Poland, 1944–1989'. In *Catholicism and Politics in Communist Societies*, ed. P. Ramet, 117–41. Durham: Duke University Press, 1990.

Clark, Juan. *Religious Repression in Cuba*. Miami: Cuban Living Conditions Project, 1998.

Crahan, Margaret E. 'Cuba: Religion and Revolutionary Institutionalization'. *Journal of Latin American Studies* 17 (1985): 319–40.

Crahan, Margaret E. 'Cuba'. In *Religious Freedom and Evangelization in Latin America: The Challenge of Religious Pluralism*, ed. P.E. Sigmund, 87–112. Maryknoll: Orbis Books, 1999.

Diamond, Larry. *Developing Democracy: Toward Consolidation*. Baltimore, MD: Johns Hopkins University Press, 1999.

Eberts, Mirella W. 'The Roman Catholic Church and Democracy in Poland'. *Europe-Asia Studies* 50 (1998): 817–42.

El Partido Comunista de Cuba. 'The Counterrevolutionary Adventure of the Government of Poland in Cuba', 2000, http://www.cuba.cu/gobierno/documentos/2000/ing/e160500i.html (accessed August 5, 2003).

Fukuyama, Francis. 'The End of History'. *The National Interest* (Summer 1989): 3–18.

Garton Ash, Timothy. *The Polish Revolution: Solidarity.* New Haven, CT: Yale University Press, 2002.

Geyer, Georgie Ann. 'As Fidel Fades'. *Washington Quarterly* 24, no. 1 (2001): 31–40.

Gill, Anthony James. *Rendering unto Caesar: The Catholic Church and the State in Latin America.* Chicago, IL: University of Chicago Press, 1998.

Goodwyn, Lawrence. *Breaking the Barrier: The Rise of Solidarity in Poland.* Oxford: Oxford University Press, 1991.

Herald Wire Services. 'Cuban Group Urges Dissident Unity in Apparent Swipe at Payá'. *The Miami Herald*, July 4, 2003, http://www.miami.com/mld/miamiherald/news/world/cuba/6232074.htm (accessed August 2, 2003).

Herbert, David. 'Christianity, Democratisation, and Secularisation in Central and Eastern Europe'. *Religion, State, and Society* 27 (1999): 277–93.

Huntington, Samuel. *The Third Wave.* Norman: University of Oklahoma Press, 1991.

Iannacconne, L.R. 'Religious Participation: A Human Capital Approach'. *Journal for the Scientific Study of Religion* 29, no. 3 (1996): 297–314.

Johnson, Douglas. *Faith-Based Diplomacy: Trumping Realpolitik.* New York: Oxford University Press, 2008.

Kennedy, Michael D., and Maurice D. Simon. 'Church and Nation in Socialist Poland'. In *Religion and Politics in the Modern World*, ed. P.H. Merkl and N. Smart, 121–54. New York: NYU Press, 1983.

Konrád, György. *Antipolitics: An Essay.* San Diego, CA: Harcourt Brace Jovanovich, 1984.

Kubik, Jan. *The Power of Symbols Against the Symbols of Power.* University Park: The Pennsylvania State University Press, 1994.

La Conferencia de Obispos Católicos de Cuba. 'El Amor Todo Lo Espera – Pastoral de los Obispos Cubanos – 8 de Septiembre de 1993' ['Love Hopes All Things – Pastoral Letter of the Cuban Bishops']. In *La Voz de la Iglesia en Cuba*, 399–418. México: Obra Nacional de la Buena Prensa, 1995.

La Conferencia de Obispos Católicos de Cuba. 'Nota del Comité Permanente de la Conferencia de Obispos Católicos de Cuba' ['Note of Permanent Committee of the Cuban Catholic Bishops' Conference']. *La Voz Catolica*, May 26, 2004, http://www.vozcatolica.org (accessed June 10, 2004).

La Redacción de *Palabra Nueva*. 'Sobre El Premio Sajarov 2002 a Oswaldo Payá Sardiñas' ['Regarding the 2002 Sakharov Prize to Oswaldo Payá Sardiñas']. *Palabra Nueva* Año XI (2003): 16.

Linard, André. 'Guarded Rapprochement Between Rome and Havana'. *Le Monde Diplomatique*, January 1998, http://mondediplo.com/1998/01/02habana (accessed January 24, 2004).

Linden, Ian. *Global Catholicism: Pluralism and Renewal in a World Church.* New York: Columbia University Press, 2009.

Linz, Juan, and Alfred Stepan. *Problems of Democratic Transition and Consolidation.* Baltimore, MD: Johns Hopkins University Press, 1996.

Lionet, Christian. 'Cuba: The Exception of the Church'. *Reportoires San Frontieres*, 2003, http://www.unhcr.org/refworld/docid/47fcca862c.html (accessed March 24, 2011).

Llano, Víctor. 'Entrevista al Arzobispo de Santiago de Cuba' ['Interview with the Archbishop of Santiago de Cuba']. *Boletín del Partido Demócrata Cristiano* II, 2002, http://www.pdc-cuba.org/boletin-02-02.htm#Entrevista%20al%20Arzobispo%20de%20Santiago%20de%20Cuba (accessed January 24, 2004).

López, Juan J. *Democracy Delayed: The Case of Castro's Cuba.* Baltimore, MD: Johns Hopkins University Press, 2003.

Malone, Shawn T. 'Conflict, Coexistence, and Cooperation: Church-State Relations in Cuba'. *The Cuba Briefing Paper Series* Number 10 (1996): 1–17.

Markus, Maria Renata. 'Decent Society and/or Civil Society?'. *Social Research* 68 (2001): 1011–30.

Márquez, Orlando. '¿Será Escuchada la Iglesia?' ['Will the Church be Heard?']. *Palabra Nueva* Año XII, no. 121 (2003): 6–8.

Martens, Kurt. 'The Position of the Holy See and the Vatican City-State in International Relations'. *University of Detroit Mercy Law Review* 83, no. 5 (Summer 2006): 729–60.

Michnik, Adam. *Letters From Prison*, trans. M. Latynski. Berkeley: University of California Press, 1985.

Michnik, Adam. *Letters from Freedom: Post-Cold War Realities and Perspectives*, trans. I. Grudzinska-Gross. Berkeley: University of California Press, 1998.

Michnik, Adam, 'To the Cuban Dissidents'. *TCDS/ECEP Bulletin* 13/3, no. 45 (2003): 4.

Morawska, Ewa. 'Civil Religion Versus State Power in Poland'. In *Church-State Relations: Tensions and Transitions*, ed. T. Robbins and R. Robertson, 221–31. New Brunswick, NJ: Transaction Books, 1987.

Mujal-León, Eusebio. 'Tensions in the Regime'. *Journal of Democracy* 20, no. 1 (2009): 20–35.

Nielson, Niels C. *Revolutions in Eastern Europe: The Religious Roots*. New York: Orbis Books, 1991.

O'Donnell, Guillermo, and Philippe C. Schmitter. *Transitions from Authoritarian Rule: Tentative Conclusions About Uncertain Democracies*. Baltimore, MD: Johns Hopkins University Press, 1993.

Ortega y Alamino, Cardenal Jaime. 'Carta Pastoral "Un Solo Dios Padre de Todos"' ['Pastoral Letter "One God the Father for All"']. *Palabra Nueva* Año VIII, no. 81 (1999): 1–19.

Ortega y Alamino, Cardenal Jaime. 'Misión de una publicación católica' ['The Mission of a Catholic Publication']. *Palabra Nueva* Año VIII, no. 81 (1999): 23.

Ortega y Alamino, Cardenal Jaime. 'Texto de la Carta Enviada por El Cardenal Jaime Ortega, Arzobispo de la Habana, a Oswaldo Payá Sardiñas' ['Text of the Letter Sent by Cardinal Jaime Ortega, Archbishop of Havana, to Oswaldo Payá Sardiñas']. *Palabra Nueva* Año XI, no. 115 (2003): 16.

Ortega y Alamino, Cardenal Jaime. 'Entre dos fuegos' ['Between Two Fires']. *Encuentro en la red: Diario independiente de asuntos cubanos*, 2004, http://www.cubaencuentro. com/entrevistas/20040120 (accessed January 24, 2004).

Ost, David. *Solidarity and the Politics of Anti-politics: Opposition and Reform in Poland Since 1968*. Philadelphia: Temple University Press, 1990.

Philpott, Daniel. 'The Catholic Wave'. *Journal of Democracy* 15, no. 2 (April 2004): 32–46.

Philpott, Daniel. 'Explaining the Political Ambivalence of Religion'. *American Political Science Review* 101, no. 3 (2007): 505–25.

Palous, Martin. 'I Add My Voice to Support Cuban Dissidents'. *The Miami Herald*, 2004, http://www.miami.com/mld/miamiherald/news/opinion/8131736.htm?1c (accessed March 12, 2004).

Pope John Paul II. 'Homily in Santiago de Cuba', January 28, 1998, http://www.vatican.va/holy_father/john_paul_ii/travels/documents/hf_jp-ii_hom_24011998_lahavana-santiago_en.html (accessed May 4, 2004).

Ratzinger, Joseph Cardinal. *Letter to the Bishops of the Catholic Church on Some Aspects of the Church Understood as Communion*. The Roman Curia: Congregation for the Doctrine of the Faith, May 28, 1992, http://www.vatican.va/roman_curia/congregations/cfaith/documents/rc_con_cfaith_doc_28051992_communionis-notio_en. html (accessed March 1, 2005).

Robles, Frances. 'Cuba's "Ladies in White" Wins Prestigious Prize', 2005, http://www. cubanet.org/CNews/y05/oct05/28e1.htm (accessed March 1, 2010).

Smith, Brian H. 'Religion and Politics: A New Look Through an Old Prism'. In *Politics, Society and Democracy*, ed. H.E. Chehabi and A. Stepan, 74–87. Boulder, CO: Westview Press, 1995.

Smith, Christian. 'Correcting a Curious Neglect, or Bringing Religion Back In'. In *Disruptive Religion: The Force of Faith in Social-Movement Activism*, ed. C. Smith, 1–28. New York: Routledge Press, 1996.

Smith, Donald Eugene. *Religion and Political Development*. Boston, MA: Little, Brown and Company, 1970.

Stepan, Alfred. 'Religion, Democracy, and the "Twin Tolerations"'. *Journal of Democracy* 11, no. 4 (2000): 37–57.

Steinberg, Niki, and Daniel Wilkinson, 'The Heroes of Cuba'. *New York Review of Books* LVII, no. 9 (May 27, 2010): 20–3.

Sullivan, Kevin. 'Cuba: Anti-Castro Forces Mount Petition Drive'. *The Washington Post*, April 28, 2002, A24.

Szajkowski, Bogdan. *Next to God...Poland: Politics and Religion in Contemporary Poland*. New York: St. Martin's Press, 1983.

Tamayo, Juan O. 'Pope Likens Cuba Trip to Fateful Poland Visit'. *Miami Herald*, January 29, 1998, 1A.

Treto, Raúl Gómez. *The Church and Socialism in Cuba*, trans. Phillip Berryman. Maryknoll: Orbis Books, 1988.

Thomas, Daniel C. *The Helsinki Effect: International Norms, Human Rights, and the Demise of Communism*. Princeton, NJ: Princeton University Press, 2001.

US Department of State's Bureau of Democracy, Human Rights and Labor, '2005 Annual Report on International Religious Freedom', 2005, http://www.state.gov/g/drl/rls/irf/2005/ (accessed November 1, 2006).

Valdés, Nelson P. 'The Varela Project and the Clash Within the Catholic Church in Cuba'. *Progreso Weekly*, August 1, 2002, http://www.progresoweekly.com/RPW_Archives/RPWeekly080102/neighborsValdesVarelaProject080102.htm (accessed May 19, 2004).

Werlau, Maria C. 'Foreign Investment in Cuba: The Limits of Commercial Engagement'. *World Affairs* 160 (Fall 1997): 51–69.

Does faith limit immorality? The politics of religion and corruption

Udi Sommer[a], Pazit Ben-Nun Bloom[b] and Gizem Arikan[c]

[a]Department of Political Science, Tel Aviv University, Tel Aviv, Israel; [b]Department of Political Science, Hebrew University, Jerusalem, Israel; [c]Department of International Relations, Yasar University, Izmir, Turkey

Critically considering scholarship relating religiosity to ethical behaviour, we contend that religion is systematically related to levels of corruption, and that the nature of this relationship is contingent on the presence of democratic institutions. In democracies, where political institutions are designed to inhibit corrupt conduct, the morality provided by religion is related to attenuated corruption. Conversely, in systems lacking democratic institutions, moral behaviour is not tantamount to staying away from corrupt ways. Accordingly, in non-democratic contexts, religion would not be associated with decreased corruption. Time-series cross-sectional analyses of aggregate data for 129 countries for 12 years, as well as individual level analyses of data from the World Values Surveys, strongly corroborate the predictions of our theory. The correlation of religion with reduced corruption is conditional on the extent to which political institutions are democratic.

Country A prides itself on its democratic form of government, but highly regulates religion. Country B is a non-democracy, but public officials are free to express their faith publicly. Which would you expect to show more government-level corruption? This is an easy question. Decades of democratic theories and corruption studies (as well as the daily news) indicate that on average non-democracies are more corrupt. However, which would you predict to have higher levels of corruption of the following two *democracies*: Country A, where religion is highly regulated, or Country C, which regulates religion only to a limited extent? The key argument in this article is that a democratic form of government conditions the effects of religion on moral behaviour. Country A-type democracies would experience less corruption than non-democracies. Yet, *ceteris paribus*, corruption levels in Country A would be higher compared to Country C, due to higher levels of religion regulation in the former. Hence, with the appropriate institutional platform, religion may be instrumental in the eradication of corruption.

Based on existing studies that show a positive relationship between religion and ethical behaviour, this article first posits that limiting religious elements in the nation's institutions leads to an increase in the prevalence of corrupt behaviour. However, we also contend that the institutional context is crucial. It moderates the effect of religious cues on corruption. In a democratic environment, corruption is viewed as unethical and inappropriate. In such a context, the effect of religion, which is to increase the kind of behaviour that is perceived as ethical, would translate into decreased corruption. In the absence of a democratic infrastructure, behaving morally does not necessarily connote staying away from corrupt ways. Hence, we expect religion to interact with democratic institutions such that in the absence of democratic institutions, the limiting effect of religious freedom on corruption would wane.

Using cross-national time-series data from 129 countries, collected between 1990 and 2002, we show that freedom of religion (measured as the lack of religious regulation and religious discrimination towards minorities) contributes to decreasing corruption, and that this beneficial effect of freedom of religion is contingent on a democratic environment. Further, our argument rests on the assumption that for religious cues to reduce corruption, the public must internalize democratic values and perceive corruption as being destructive to a democratic form of government. To test this individual-level component of our theory, we conduct individual level analyses with data from the fifth wave of the World Values Surveys. The individual-level analyses indicate that holding democratic values boosts the effect of religiousness on attitudes towards corruption.

Explaining corruption

Corruption is the use of government powers by government officials for illegitimate private gain.[1] By far the most widely examined antecedent of corruption in the political science literature is institutional design. This is true particularly insofar as those institutions increase competition.[2] One aspect of institutional design that instigates healthy competition and thus also affects corruption is the clarity with which accountability may be assigned. Through their effects on the clarity of governmental responsibility, political institutions influence the level of corruption.[3]

The types of institutions whose effects on corruption have been examined are varied. The size of the government is one key institutional predictor of corruption.[4] How accountability is formally enforced[5] and the electoral rules[6] also affect corruption.[7] The constitutional structure may also lead to corruption, with more centralized constitutions (for example, unitary as opposed to federal systems) decreasing the likelihood of corruption[8] and with district magnitude also having an effect.[9] Further, legal reforms,[10] the type of party system,[11] and the institutional organization of the public sector[12] influence corruption as well, together with a range of additional economic and institutional variables.[13]

On the other hand, some scholars have gone beyond the scholarship that emphasizes the institutional antecedents for corruption. For example, while Uslaner acknowledges the role of poor policy choices in increasing corruption his main emphasis is on the economic or social sources of corruption.[14] According to Uslaner, inequality works its way through low interpersonal trust to increase corrupt conduct. In addition to social capital and trust, cultural value orientations have also been suggested as important factors underlying corruption. For instance, Hofstede's individualism and Schwartz's autonomy and egalitarianism dimensions were positively related to non-corruption and the rule of law.[15] Cultural values that legitimize the use of power and the exploitation of others (for example, Hofstede's power distance and Schwartz's hierarchy dimension) have been associated with more corruption.[16] Conversely, trust has been regarded as a key factor in promoting good governance, as it facilitates collective action, which is key for limiting corruption.[17]

Most pertinent to our investigation, some research has considered the role of specific religious beliefs in promoting or deterring corruption.[18] Following Weber's perspective on the values and beliefs embedded in Protestant religion, most of these studies have posited that religion could play a role in either reducing or increasing corruption, depending on the values and belief systems dominant in the particular denomination. Protestantism is usually associated with lower levels of corruption because it promotes the values of individualism and is less hierarchical and authoritarian than other religions.[19] On the other hand, Confucian or Islamic societies are more collectivist and hierarchical[20] and therefore are associated with more corruption. Putnam[21] and Landes[22] have argued that Catholic religion has historically had an adverse effect on good governance, hence increasing corruption because it promotes 'vertical bonds of authority'.[23] What is more, Catholicism has historically acquired a culture of intolerance and closed-mindedness that has retarded development.[24] According to Landes, as intolerance is present in Islam as well, Muslim societies tend to be more susceptible to corruption. Finally, some scholars have argued that corruption is the result of social norms and exists in cultures where loyalty to clan trumps loyalty to the state.[25]

In this article, we attempt to go beyond existing arguments concerning the effect of religious values on good governance. First, we seek to emphasize the role of religion in general in affecting corruption, rather than the teachings of specific denominations. This is one key advance upon extant literature – we go beyond religious identity as a basis for determining the influence of religion on corruption. Second, we are interested in the role of religious elements in the state's institutions. We contend that the ability to freely exercise religion by the masses as well as by public employees in state institutions (for example, observing religious practices, engaging in various public religious activities, freedom to display religious symbols) deters corruption, as long as corruption is viewed as an immoral behaviour in the specific political setting. Therefore, crucially important for the theoretical framework developed below is the interaction between institutions and religion; the effect of religious worldviews on corruption is contingent on the institutional platform in place. Whether the polity is a consolidated democracy would influence the extent to which the use of government powers for private gain is legitimate. Consequently, only in a democratic environment would religious elements in the political institutions reduce corruption. In a departure to some of the literature cited above, we contend that, regardless of its specific beliefs and teachings, *any* religion has the potential to promote ethical and moral behaviour. For this to happen, though, the state must provide an environment in which religious views can be expressed and practiced freely and the political system should be democratic.

Religion and moral behaviour

Religion provides a language of ethics, as it serves as a constant reminder of what is considered good and evil. As such, religion may be translated into political virtuousness and integrity. Indeed, studies show that individual level religiosity is usually connected to ethical political behaviour. For example, an analysis of data from more than 30 countries shows higher levels of tax morale among religious participants.[26] Along the same lines, there is also a vast literature connecting religiosity to philanthropy and charity.[27]

An emerging body of experimental literature suggests that moral conduct is promoted in an environment with religious elements. In fact, current studies argue and demonstrate that subtle and even subliminal religious cues in the environment can boost ethical behaviour among both the devout and the secular. Mazar, Amir, and Ariely argue that religious cues increase attention to moral standards, notwithstanding how devout one is.[28] The amplified attention to one's moral compass, in turn, increases the tendency to act in accordance with these moral standards.

Presenting participants with religious concepts promotes moral behaviour,[29] the punishment of unfair behaviour,[30] and pro-social behaviour.[31] What is more, religious cues were found to increase one's ethical standards; a recent experimental study shows that mere exposure to religious concepts significantly decreases the likelihood of cheating in a difficult task[32] and increases ethical behaviour more generally.[33] To explain why exposure to religious content increases ethical behaviour, some argue that religious cues increase the accessibility of thoughts about a supernatural watcher[34] or about the moral behaviour of religious figures.[35]

Applying these findings to the realm of politics, religious cues in the political environment may boost the standards of honesty among decision-makers. The morally purifying effect of religion in Mazar, Amir, and Ariely is not contingent on a person's religiosity[36]; simply knowing that the Ten Commandments are about moral rules proved to be sufficient to increase attention to moral standards in individuals. This, in turn, increased the likelihood of behaviour consistent with these standards. In sum, it is not just the religiosity of decision-makers that affects their moral behaviour. Rather, it is the presence of religious cues in the institutional environment in which they operate that would have this effect. We first argue, therefore, that the presence of religious cues in state institutions will work to increase moral behaviour on the part of decision-makers. Therefore, corruption should decline with the salience and presence of religion in state institutions. Conversely, restrictions on the freedom to express religious beliefs or practice religion may hinder the positive effect of religiosity on reducing corrupt behaviour. Therefore, regulation of religion by the state is expected to be associated with higher levels of corruption:

> H1: Higher levels of religious regulation should be associated with increased corruption.

While religious priming has a robust effect on pro-social behaviour in some contexts, religion has a darker side too. The political science literature has long documented religion as connected to prejudice and political intolerance.[37] While most of these works are concerned with the effect of individual religious beliefs, the effect of religion–state relationship on religious tolerance, religious freedom, and human rights records is also revealed in some aggregated cross-national analyses. For instance, state regulation of religious activity[38] as well as legislation of religion into law and state support for one or more religions[39] are found to increase discrimination against minority religions and worsen a state's level of human rights practice.

Similarly, experimental work indicates that religion may activate anti-social behaviour towards out-groups[40] and increase support for suicide attacks against the out-group.[41] Thus, for religion to be associated with reduced corruption, it should increase self-transcendence (rather than in-group favouritism and out-group resentment). For that matter, the political environment should not only provide freedom to express religious worldviews, engage in religious activities, and display religious symbols, but also allow for religious pluralism. When the state discriminates against certain religious groups, we do not expect religion to motivate ethical behaviour. Therefore, religious discrimination is expected to be correlated with increased levels of corruption in a country:

> H2: Higher levels of religious discrimination should be associated with increased corruption.

Religion and corruption: the moderating role of democracy

While we hypothesize that religious cues in general have the potential to reduce corruption by increasing accessibility to one's moral standards, we also posit that the effect of religion on corruption is dependent on the institutional environment within which the individual is located. For religious cues to reduce corruption, public servants have to see their ethics as relevant to their work. Increased attention to one's moral compass brought about by religious cues should reduce corruption only to the extent that such behaviour is perceived by the individual as normatively wrong. This would be a function of how democratic one's context is.[42]

One of our key arguments is that democratic institutions have an indirect effect on reducing corrupt behaviour via their effect on the relationship between religion and corruption. In a democratic system, corruption is perceived as an immoral act. In consolidated democracies where checks and balances function, elements crucial for deterring corruption such as an independent judiciary, a political culture, and free media that stress integrity are all in place. In addition, public opinion is prone to concern with post-materialistic needs of self-actualization, quality of life, and self-expression, which underlie anti-corruption pressures.[43] Put together, these characteristics of democracies make clear that the use of government powers for private gain is unethical and normatively wrong. Thus, in such an environment, activation of moral standards through religious cues is expected to reduce the likelihood of corruption. Conversely, in an institutional context where corruption is not viewed as morally wrong, religious cues that activate one's moral compass are not expected to decrease corruption. In a political environment where corruption is not viewed as categorically wrong, religious cues cannot be expected to hold it back.

H3: Democratic governance moderates the relationship between religious freedom and corruption such that higher levels of democracy are expected to strengthen the effect of religion on reduced corruption, while lower levels of democracy would attenuate the effect of religion on corruption.

Apart from the interactive effect, it is generally expected that democratic conditions depress corruption. First, knowing that their conduct is subject to scrutiny constrains officials to loyally carry out their duty.[44] A democratic form of government increases the likelihood of institutionalized penalty, which in turn shapes the cost-benefit analysis of elites. In addition to its effects via political institutions, democracy also moulds the political culture and the prevailing values, affecting both the public's tolerance for corruption and the elite's belief system.

H4: Democracies will show lower levels of corruption.

Finally, we control for variables traditionally associated with corruption. These include history as a British colony,[45] gross domestic product (GDP), openness to trade, and globalization. We also control for the size of different religious groups in the nation.

Data and methods

We test our core hypotheses concerning the effect of religious freedoms on corruption using cross-sectional time-series data collected between 1990 and 2002. The time period under study is dictated more by the data than theoretical constraints. While data on other variables are widely available from many sources, time-series data for religious freedom measures (such as religious regulation and discrimination towards minorities) is compiled by Religion and the State (RAS) Project and is currently only available for the period between 1990 and 2002.

Data for the dependent variable, *Level of Corruption*, are taken from International Country Risk Guide's Political Risk Ratings. The scale is 0 to 1, with values closer to 1 indicating a political system with higher levels of corruption. The Political Risk Ratings are taken from the Political Risk Services (PRS) data available for purchase from the PRS group, a research group focused on political risk analysis, whose ratings are used extensively in academic work.[46] This type of data is the most appropriate for the time-series aspect of the empirical tests conducted here. As Thompson and Shah suggest, those indicators suggesting limited variance over time (for example, Transparency International's index) are not adequate to gauge temporal change because of the measurement strategy used to compile them.[47]

Data for the predictors are taken from several sources. Data on state activity in the area of religion come from the Religion and State (RAS) project as mentioned above. This is a university-based project that includes a set of measures used to systematically gauge the intersection between government and religion. Three independent variables are used based on the RAS data.[48] *Religious Regulation* is the first of these and addresses whether the state regulates either all religions or the majority religion. The measure combines specific types of religious restrictions that a government may place on the majority religion, or on all religions, including but not limited to restrictions on religious political parties, formal religious organizations, restrictions on public observance of religious practices, and public religious speech. *Religious Discrimination against Minorities* is the second outcome variable that measures the extent of religious freedom, and ranges from 0 (no restrictions on minorities) to 48 (minorities are prohibited or sharply restricted from public observance of religious services, building and maintaining places of worship, are forced to observe religious laws of other groups, their religious organizations are restricted, religious education restricted, there is arrest or harassment of religious figures, restrictions on the ability to make materials necessary for religious rites, restrictions on ability to write, disseminate, or publish religious material, restrictions on observance of religious laws concerning personal status, forced conversions, restrictions on proselytizing, and requirement for the minority religions to register in order to be legal or receive special tax status).[49] To facilitate interpretation by allowing a comparison of effect sizes, both variables are recoded to vary between 0 and 1. Higher values were coded to indicate higher levels of regulation and discrimination.

To measure *Democratic Conditions*, we utilize the Freedom House/Polity measure, which transforms the average of Freedom House and Polity scales to one that varies between 0 (least democratic) and 10 (most democratic) and imputes the values where data on Polity is missing by regressing Polity on the average.[50] In addition, we control for variables traditionally associated with corruption. *Globalization Scale* is the weighted average of three variables: social globalization, economic globalization, and political globalization.[51] The *Social Globalization* measure includes three categories of indicators: personal contacts (for example, telephone traffic and tourism), information flows (for example, number of internet users), and cultural proximity (for example, trade books and number of IKEA warehouses per capita). *Economic Globalization* is measured by restrictions on trade and capital such as tariff rates, and by actual flows of trade and investments. The index of *Political Globalization* is measured by the number of embassies and high commissions in a country, the number of memberships the country has in international organizations, participation in UN peace-keeping missions, and the number of international treaties signed since 1945. Predictors for *Percent From Religious Denomination* reflect the share of each of those denominations in the population (RAS dataset). GDP per capita in constant US dollars at base year 2000 was used as a proxy for levels of modernization. Missing data were imputed using the CIA World Fact Book.[52] *Postcommunism* is a dummy variable coded 1 if the country has a communist legacy.

We use time-series cross-sectional data, listing all states in the abovementioned datasets for which data were available for the period 1990–2002. We employ a generalized estimating equation (GEE) model.[53] A marginal approach, such as the GEE, is appropriate in this case since we are interested in the variables that influence corruption.[54] We employ a GEE model with first-order autoregressive component. We use robust standard errors clustered on the nation.

Results

What is the relation between religion and corruption? Table 1 presents the results of the cross-national time-series portion of the analysis. Model I examines the effects of religious regulation and religious discrimination against minorities, controlling for the effects of other independent variables. In Model II we add controls for the dominance of a range of religious denominations in the nation. The results of these models provide strong empirical support for Hypotheses 1 to 4.

Model I lends support to both H1 and H2. We find that as freedom of religion increases (that is, as religious regulation and discrimination against minorities decrease), corruption declines. Thus, all else being equal, nations that regulate religion more tend to have higher levels of corruption. In addition, religious discrimination also boosts corruption. In countries where the rights and freedoms of minority religions are not respected, corrupt behaviour tends to increase. Next, we find evidence that more democratic states are less corrupt than less democratic nations on average, which lends support to H4. In addition, control variables show that economic development measured as GDP per capita has the effect of deterring corruption, and that former British colonies suffer from corruption to a greater extent than countries not formerly under British rule. While this result is contrary to theoretical claims that link the tradition of British civil service to lower levels of corruption,[55] at the same time, it is in line with some recent evidence that does not find a significant effect of British colonial heritage on levels of corruption.[56]

Model I provides strong empirical support for the argument that the fewer the religious cues within state institutions – captured as an increased regulation of the religious activities of majority and minority religions as well as attempts to prevent

Table 1. The effect of state-level religion on corruption.

	Model I	Model II
Religious regulation	0.223 (0.099)**	0.196 (0.101)**
Religious discrimination	0.271 (0.078)***	0.256 (0.072)***
Democratic conditions	−0.366 (0.200)*	−0.358 (0.211)*
GDP in real $s – logged	−0.065 (0.012)***	−0.062 (0.013)***
British colony	0.048 (0.027)*	0.081 (0.032)**
Post communism	0.040 (0.029)	0.009 (0.033)
Globalization	−0.023 (0.073)	−0.024 (0.077)
% Catholics	−	0.001 (0.000)
% Orthodox	−	0.000 (0.001)
% Protestant	−	−0.002 (0.001)***
% Muslim	−	−0.000 (0.000)
% Buddhist	−	−0.001 (0.001)
% Hindu	−	0.008 (0.004)**
% Jewish	−	−0.024 (0.054)
% Confucians	−	−0.014 (0.006)**
% Sikhs	−	−0.007 (0.013)
% Bahais	−	−0.061 (0.054)
Constant	1.028*** (0.091)	1.026 (0.092)***
N	1566	1566
N of groups	129	129
Observations per group	Min 4; Average 12.1; Max 13	Min 4; Average 12.1; Max 13
Wald χ^2	$\chi^2(7) = 114.82$ Prob $> \chi^2 = 0.000$	$\chi^2(17) = 382.67$ Prob $> \chi^2 = 0.000$

Notes: Table entries are unstandardized coefficients with standard errors in parentheses. *$P < 0.10$, **$P < 0.05$, ***$P < 0.01$.

minority religions from freely exercising their religions – the stronger the deterring effect on moral behaviour, thus increasing corruption.

In Model II, we also control for the percentage of adherents to major religious traditions. The key results in Model I still hold when controlling for the effect of religious denominations, thus showing that the findings are robust to model specification and the addition of further control variables. We also find that, in general, levels of corruption are not necessarily affected by the presence of the adherents of specific religious traditions. The coefficients for percent of religious adherents are usually not statistically significant with the exception of Protestants and Hindus. The results show that as the percentage of Protestants in a nation increases, corruption is likely to decrease. This result is in line with historical debates and previous empirical evidence concerning the effect of Protestant values on deterring corruption. On the other hand, we do not find support for the argument that Islam or Catholicism are related to more corruption because such religions promote hierarchy and collectivist values that may have the effect of encouraging corrupt behaviour. In sum, religious traditions in a country do not have consistent effects on levels of corruption.

In order to test our argument concerning the moderating role of levels of democracy on religious freedom and corruption (H3), we added two interaction terms to Model II: level of democracy x religious regulation and level of democracy x religious discrimination towards minorities, of them only the former returned statistical significance, and it is depicted in Figure 1. The predicted level of corruption is calculated given changing levels of democratic conditions for religious freedom. The thick gray line in the panel represents established democracies, the darker gray line represents the conditions in developing democracies and the narrow black line indicates the effect of religious freedom in non-democracies. The coefficients of each of the lines and their corresponding confidence intervals are presented in Appendix Table A1.

As Figure 1 indicates, freedom of religion has a negative effect on corruption in democratic countries: as regulation increases, all else being equal, corruption is bound to increase. However, this effect is reversed in non-democracies, where freedom of religion slightly increases corruption. This result confirms our hypothesis that the effect of religious freedom on decreasing corruption is conditional on being a consolidated democracy.

We also test whether economic development and modernization, which are associated with democratization, likewise condition the effect of religious freedom on decreasing corruption. To this end, we again rerun Model II, this time adding the interaction of two religious freedom variables with GDP per capita (as proxies for development and modernization). Figure 2 shows the statistically significant interaction terms. On the x-axis in each of the panels is religion, with 1

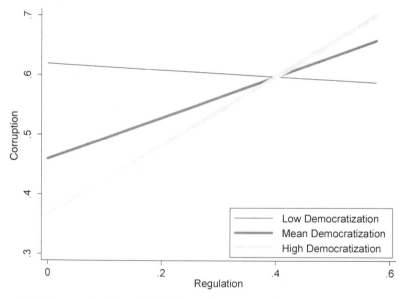

Figure 1. The interactive effect of religiosity and democratization on corruption

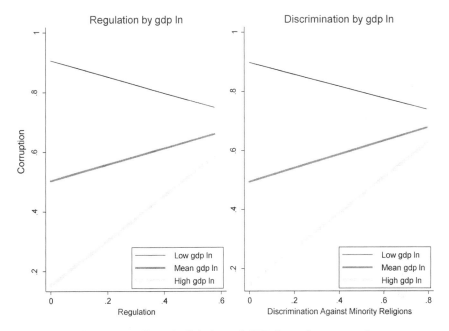

Figure 2. The interactive effect of religiosity and GDP (logged) on corruption

being no freedom of religion (highest regulation, highest discrimination). Regulation is at the left-hand panel, and discrimination to its right. The thick gray line in each panel represents the most affluent countries, the darker gray line represents the mean GDP and the narrow black line indicates the effect of religion in poor countries. The coefficients of each of the lines and their corresponding confidence intervals are presented in Appendix Table A1.

As hypothesized, freedom of religion has a negative effect on corruption in affluent countries; as regulation and discrimination increase, there will be more corruption. However, as Figure 1 indicates, this effect is reversed in poor countries, where freedom of religion does not affect, or even increases, corruption.

Therefore, both Figure 1 and Figure 2 lend strong support to H3. Since our conditional hypothesis assumes that the positive effect of religious freedoms on corruption rests on a public that internalizes democratic values, we also provide below some supporting evidence using analysis of individual-level data.

Supporting analysis: individual-level models

For religious cues to reduce corruption, the public has to consider religion as tied to ethical behaviour and good governance. We contend that, in a democratic country, corruption is perceived as an immoral act. But this should be relevant only to the extent that a person internalizes the democratic values. As a person internalizes democratic values, s/he is more likely to view corruption as a threat to democracy. Therefore, we expect democratic values to condition the effect of religious cues on how corrupt behaviour is perceived. We therefore hypothesize that the effect of religiosity on corrupt behaviour is contingent on whether the individual supports a democratic form of government or not. To directly test the mechanism through which religiosity and corruption may be related at the individual level, we use data from the latest wave of the World Values Surveys, which were conducted in 57 countries during 2005. Due to missing items, some countries were not included in the analysis. As a result, the final analysis includes observations from 36 countries. Random intercept multilevel modelling is used to account for the hierarchical nature of the data.[57]

The dependent variable is an additive scale of four variables on the justifiability of the following actions: 'Claiming government benefits to which you are not entitled', 'Avoiding a fare on public transportation', 'Cheating on taxes if you have a chance', and 'Someone accepting a bribe in the course of their duties'. The items are measured as a Likert scale from 1 (never justifiable) to 10 (always justifiable). The scale reliability coefficient of the items, measured by Cronbach's alpha is 0.79. The final measure is coded to vary between 0 to 1, where higher values indicate a tendency to justify corrupt behaviour.

As for the predictors, religiosity is measured using three variables. The first variable is a self-assessed religiosity variable. This is a dummy variable coded 1 if the respondent considers herself a religious person, and 0 otherwise. Although far from being ideal, we still include this variable in our analysis. The second is the importance of God in the respondent's life, measured on a Likert scale from 1 (not important) to 10 (very important). Finally, we also include the frequency of church attendance. These variables are recoded to vary between 0 and 1. We also control for respondents' religious denomination.[58] Finally, we control for age, level of education, income, gender, ideological orientation, national pride, trust, satisfaction with household income, and confidence in institutions. All these variables, with the exception of age, are normalized to vary between 0 and 1.

The results in Table 2 largely support the hypotheses that while both religiosity and democratic attitudes are crucial to the justifiability of corruption, support for democratic institutions bolsters the positive effect of religiosity on deterring corrupt behaviour. In Model I, we find that both the importance of God in a respondent's life and attendance at religious services decrease the justifiability of corruption. Support for democracy is significantly and negatively related to justification of corrupt behaviour. Indeed, support for democracy has the strongest effect on support for corrupt behaviour. Model II in Table 2 considers the interaction of self-assessed religiosity and support for democracy on justifiability of corruption. Although the coefficient of religiosity in this model is positive, the interaction effect is negative and statistically significant, indicating that, all else being equal, for a religious person, the marginal effect of supporting democracy on justifiability of corruption is -0.121. Similar results emerge when we consider the interactive effects of the importance of God and frequency of attendance at religious services. In both Models III and IV, the coefficients of importance of God

Table 2. Religiosity, democratic attitudes, and justifiability of corruption: individual-level supporting analysis.

	Model I	Model II	Model III	Model IV
Within-level effects				
Religious person	−0.001 (0.003)	0.013 (0.008)*	−0.001 (0.003)	−0.001 (0.003)
Importance of God	−0.021 (0.005)***	−0.020 (0.005)***	0.000 (0.011)	−0.020 (0.005)***
Religious attendance	−0.014 (0.004)**	−0.014 (0.004)**	−0.014 (0.004)**	0.008 (0.010)
Endorsing democracy	−0.127 (0.005)***	−0.113 (0.009)***	−0.107 (0.011)***	−0.113 (0.008)***
Religious x Endorse dem.	—	−0.021 (0.010)**	—	—
Imp. God x Endorse dem.	—	—	−0.028 (0.014)**	—
Rel. attendance x Endorse dem.	—	—	—	−0.031 (0.013)**
Buddhist	0.008 (0.007)	0.008 (0.007)	0.008 (0.007)	0.008 (0.007)
Catholic	0.010 (0.004)**	0.010 (0.004)**	0.010 (0.004)**	0.010 (0.004)**
Hindu	0.003 (0.012)	0.003 (0.012)	0.003 (0.012)	0.003 (0.012)
Independent/other	−0.003 (0.006)	−0.003 (0.006)	−0.003 (0.006)	−0.003 (0.006)
Jewish	0.035 (0.023)	0.035 (0.023)	0.035 (0.023)	0.035 (0.023)
Muslim	−0.007 (0.008)	−0.007 (0.008)	−0.007 (0.008)	−0.007 (0.008)
Orthodox	0.030 (0.008)***	0.030 (0.008)***	0.030 (0.008)***	0.030 (0.008)***
Protestant	−0.006 (0.004)	−0.005 (0.004)	−0.005 (0.004)	−0.005 (0.004)
Evangelical	0.003 (0.006)	0.003 (0.006)	0.003 (0.006)	0.003 (0.006)
National pride	−0.056 (0.005)***	−0.056 (0.005)***	−0.056 (0.005)***	−0.056 (0.005)***
Trust	0.007 (0.003)**	0.007 (0.003)**	0.007 (0.003)**	0.007 (0.003)**
Confidence in institutions	0.009 (0.006)	0.009 (0.006)	0.009 (0.006)	0.009 (0.006)
Satisfaction with financial situation	−0.016 (0.005)**	−0.016 (0.005)**	−0.016 (0.005)**	−0.016 (0.005)**
Ideology	0.018 (0.005)***	0.018 (0.005)***	0.018 (0.005)***	0.018 (0.005)***
Age	−0.002 (0.000)***	−0.002 (0.000)***	−0.002 (0.000)***	−0.002 (0.000)***
Low education	0.028 (0.003)***	0.028 (0.003)***	0.028 (0.003)***	0.028 (0.003)***
Middle education	0.006 (0.003)**	0.006 (0.003)**	0.007 (0.003)***	0.007 (0.003)***
Income	0.021 (0.005)***	0.021 (0.005)***	0.021 (0.005)***	0.021 (0.005)***
Male	0.011 (0.002)***	0.011 (0.002)***	0.011 (0.002)***	0.011 (0.002)***

(*Continued*)

Table 2. Continued.

	Model I	Model II	Model III	Model IV
Intercept	0.336 (0.013)***	0.326 (0.014)***	0.321 (0.015)***	0.325 (0.014)***
Variance components				
Country level constant	0.063 (0.008)***	0.063 (0.008)***	0.063 (0.008)***	0.063 (0.008)***
Individual level constant	0.176 (0.001)***	0.176 (0.001)***	0.176 (0.001)***	0.176 (0.001)***
N (level 1)	27398	27398	27398	27398
N (level 2)	36	36	36	36
Wald chi-sq.	1521.55	1525.88	1525.91	1527.70
Prob > chi-sq.	0.000	0.000	0.000	0.000
−2x LL	−17361.58	−17365.66	−17365.69	−17367.38

Notes: Table entries are unstandardized coefficients with standard errors in parentheses. *P <0.10, **P < 0.05, ***P < 0.01.

and attendance at religious services are positive, but, again, the interaction effects are negative and statistically significant – higher support for democracy bolsters the positive effect religiosity has on deterring corrupt behaviour. Once religious belief and religious social behaviour are taken into account, specific religious beliefs do not necessarily have a substantive effect on corrupt behaviour. We systematically find that Catholic and Orthodox identifications tend to increase justifiability of corruption, but, with the exception of these, the rest of the denominations do not have a statistically significant effect on support for corrupt behaviour.

Discussion and conclusions

For years, religion has been largely ignored in the study of politics. Yet, as political occurrences worldwide indicate, religion plays an important role in many aspects of social and political life. This article contributes to the extant literature by showing that religion can be a source of good governance. The presence of religious cues in state institutions systematically decreases levels of corruption. This effect, however, is conditional on the institutional framework in place. In a democratic context, corruption is viewed as unethical and inappropriate. The effect of freedom of religion, which is to increase the type of behaviour that is perceived as ethical, would in this context translate into a reduction in corrupt behaviour. Conversely, in a non-democratic context, behaving morally does not always mean staying away from corruption. Where political corruption is not viewed as an unethical behaviour, religious cues are unlikely to suppress it.

We tested the interactive effect of democratic institutions and religion on corruption with two independent sets of data at two levels of analysis, and found robust support. At the macro level, analysis of data from 129 nations over a period of 12 years indicates that the positive effect of religious freedom on limiting corruption is conditional on the level of democracy in a country. Further, our hypothesis rests on the notion that the positive effect of religion on reducing corruption depends on the extent to which the individual internalizes democratic values. Accordingly, we also conducted an individual-level analysis using data from the latest wave of the World Values Surveys. The results provide strong empirical support for our contention that, for religious cues to have a beneficial effect on non-corrupt behaviour, the public should be supportive of democratic norms promoting good governance.

This work makes several significant contributions to the literature. At the level of theory, we combine institutional and political-psychological approaches to study the antecedents of corruption. We posit that religious cues in the context of the political apparatus would affect decision-makers to act morally. Yet, acting morally would depend on the institutional context. In a democracy, being morally virtuous would mean avoiding corruption. At the empirical level, while important lessons about ways to limit corruption are gleaned from institutional analysis, this work sheds new light on the topic. We demonstrate empirically how the psychological effects of religion and the institutional environment interact to influence corruption.

This work offers some important observations and empirical predictions to be further developed and tested in future work. The combination of insights from political-psychological scholarship on the one hand and institutional scholarship on the other provides a theoretical framework that is not only more nuanced, but also offers considerably more explanatory power. The psychological effects are contingent on the institutional context, and the institutional consequences are a function of certain mental processes. This would be a fertile theoretical framework not only for the study of religion and corruption, but also for the examination of a host of other political phenomena, traditionally studied discretely using either theories from the political-psychological realm or accounts from the world of political institutions.

Finally, the conclusions of the analyses presented here are pertinent to the work of scholars as well as to leaders – religious and otherwise. Religion is playing an increasingly larger role in politics worldwide; religious movements in the Middle East are gaining power, some of the political violence in Europe has religious overtones, and some of the key ongoing conflicts, both between nations and within them, are related to religion. Yet, as the findings of this study illustrate, some of the implications of religion within the political realm may in fact be positive. At least as far as corruption is concerned, the effects of religion on politics are conditional on the institutional framework in place. Religion as such does not have the power to purge the political system of corruption. Yet, with the appropriate institutional platform, religion may be instrumental in the eradication of corruption.

Notes

1. Peters and Welch, 'Political Corruption in America'.
2. Nas, Price, and Webber, 'A Policy-oriented Theory of Corruption'; Meier and Holbrook, '"I Seen My Opportunities and I Took 'Em": Political Corruption in the American States'; Lederman, Loayza, and Soares, 'Accountability and Corruption: Political Institutions Matter'; Alt and Lassen, 'The Political Economy of Institutions and Corruption in American States'; Kunicova and Rose-Ackerman, 'Electoral Rules as Constraints on Corruption'.
3. Powell and Whitten, 'A Cross-national Analysis of Economic Voting'; Tavits, 'Clarity of Responsibility and Corruption'.
4. Golden, 'Electoral Connections'.
5. Heilbrunn, 'Oil and Water? Elite Politicians and Corruption in France'; Tavits, 'Clarity of Responsibility and Corruption'.
6. Persson, Tabellini, and Trebbi, 'Electoral Rules and Corruption'.
7. Chang, 'Electoral Incentives for Political Corruption under Open-List Proportional Representation'.
8. Gerring and Thacker, 'Political Institutions and Corruption'.
9. Chang and Golden, 'Electoral Systems, District Magnitude and Corruption'.
10. Cox and Kousser, 'Turnout and Rural Corruption'.
11. Davis, Camp, and Coleman, 'The Influence of Party Systems on Citizens' Perceptions of Corruption and Electoral Response in Latin America'.
12. Gillespie and Okruhlik, 'The Political Dimension of Corruption Cleanups'.
13. For instance, economic structure and population density (Banerjee, 'A Theory of Misgovernance'; Herbst, *States and Power in Africa*), colonial legacy (Treisman, 'The

Causes of Corruption'), the independence of the media (Peters and Welch, 'The Effects of Charges of Corruption on Voting Behavior in Congressional Elections'; Giglioli, 'Political Corruption and the Media') and levels of globalization and international integration (Sandholtz and Gray, 'International Integration and National Corruption'; Sandholtz and Koetzle, 'Accounting for Corruption') have also been noted as influencing such violation of norms of public service.

14. Uslaner, *Corruption, Inequality, and the Rule of Law.*
15. Basabe and Ros, 'Cultural Dimensions and Social Behavior Correlates'.
16. Licht, Goldschmidt, and Schwartz, 'Culture Rules', 665.
17. La Porta et al., 'Trust in Large Organizations'; Putnam, *Making Democracy Work*; Uslaner, 'Trust and Corruption'.
18. Putnam, *Making Democracy Work*; Treisman, 'The Causes of Corruption'; Landes, *The Wealth and Poverty of Nations*; La Porta et al., 'The Quality of Government'; Lipset and Lenz, 'Corruption, Culture and Markets'; Paldam, 'Corruption and Religion'; Basabe and Ros, 'Cultural Dimensions and Social Behavior Correlates'; Licht, Goldschmidt, and Schwartz, 'Culture Rules'.
19. For example, Licht, Goldschmidt, and Schwartz, 'Culture Rules'.
20. Basabe and Ros, 'Cultural Dimensions and Social Behavior Correlates'.
21. Putnam, *Making Democracy Work.*
22. Landes, *The Wealth and Poverty of Nations.*
23. Putnam, *Making Democracy Work*, 107.
24. Landes, *The Wealth and Poverty of Nations.*
25. Banfield, *The Moral Basis of a Backward Society*; Wraith and Simkins, *Corruption in Developing Countries*; Heidenheimer, *Political Corruption.*
26. Torgler, 'The Importance of Faith: Tax Morale and Religiosity'.
27. For example, Hoge and Yang, 'Determinants of Religious Giving in American Denominations'; Forbes and Zampelli, 'Religious Giving by Individuals'; Brooks, 'Religious Faith and Charitable Giving'; Chang, 'Religious Giving, Non-religious Giving, and After-life Consumption'.
28. Mazar, Amir, and Ariely, 'The Dishonesty of Honest People'.
29. Fishbach, Friedman, and Kruglanski, 'Leading Us Not Unto Temptation'; Randolph-Seng and Nielsen, 'Honesty: One Effect of Primed Religious Representation'.
30. McKay et al., 'Wrath of God'.
31. Shariff and Norenzayan, 'God is Watching You'; Pichon, Boccato, and Saroglou, 'Nonconscious Influences of Religion on Prosociality'.
32. Randolph-Seng and Nielson, 'Honesty: One Effect of Primed Religious Representation'.
33. Mazar, Amir, and Ariely, 'The Dishonesty of Honest People'.
34. Shariff and Norenzayan, 'God is Watching You'.
35. Randolph-Seng and Nielsen, 'Honesty: One Effect of Primed Religious Representation'.
36. Mazar, Amir, and Ariely, 'The Dishonesty of Honest People'.
37. Adorno et al., *The Authoritarian Personality*; Gibson, 'The Political Consequences of Intolerance'; Hunsberger, 'Religion and Prejudice'; Karpov, 'Religiosity and Tolerance in the United States and Poland'. These effects are a result of religion's ability to enhance commitment to coalitional identities and strongly differentiate between in- and out-group interests (Atran, 'Genesis of Suicide Terrorism'; Irons, 'Religion as a Hard-To-Fake Sign of Commitment'; Choi and Bowles, 'The Coevolution of Parochial Altruism and War').
38. Grim and Finke, *The Price of Freedom Denied.*
39. Fox, *A World Survey of Religion and the State*; Fox, 'State Religious Exclusivity and Human Rights'.

40. Johnson, Rowatt, and LaBouff, 'Priming Christian Religious Concepts Increases Racial Prejudice'.

41. Ginges, Hansen, and Norenzayan, 'Religion and Support for Suicide Attacks'.

42. Thus, religiosity may enhance altruistic or morally oriented behaviour that may be viewed normatively as negative by an outsider, such as in-group favouritism and out-group prejudice (on parochial altruism see Choi and Bowles, 'The Coevolution of Parochial Altruism and War'). A typical example that the effect of religion depends on what is viewed as moral in some context is the case of suicide bombing. Such behaviour can be seen as altruistic in some political and social context, and categorically immoral in some other context (see Ginges, Hansen, and Norenzayan, 'Religion and Support for Suicide Attacks', for the positive relationship between religious primes and approval of suicide attacks).

43. Inglehart, 'Post-Materialism in an Environment of Insecurity'; Abramson and Inglehart, *Value Change in Global Perspective*.

44. Bentham, 'Essay on Political Tactics'; Mill, *Considerations on Representative Government*.

45. It has been suggested that the British passed on the powerful norm of compliance with established procedures as opposed to personal authority (Treisman, 'The Causes of Corruption'). As a result, this better civil service code is expected to be associated with lower levels of corruption (although this expectation was challenged by some scholars, see for example Pellegrini and Gerlagh, 'Causes of Corruption'), while no similar theory applies to other former colonies. We thus control solely for being a former British colony. In fact, addition of a French colony dummy does not lead to any substantive change in results, and shows a statistically insiginficant coefficient.

46. See details on methods used in data collection and use in academic work on the PRS website at http://www.prsgroup.com. Data were purchased on the website in January 2011.

47. Thompson and Shah, 'Transparency International's Corruption Perceptions Index'.

48. Data were taken from the RAS website in October 2010 – http://www.thearda.com/ras/.

49. For a more detailed review of the measures, see Fox, *A World Survey of Religion and the State*, chapter 3.

50. See Hadenius and Teorell, 'Cultural and Economic Prerequisites of Democracy', for the advantages of this measure.

51. Dreher, 'Does Globalization Affect Growth?'; Dreher et al., *Measuring Globalization*.

52. Gleditsch, 'Expanded Trade and GDP Data'.

53. Zorn, 'Generalized Estimating Equation Models for Correlated Data'.

54. Ibid., 475.

55. Treisman, 'The Causes of Corruption'.

56. See, for example, Pellegrini and Gerlagh, 'Causes of Corruption'.

57. See Steenbergen and Jones, 'Modeling Multilevel Data Structures'.

58. The classification of religious denominations used in the analysis is based on Ben-Nun Bloom and Arikan, 'A Two-edged Sword'.

Notes on contributors

Udi Sommer is assistant professor at the political science department at Tel Aviv University. He specializes in the analysis of political institutions. Sommer's scholarship has appeared or is forthcoming in publications such as *Comparative Political Studies, Rationality and Society, Judicature* and *Justice System Journal*. Sommer is a recipient of the Marie Curie Grant, the Fulbright Doctoral Fellowship and a grant from the American National Science Foundation.

Pazit Ben-Nun Bloom is Assistant Professor in the Department of Political Science at the Hebrew University of Jerusalem, Israel. Her research examines the role of morality, religiosity and values in political behaviour.

Gizem Arikan is Assistant Professor in the Department of International Relations at Yasar University, Izmir, Turkey. Her research focuses on the effect of political culture and values on public opinion and policy. She also conducts research on religiosity and attitudes towards democracy.

Bibliography

Abramson, P.R., and R. Inglehart. *Value Change in Global Perspective*. Ann Arbor, MI: University of Michigan Press, 1995.

Adorno, T.W., E. Frenkel-Brunswik, D.J. Levinson, and R.N. Sanford. *The Authoritarian Personality*. New York: Harper and Row, 1950.

Alt, J.E., and D.D. Lassen. 'The Political Economy of Institutions and Corruption in American States'. *Journal of Theoretical Politics* 15, no. 3 (2003): 341–65.

Atran, S. 'Genesis of Suicide Terrorism'. *Science* 299 (2003): 1534–9.

Banerjee, A. 'A Theory of Misgovernance'. *Quarterly Journal of Economics* 112 (1997): 1289–332.

Banfield, E.C. *The Moral Basis of a Backward Society*. New York: Free Press, 1958.

Basabe, N., and M. Ros. 'Cultural Dimensions and Social Behavior Correlates: Individualism-Collectivism and Power Distance'. *Revue Internationale de Psychologie Sociale* 1, no. 1 (2005): 189–225.

Ben-Nun Bloom, P., and G. Arikan. 'A Two-edged Sword: The Differential Effect of Religious Belief and Religious Social Context on Attitudes towards Democracy'. *Political Behavior* (forthcoming 2012).

Bentham, J. 'Essay on Political Tactics'. In *The Works of Jeremy Bentham*, ed. John Browning, 310–17. Edinburgh: William Tait, 1839.

Brooks A.C. 'Religious Faith and Charitable Giving'. *Policy Review* 121 (2003): 39–48.

Chang, E.C.C. 'Electoral Incentives for Political Corruption under Open-List Proportional Representation'. *The Journal of Politics* 67, no. 3 (2005): 716–30.

Chang, E.C.C., and M.A. Golden. 'Electoral Systems, District Magnitude and Corruption'. *British Journal of Political Science* 37, no. 1 (2007): 115–37.

Chang W.C. 'Religious Giving, Non-religious Giving, and After-life Consumption'. *Topics in Economic Analysis and Policy* 5, no. 1 (2005): 13.

Choi, J., and S. Bowles. 'The Coevolution of Parochial Altruism and War'. *Science* 318 (2007): 636–40.

Cox, G.W., and J.M. Kousser. 'Turnout and Rural Corruption: New York as a Test Case'. *American Journal of Political Science* 25, no. 4 (1981): 646–63.

Davis, C.L., R. Ai Camp, and K.M. Coleman. 'The Influence of Party Systems on Citizens' Perceptions of Corruption and Electoral Response in Latin America'. *Comparative Political Studies* 37, no. 6 (2004): 677–703.

Dreher, A. 'Does Globalization Affect Growth? Evidence from a New Index of Globalization'. *Applied Economics* 38, no. 10 (2006): 1091–110.

Dreher, A., N. Gaston, P. Martens, and W.J.M. Martens. *Measuring Globalization: Gauging its Consequences*. New York: Springer, 2008.

Fishbach, A., R.S. Friedman, and A.W. Kruglanski. 'Leading Us Not Unto Temptation: Momentary Allurements Elicit Overriding Goal Activation'. *Journal of Personality and Social Psychology* 84 (2003): 296–309.

Forbes, K.F., and E.M. Zampelli. 'Religious Giving by Individuals: A Cross Denominational Study'. *The American Journal of Economics and Sociology* 56, no. 1 (1997): 17–30.

Fox, J. *A World Survey of Religion and the State*. Cambridge: Cambridge University Press, 2008.

Fox, J. 'State Religious Exclusivity and Human Rights'. *Political Studies* 56, no. 4 (2008): 928–48.

Gerring, J., and S.C. Thacker. 'Political Institutions and Corruption: The Role of Unitarism and Parliamentarism'. *British Journal of Political Science* 34, no. 2 (2004): 295–330.

Gibson J.L. 'The Political Consequences of Intolerance: Cultural Conformity and Political Freedom'. *American Political Science Review* 86 (1992): 338–56.

Giglioli, P.P. 'Political Corruption and the Media: The Tangentopoli Affair'. *International Social Science Journal* 48 (1996): 381–94.

Gillespie K., and G. Okruhlik. 'The Political Dimension of Corruption Cleanups: A Framework for Analysis'. *Comparative Politics* 24 (1991): 77–95.

Ginges, J., I. Hansen, and A. Norenzayan. 'Religion and Support for Suicide Attacks'. *Psychological Science* 20 (2009): 224–30.

Gleditsch, K.S. 'Expanded Trade and GDP Data'. *Journal of Conflict Resolution* 46 (2002): 712–24.

Golden, M.A. 'Electoral Connections: The Effects of the Personal Vote on Political Patronage, Bureaucracy and Legislation in Postwar Italy'. *British Journal of Political Science* 33, no. 2 (2003): 189–212.

Grim, Brian J., and Roger Finke. *The Price of Freedom Denied: Religious Persecution and Conflict in the Twenty-First Century*. Cambridge: Cambridge University Press, 2011.

Hadenius A., and Jan Teorell. 'Cultural and Economic Prerequisites of Democracy: Reassessing Recent Evidence'. *Studies in Comparative International Development* 39 (2005): 87–106.

Heidenheimer, A.J. *Political Corruption: Readings in Comparative Analysis*. New Brunswick, NJ: Transaction Books, 1970.

Heilbrunn, J.R. 'Oil and Water? Elite Politicians and Corruption in France'. *Comparative Politics* 37, no. 3 (2005): 277–96.

Herbst, J. *States and Power in Africa: Comparative Lessons in Authority and Control*. Princeton, NJ: Princeton University Press, 2000.

Hoge, D.R., and F. Yang. 'Determinants of Religious Giving in American Denominations: Data from Two Nationwide Surveys'. *Review of Religious Research* 36 (1994): 123–48.

Hunsberger, Bruce. 'Religion and Prejudice: The Role of Religious Fundamentalism, Quest, and Right-wing Authoritarianism'. *Journal of Social Issues* 51 (1995): 113–29.

Inglehart, R. 'Post-Materialism in an Environment of Insecurity'. *The American Political Science Review* 75, no. 4 (1981): 880–990.

Irons, W. 'Religion as a Hard-To-Fake Sign of Commitment'. In *Evolution and the Capacity for Commitment*, ed. R. Nesse, 292–309. New York: Russell Sage Foundation, 2001.

Johnson, M.K., W.C. Rowatt, and J. LaBouff. 'Priming Christian Religious Concepts Increases Racial Prejudice'. *Social Psychological and Personality Science* 1, no. 2 (2010): 119–26.

Karpov, V. 'Religiosity and Tolerance in the United States and Poland'. *Journal for the Scientific Study of Religion* 41, no. 2 (2002): 267–88.

Kunicova, J., and S. Rose-Ackerman. 'Electoral Rules as Constraints on Corruption'. *British Journal of Political Science* 35, no. 4 (2005): 573–606.

La Porta, R., F. Lopez-de-Silanes, A. Shleifer, and R.W. Vishnv. 'The Quality of Government'. *Journal of Law, Economics and Organization* 15, no. 1 (1999): 222–79.

La Porta, R., F. Lopez-De-Silanes, A. Shleifer, and R.W. Vishny. 'Trust in Large Organizations'. *American Economic Review Papers and Proceedings* 87 (1997): 333–8.

Landes, D. *The Wealth and Poverty of Nations*. New York: W.W. Norton, 1998.

Lederman, D, M. Loayza, and R. Soares. 'Accountability and Corruption: Political Institutions Matter'. *World Bank Working Paper No. 2708*. Washington DC: World Bank, 2001.

Licht, A., C. Goldschmidt, and S. Schwartz. 'Culture Rules: The Foundations of the Rule of Law and Other Norms of Governance'. *Journal of Comparative Economics* 35 (2007): 659–88.

Lipset, S.M., and G.S. Lenz. 'Corruption, Culture and Markets'. In *Culture Matters: How Values Shape Human Progress*, ed. L.E. Harrison and S.P. Huntington, 112–24. New York: Basic Books, 2000.

Mazar, N., O. Amir, and D. Ariely. 'The Dishonesty of Honest People: A Theory of Self-Concept Maintenance'. *Journal of Marketing Research* 45, no. 6 (2008): 633–44.

McKay, R., C. Efferson, H. Whitehouse, and E. Fehr. 'Wrath of God: Religious Primes and Punishment'. *Proceedings of the Royal Society Series B – Biological Sciences* 278, no. 1713 (2011): 1858–63.

Meier, K.J., and T.M. Holbrook. '"I Seen My Opportunities and I Took 'Em": Political Corruption in the American States'. *The Journal of Politics* 54, no. 1 (1992): 135–55.

Mill, J.S. *Considerations on Representative Government*. South Bend: Gateway, 1962.

Nas, T.F., A.C. Price, and C.S. Weber. 'A Policy-oriented Theory of Corruption'. *The American Political Science Review* 80, no. 1 (1986): 107–19.

Paldam, M. 'Corruption and Religion: Adding to the Economic Model'. *Kyklos* 54, nos 2–3 (2001): 383–413.

Pellegrini, R., and R. Gerlagh. 'Causes of Corruption: A Survey of Cross-country Analyses and Extended Results'. *Economics of Governance* 9 (2008): 245–63.

Persson, T., G. Tabellini, and F. Trebbi. 'Electoral Rules and Corruption'. *NBER Working Paper No. 8154*. Cambridge, MA: NBER, 2001.

Peters, J.G., and S. Welch. 'The Effects of Charges of Corruption on Voting Behavior in Congressional Elections'. *The American Political Science Review* 74, no. 3 (1980): 697–708.

Peters, J.G., and S. Welch. 'Political Corruption in America: A Search for Definitions and a Theory or If Political Corruption is in the Mainstream of American Politics Why is it not in the Mainstream of American Politics Research?'. *The American Political Science Review* 72, no. 3 (1978): 974–84.

Pichon, I., G. Boccato, and V. Saroglou. 'Nonconscious Influences of Religion on Prosociality: A Priming Study'. *European Journal of Social Psychology* 37, no. 5 (2007): 1032–45.

Powell, B.G., and G.D. Whitten. 'A Cross-national Analysis of Economic Voting: Taking Account of the Political Context'. *American Journal of Political Science* 37, no. 2 (1993): 391–414.

Putnam, R. *Making Democracy Work: Civic Traditions in Modern Italy*. Princeton, NJ: Princeton University Press, 1993.

Randolph-Seng, B., and M.E. Nielsen. 'Honesty: One Effect of Primed Religious Representation'. *International Journal for the Psychology of Religion* 17 (2007): 303–15.

Sandholtz, W., and M. Gray. 'International Integration and National Corruption'. *International Organization* 57, no. 4 (2003): 761–800.

Sandholtz, W., and W. Koetzle. 'Accounting for Corruption: Economic Structure, Democracy, and Trade'. *International Studies Quarterly* 44, no. 1 (2000): 31–50.

Shariff, A.F., and A. Norenzayan. 'God is Watching You: Supernatural Agent Concepts Increase Prosocial Behavior in an Anonymous Economic Game'. *Psychological Science* 18 (2007): 803–9.

Steenbergen, M., and B. Jones. 'Modeling Multilevel Data Structures'. *American Journal of Political Science* 46, no. 1 (2002): 218–37.

Tavits, M. 'Clarity of Responsibility and Corruption'. *American Journal of Political Science* 51, no. 1 (2007): 218–29.

Thompson, T., and A. Shah. 'Transparency International's Corruption Perceptions Index: Whose Perceptions Are They Anyway?', 2005, http://siteresources.worldbank.org/PSGLP/Resources/ShahThompsonTransparencyinternationalCPI.pdf (accessed March 1, 2011).

Torgler, B. 'The Importance of Faith: Tax Morale and Religiosity'. *Journal of Economic Behavior and Organization* 61 (2006): 81–109.

Treisman, D.S. 'The Causes of Corruption: A Cross-national Study'. *Journal of Public Economics* 76 (2000): 399–457.

Uslaner, E. *Corruption, Inequality, and the Rule of Law: The Bulging Pocket Makes the Easy Life*. New York: Cambridge University Press, 2008.

Uslaner, E. 'Trust and Corruption'. In *The New Institutional Economics of Corruption – Norms, Trust, and Reciprocity*, ed. J.G. Lambsdorff, M. Schramm, and M. Taube, 76–92. London: Routledge, 2004.

Wraith, R.E., and E. Simkins. *Corruption in Developing Countries*. London: Allen and Unwin, 1963.

Zorn, C.J.W. 'Generalized Estimating Equation Models for Correlated Data: A Review With Applications'. *American Journal of Political Science* 45, no. 2 (2001): 479–90.

Appendix

Table A1. Simple effects of the interactions in Figures 1 and 2.

		Coefficient	Std. error	Z	CI 95%		CI 90%	
					Lower	Upper	Lower	Upper
Regulation	Democratization low	-0.229	0.220	-1.04	-0.660	0.203	-0.591	0.133
	Democratization medium	0.334	0.299	1.12	-0.251	0.920	-0.157	0.826
	Democratization high	1.060	0.530	2.00	0.022	2.098	0.189	1.931
	GDP low	-0.301	0.161	-1.87	-0.617	0.014	-0.566	-0.036
	GDP medium	0.154	0.241	0.64	-0.317	0.626	-0.241	0.550
	GDP high	0.948	0.504	1.88	-0.040	1.937	0.119	1.778
Discrimination	GDP low	0.186	0.363	0.51	-0.527	0.898	-0.412	0.783
	GDP medium	0.027	0.190	0.14	-0.346	0.399	-0.286	0.339
	GDP high	1.002	0.379	2.64	0.259	1.744	0.379	1.625

Notes: Table entries are coefficients, standard errors, Z value and confidence intervals for the effect of regulation/discrimination when democratization/GDP is at the lowest 20%, between 40–60%, and highest 20%.

Political Islam in the Mediterranean: the view from democratization studies

Frédéric Volpi

School of International Relations, University of St. Andrews, St. Andrews, KY16 9AX, Scotland

Contemporary perceptions of, and responses to, the growth of political Islam on the southern shores of the Mediterranean are still heavily influenced by traditional orientalist views on 'Islam' and by realist notions of regional security. This situation contributes to the formation of predominantly state-centric responses to what is perceived to be a monolithic Islamist threat. The issues of democratization and democracy promotion are downplayed in the face of security concerns. When addressed, liberal-inspired views of democracy and civil society are nonetheless problematically deployed in a social and political context that does not duplicate well the conditions met in previous 'waves' of successful democratization elsewhere. The prospects for democratization are linked to a situation where moderate Islamist movements are expected to endorse liberal-democratic values – albeit reluctantly and by default – and where state-imposed constraints on political liberalization can only slow down the process of implementation of electoral democracy. Far too little attention is paid to the alternative forms of participation that are devised locally by Islamists, as well as to the relevance of standard electoral processes in the context of refined authoritarian systems.

Introduction: influences on the study of democratization in the Middle East and North Africa (MENA)

Over the last few decades, the issue of the absence of recognizable forms of liberal democracy in most Muslim-majority countries has been at the centre of much debate in both political science and foreign policy. In the preceding decades, political Islam was not deemed to be a research topic worthy of much social science inquiry and was seen as something better left to orientalist scholars with regional interests. The most emblematic Islamic political movement of the twentieth century, the Muslim Brotherhood, hardly featured on the political science landscape until the 1960s.[1] In practice, political science studies on Islamic movements, when they existed, received little attention before the 1979 Iranian revolution. Then, in the space of two decades, political Islam moved from being viewed as an anachronism to being considered one of the leading features of political life and institutional change in the region.[2] From the mid-1980s onward, there has been an exponential growth of two comparatively new bodies of literature attempting to explain political change in the Muslim world: democratization studies and studies of Islamism. These two types of expertise met after the end of the cold war in the so-called 'third wave' of democratization, when many believed that authoritarian regimes worldwide would quickly disappear to be replaced by Western-style, liberal democracies.[3]

Due to the largely disappointing results of democratization in most Muslim-majority polities, and in particular in the Middle East and North Africa, scholars and policy-makers have concentrated their attention on what might cause the continuing absence of substantial democratic reforms in those parts of the world.[4] Repeatedly, the most conspicuous answers to the lack of 'progress', liberalism, and democracy in Muslim polities have been that it is a consequence of the intrinsically regressive and authoritarian precepts of Islam as a system of belief(s) and social organization, and/or a result of the political and socio-economic backwardness of these countries. These issues became a global concern in the post-9/11 period when the radical edge of political Islam began to present itself as a new international security challenge for the dominant state actors.

At about the same time, many analyses of democratization began to shift the grounds of their inquiries toward more empirical methods of political assessment. They refocused their attention to practical dilemmas about political Islamization and democratization, rather than meta-questions about Islam and democracy.[5] These analyses became concerned with the issue of the practical role played by Islamist movements as institutional actors for political mobilization, and not with the more diffuse cultural and religious underpinnings of social identification. In the years of the 'war on terror', democracy and democracy promotion were reaffirmed in connection with the dominant institutions and practices of 'really existing' liberal democracies. Serious considerations on what might constitute viable, democratic alternatives to this prevailing model receded into the background.

In the following, I analyse the above mentioned trends in order to highlight the internal dynamics of the study of democratization in Muslim polities, particularly those on the southern shores of the Mediterranean, and how this is relayed into the field of policy-making. In the first section, I look at the heritage of orientalism and its role in constructing Islam and, later, political Islam as unitary objects of analysis in the region. In the second section, I examine the 'realist' legacy of the Cold War, as a power-focused, state-centric set of narratives, and its influence on the growth of democratization studies from the mid-1980s onwards. In the third section, I assess the debates on civil society that are prevalent in the 'third wave' of democratization and outline how this idea (and ideal) is deployed in connection to political Islam in MENA polities. In the fourth section, I detail the mechanisms that are commonly invoked to explain how and why democratization is currently caught up in a 'grey zone' in the Muslim world, and particularly on the southern shores of the Mediterranean.

Legacies of orientalism

It is instructive first to approach the issue of political Islam and democracy in the Muslim context from an orientalist perspective. By orientalism, I mean an approach to Islam that tries to build a comprehensive and systematic picture of an Islamic civilization, with its own logic and system of values.[6] Admittedly, this Islamic narrative is being analysed and explained through the lenses of western concepts and methodologies. Yet, as long as these concepts and methods are presented as rational universals, orientalist accounts have no particular difficulty in making their case. They are firmly in the lineage of the positivist social sciences of the nineteenth century and have a clear, realist epistemology. There is an object out there called 'Islam', or the 'Muslims', which can be the object of systematic study; and the task of orientalist scholarship is precisely to contribute, little by little, to providing the grand picture of the internal workings of this phenomenon or society.

As both critiques and proponents of this scholarship have argued repeatedly, there is little doubt that traditional orientalists had (and in some cases have) a sophisticated knowledge of many aspects of the fields that they studied. Indeed, in the early days of social science investigation of the Middle East, it seemed difficult to move beyond orientalism. Manfred Halpern's approach in the 1960s is a clear illustration of this trend.[7] Rather than directly questioning the narratives put forward by traditional orientalists, he attempted to supplement them with more empirical analyses of political behaviour in the postcolonial states of the region. Reviewing the orientalist scholarship of the 1950s, Halpern stated unambiguously that in his view, 'it would be quite impossible for students of political modernization to do any sensible work without, for example, drawing upon the works of H.A.R. Gibb, Gustave von Grunebaum, or Wilfred Cantwell Smith'.[8] Hence, he was concerned with developing a 'new orientology', more attuned to the paradigms of modern political science and based more in quantitative methods of analyses than was previously the case. Halpern did not see a fundamental contradiction between these two approaches; rather, he envisioned a complementary relationship – one that fully appreciated the orientalist heritage. Indeed, social and political science experts in the 1960s and 1970s, from Leonard Binder to Dankwart Rustow, would mainly provide more empirically grounded elaboration of traditional, 'ex cathedra' orientalist arguments about the dynamics of the political culture of the MENA.[9]

For those authors in the political science tradition, the main legacy of orientalism has a dual philosophical and political set of implications. First, from a philosophical perspective, orientalist scholarship seeks to (re)construct a paradigmatic reading of Islam that structures the freedom of action of Muslim social and political actors; what they can or cannot do and say, what they should or should not do and say. This is contrasted to a similarly rigid account of liberal democratic principles that cannot accommodate, or be accommodated by, the Islamic tradition in some of its most fundamental characteristics. While traditional orientalism focused on religious and theological exegesis, contemporary, 'neo-orientalist' analysts concentrate instead on the politicized pronouncements of various Islamic ideologues, as well as the performative media dimension of their discourse. Second, from a political perspective, orientalist approaches are connecting these philosophical/theological interpretations directly to political practice. This perspective argues that because this is what the leaderships of Islamist movements think, this is how politics will be organized by an Islamist regime, therefore, this is what foreign policy and international alignment will be like, and so on. This (neo-)orientalist take on Islam accommodates itself well to, and is also constitutive of, a traditional realist (or neorealist) account of power construction and projection in international relations theory.

Seen from outside the region, political Islam was, for most of the Cold War, merely a dependent variable of political change. In MENA settings, where 'realist' theories of international relations appear to be quite adequate to account for external state behaviour, and where modernization theory was meant to encapsulate the direction of societal change internally. In this context, for decidedly orientalist scholars like Elie Kedourie or Bernard Lewis, the democratization debate is a non-starter, both because of the weight of the Islamic tradition and because Islamist ideologues and leaders repeatedly speak openly against the idea of democracy.[10] Such analyses emphasize the utilization of key theological resources of Islam to undermine the basic concepts of democratic organization, like popular sovereignty. As such, these approaches are attempting to frame the domestic and international politics of Muslim-majority societies in relation to a fairly unitary notion of 'national interest', defined on the basis of Islamist ideology.

For more political science-minded authors, the merging of orientalist scholarship and the study of political behaviour remains largely under-scrutinized and/or is waved away as commonsensical. Thus, in an often-consulted textbook about Middle Eastern politics from the 1970s and 1980s, James Bill and Carl Leiden could argue that 'despite all the differences that separate Middle Eastern leaders and elites, there are in the Muslim world a number of deep seated and persisting similarities in rule'.[11] They suggested that these similarities 'have existed throughout Islamic history and can be traced to the days of the Prophet Muhammad, himself the model par excellence of political leadership'. Thus Bill and Leiden could conclude that since 'millions of Muslims continue to pattern their lives after his, it is not surprising, therefore, that twentieth-century Muslim political leaders often have styles and use strategies that are very similar to those instituted by the Prophet Muhammad in Arabia some 1,400 years ago'.[12] These 'commonsense' approaches to political culture in the MENA were not, in fact, proposing an analysis of political elites and of the institutional organization of the postcolonial state in the region. Yet, there were already accounts, such as Michael Hudson's study of the legitimization crisis in the Arab world, which actually did provide this kind of detailed and careful explanation of political order (and its failures) in the region.[13] Nor did these narratives propose a more historically-construed investigation into the survival and modernization of tribal and religious modes of governance, which various studies of 'neo-*asabiyya*' processes provided.[14] Rather, what was invoked in the kind of analyses that Bill and Leiden (and many others) proposed at that time was a set of culturalist assumptions, which are at best supported by tenuous historical correlations. For example, how does the above-mentioned argument apply to secularized, modernist Middle Eastern elites, who only make perfunctory and rhetorical uses of the examples set by the Prophet? Alternatively, how is one able to specify what constitutes a specifically Islamic model of leadership: Is it to be a reference to the constitution of Medina? Is it the entire life of the Prophet himself? Does it include the time of the first few caliphs (the so-called Golden Age of Islam)? And so on.

For domestic politics, because the notion that modernization and secularization of institutions and, more generally, of social life was the preferred, developmental paradigm for Muslim polities, a comparison of these transformations with democratic developments in the 'West' was not only useful for understanding what was happening, but was, in fact, necessary to explain it. Resistance to the secularization and modernization of social and political life was deemed largely futile before the 1979 Iranian revolution. As Daniel Lerner's well-known comment indicated it appeared to be a straightforward choice between 'Mecca and mechanization'.[15] In effect, it was not even a choice at all since Lerner and many others fully anticipated that the religious glue of Muslim societies would be dissolved by modernization. Some less sanguine observers, like Abu-Lughod, noted however, that since these processes were often forcefully implemented by authoritarian regimes, a return of the repressed social and political forces, particularly Islamic ones, was likely to happen at some point and provide a corrective to this trend.[16] By and large, however, this corrective was not actually deemed to be significant enough to warrant much research and thinking on the topic at that time. It was not until well after the Iranian revolution that scholars began to consider the overstretching of the modernization/secularization theory, especially when it was applied to largely under-studied social forces in Muslim-majority countries.[17]

Ending the Cold War: democracy as a peculiar dilemma of Middle Eastern politics

At a substantive level, interpretations of political Islam remained on the whole a second order tool of analysis for most of the 1980s since the bipolar dynamics of the Cold War were viewed as the first order *explanandum* in the (greater) Middle Eastern context. In international relations, the specificities of Muslim-majority countries were for a long time subsumed under a regionalist approach to Middle East politics.[18] This area-study perspective was, in turn, structured for a long time by the dominant (neo)realist paradigms of the Cold War. Even when supplemented by a dose of neo-liberal analyses, such a 'realist' take on the Muslim world is key to understanding the evolution of the democratization debates from the mid-1980s onwards. Illustrative of this situation are the views on the 'third wave' of democratization that Samuel Huntington presents in his analysis of the Middle Eastern/Islamic democratization conundrums. From his 1984 article 'Will More Countries Become Democratic' to his 1991 book *The Third Wave*, Huntington views the spread of liberal democracy to the Middle East and the Muslim world as a problematic process, but not for conceptual reasons.[19] He does not see Islamism as providing a concrete and realistic alternative to liberal democratic institutional models for the region. He warns against a particularly difficult set of structural factors stacking up against a smooth and rapid democratization sequence in many key Muslim-majority countries. Yet, he argues that this situation only points to a quantitatively bigger problem rather than to a qualitatively different democratization dilemma.[20] Huntington's account from the 1980s (like his civilizational narrative in the 1990s) proposes some 'obvious' generalizations about Muslim politics, underpinned by orientalist scholarship, that rely on very little else than correlations; and these correlations remain to be explained since they do not constitute explanations in themselves.

This strand of thinking, as well as the tendency to merge *explanan* and *explanandum*, continues unabated after the Cold War when it comes to analysing Muslim polities. Many democratization specialists do not seriously revise their positions regarding the Muslim world and one notices instead an increased polarization between approaches to democratization in the region.[21] This polarization is informed by the debate in the sociology of religion that emphasizes the (partial) deprivatization of religion.[22] The undermining of the edifice of modernization theory that many analysts had used to frame their understanding of social and political change in the MENA, led to even more exceptionalist explanations of Muslim exceptionalism. In particular, there is a new set of more pessimistic interpretations of the prospects for liberal democratization in the Muslim world shaped by the idea of the emergence of a political order based on political Islam. In Huntington's narrative, this is illustrated by the revision of his argument about quantitative resistances into a qualitative clash of 'civilizations'.[23] In a not too dissimilar mould, Adrian Karatnycky's review of the Freedom House Survey trends in 2001 stresses that Muslim-majority societies remain the most resistant to the spread of democracy and, quoting Lewis approvingly on the paucity of the democratic lexicon in Arabic and Persian, refers back to the idea that it simply takes time and efforts for democratic principles to take root in an Islamic political culture.[24] This over-reliance on some vague notion of 'Islamic political culture' as a generic explanation provides a common thread between modernization accounts of the 1950s and 1960s, the realist analyses of the Cold War, and the post-Cold War narratives about Muslim democratic exceptionalism.[25]

Up to the end of the Cold War, such loose references to political Islam only served to buttress a state-centric narrative about Middle Eastern politics as *realpolitik* in a realist/neorealist regional order. Immediately after the collapse of the USSR and the rise of Islamic militancy in Central Asia, the notion of a 'Greater Middle East' even gained popularity as a means of bringing the new Central Asian republics within a known frame of reference. This meant that explanations emphasized traditional security practices, such as the role of military alliances with nationalist autocrats to secure oil resources and hold Islamism in check.[26] Although sometimes presented as an exception to the dominant realist paradigm, the activities of the European Union (EU), especially in relation to the Euro-Mediterranean Partnership, had difficulties in moving beyond a sophisticated realist model for politics in the region. This is due not least to the fact that the EU had difficulty conceiving what the Mediterranean should be as a region.[27] As Pace indicates in this special issue, the EU has considerable difficulties not only in turning theory into practice, but also in thinking through a coherent, conceptual approach for its multiple policy initiatives at the regional level. EU officials generally wish to emphasize a 'soft power' approach to reforming institutions and practices in the region instead of imposing some new rules of the game. Yet, they do resort to arm-twisting tactics whenever the circumstances appear to demand it (for example, in trade negotiations, in the recognition of Hamas). This 'realist' tendency has been more visible in EU policies after 9/11 as the dynamics of securitization became more prominent within both the EU zone and the Mediterranean region, especially when Islamist movements are involved, since they remain an unknown quantity for EU institutions.[28]

Fred Halliday noted how, in the post-Cold War context, the debates about political Islam in the Middle East became polarized between 'essentialist' and 'contingencist' strands of arguments.[29] Essentialists develop an argument with a strong orientalist flavour that posits that the 'fundamentals' of Islam are the reason for systemic and systematic clashes with western notions of liberal democracy. Contingencists, on the other hand, argue that, like any other religious doctrine, Islam is malleable enough to be conceptually and practically interpreted in such a way that the areas of frictions with liberal notions of democracy are minimal in the right circumstances. Such polarized views remain common mainly because analysts in each 'camp' have embarked upon rather different kinds of intellectual endeavours that cannot be unified by mere reference to the 'data'. From an international relations perspective, various neo-orientalist and neorealist approaches repeatedly try to establish a causal link between (liberal) democracy and political Islam (or Islam *tout court*) in order to show the incompatibility (or occasionally compatibility) of these two organizing principles of social and political life. Meanwhile, their post-orientalist and constructivist opponents engage with them on those same terms. For the former, the task is to construct a usable framework for constructing/representing 'national interests' from the discourse on political Islam and, therefore, to find unity in diversity. For the latter, the task is to unmask the alternative articulations of Islamic discourses and show where and when the resources of the Islamic tradition can be re-articulated synergistically with other resources, including those from the liberal democratic tradition.

These opposing perspectives parallel the disagreements in democratization studies between, on the one hand, those agency-based, transitology studies in the fashion of Guillermo O'Donnell and Phillipe Schmitter that became fashionable in the mid-1980s and, on the other hand, those slightly older, structure-based accounts of democratization that have their roots in modernization theory.[30] For essentialist-minded writers, the core characteristics of the Islamic and liberal-democratic tradition are simply too dissimilar to ever allow individuals to build a polity that would satisfy both sets of skills and expectations; no matter how much *fortuna* and *virtu* one may have. For contingencist-minded authors, given the right circumstances, individuals and groups can find interpretations of their religious principles that interact synergistically, rather than conflict with, liberal-democratic practices and institutions. Evidently, the mere possibility of a convergence does not imply that it will necessarily happen in practice. Some of the key post-orientalist narratives of the 1990s, from Kepel's *The Revenge of God* to Roy's *The Failure of Political Islam*, did in fact emphasize a sizeable chasm between the two traditions, as well as the continuing relevance of an 'Iranian model' or an 'Algerian scenario' type of Islamist takeover.[31] As ever, simply referring to the 'facts of life' in the region does not provide a way of resolving such a dilemma. Because of the limited numbers of examples and counter examples invoked in each instance, what counts as meaningful generalization and what is meant to be an exception is strongly determined by the type of explanation that the analysts want to put forward in the first instance.

Democratization in Turkey can be used as a useful illustration of how either narrative can be supported by political transformations in a polity. For analysts attributing a benign role to political Islam, the fact that the country has been governed by political parties with strong Islamist inclinations in 1996–1997 and since 2002 is a clear indication that democratization can proceed smoothly even in the presence of a substantial Islamic political discourse. Yet Turkey also proclaims its republican credentials loud and clear, and it promotes its own brand of republicanism, Kemalism, as the state ideology. On the basis of the latter aspects of the political evolution of Turkey, some authors are able to articulate developmentalist and primordialist arguments about the relationship between Islamism and modern liberal democracies. Lewis has long argued that there is a prior requirement for a radical change in frames of reference for the conduct of democratic politics, since even words such as 'citizen' and 'citizenship' had, until recently, no direct equivalent in the Arabic, Persian or Turkic languages.[32] From this perspective, the current situation in Turkey is not an example of Islamic moderation, but an illustration of the successes of political secularization. Even though one may agree with some of the historical points made by orientalist scholars, it should be noted that such a developmentalist approach is linked to the construction of an 'oriental' approach to modern liberal democracy. 'Contingencists' might reply that actual words are less important than the meanings that they acquire politically over time. Clearly, the western political lexicon has long possessed those terms, but their political meaning has been changed and recreated from the Enlightenment onwards to resonate with the new practices corresponding to the modern liberal democratic ethos.[33]

To avoid such conceptual dilemmas, some comparative studies within political science have attempted to leave semantic issues behind and simply to take into account political and social preferences in the contemporary context. From the mid-1990s onward, there has been an increasingly fashionable strand of survey-based studies that investigate the attitudes of 'Muslims' toward 'democracy' in order to assess the degree of compatibility between the two. A wide array of more or less well-designed surveys, as well as more rigorous political analyses, outline how the religious beliefs held by the citizenry in various parts of the Muslim world do not in themselves seem to preclude people from taking an interest in 'democracy'.[34] Although this approach has the advantage of avoiding the pseudo-philosophical problems that flourished in the earlier debates by focusing on what a substantial number of people actually say, it faces a different kind of definitional problem. Repeatedly the notion of democracy is taken to be not only a fixed concept, but also a self-evident one. Hence, these analyses do not particularly focus on what respondents actually mean when they use the words that are put in front of them by researchers. Rather, a very malleable notion of liberal democracy is alluded to in connection to a set of basic social and political preferences that are put forward for consideration by the surveys' respondents. Because of the very nature of data obtained, these analyses do not and cannot describe the deliberative processes that produce a substantive account of what a word such as 'democracy' actually means. The lack of characterization of these key concepts undermines the explanatory powers of the analyses, regardless of their descriptive capabilities. Clearly, 'democracy' and 'democratization' are far more fashionable political terms than they were 20 years ago. Yet the mere presence of a practical interest in democratization throughout the Muslim world today does not allow analysts to make many direct political forecasts.

Beyond the 'democratization paradigm' for political Islam in the MENA

Trying to measure 'really existing democracy' in the Muslim world has created a new set of dilemmas. Two types of related, but distinct, contemporary debates have emerged to address these new issues, as illustrated by the contributions to this volume. The first set of arguments is attuned to the development of democratization studies in the 1980s and 1990s and focuses on civic activism and the role of civil society in political transformations. The second type of debate has a longer tradition in development studies and focuses on the structural impediments to democratization, primarily from socio-economic and politico-military perspectives.

There are evidently different types of 'civil society' or 'civil sphere' in different parts of the Muslim world, but the debates have commonly been polarized between those who view the MENA region as just another setting for the kind of civil society revival that was witnessed in Latin America and in Eastern and Southern Europe, and those who emphasize the distinctiveness of the Muslim and/or MENA context. Thus, for the followers of Ernest Gellner's *Conditions of Liberty*, whatever associative life there may exist in Muslim polities, they are not of the 'right' kind and, therefore, unpropitious to the emergence of a genuine liberal democratic order.[35] By contrast, those influenced by the work of Augustus Norton and his collaborators in *Civil Society in the Middle East* emphasize the presence of a recognizably liberal civil society impulse, even when it remains the project of a small but active minority.[36] The debates to date on the practical and conceptual developments in civil society in the Muslim world remain tentatively optimistic, but proponents of a progressive 'civil society' paradigm advance their argument with extreme prudence.[37] In the cases of Latin America and Eastern Europe, there had been a tendency to let one's own normative preferences and teleological inclinations brush aside some serious inconsistencies of the process of democratic consolidation.[38] For these particular democratic transitions, such conceptual lapses appear not to have had significant consequences because the voluntarist drive of the analyses, more often than not, reflected the views of the civil society groups and political counter-elites that were on the ascendancy in those polities at that time. In most of the Muslim world, however, similar assumptions about the liberal nature of civil society and of the political counter-elite cannot be taken for granted today.

In effect, even for those scholars who do not endorse Gellner's negative assessment of the prospect for civil society in the region, the common view appears to be that civil society cannot play the role of a dominant democratization paradigm in the Muslim context in the same way that it could be invoked in the 1980s and 1990s in Latin America and Eastern Europe.[39] Only in a few specific cases is this factor being invoked as one of the main explanatory tools for democratic transition, as in Robert Hefner's analysis of the Indonesian case.[40] From this perspective there are fewer opportunities for the authoritarian elites to hand over power 'gracefully' on the model of the Latin American 'pacted' transitions because of the ideological positions of the most powerful Islamist opposition movements in the MENA countries. The situation in Southeast Asia might have been the most propitious for such a process; but elsewhere in the Muslim world, only the better-run parliamentary monarchies, like Morocco or Jordan, appear to provide the kind of exit strategy for the ruling elite that might avoid a brutal democratic transition.

Yet, as the articles on Morocco by Cavatorta and by Wegner and Pellicer-Gallardo in this special issue illustrate, even in a reforming authoritarian system, the opportunities for full democratization are dependent upon the goodwill of the monarchy. Whatever incentives a powerful regional player like the EU can devise, the limits of its effectiveness are principally dictated by the willingness of the regime to allow a degree of political pluralism. In other cases, clearly, what emboldens the determination of the ruling elite to stay in power is simply the perception that dramatic consequences would follow were they to relinquish power to the Islamist opposition, as the Algerian scenario illustrates. The contributions by Wolff and by Demmelhuber in this volume, regarding the situation in Egypt, exemplify quite well the inadequacy of EU incentives in the face of a regime that places survival and continuity at the core of its system of governance. Optimistically, one could view this situation as creating reserves of good democratic practices in civil and political society, waiting only for a weakening of authoritarian institutions in order to come out in the open and reshape domestic and regional politics.[41] A less sanguine assessment would be that not only democratic skills are being built up and refined, but also authoritarian views and practices. Hence, were a specific authoritarian system to go bust, democratic alternatives would not be the only ones available on the ground for political entrepreneurs.[42]

In many countries of the Muslim world, the limited liberal democratic civil society impulse contributes to creating an enduring situation of stalled transitions, which analysts then evaluate in connection to more structural, socio-economic, political and security factors. As Thomas Carothers points out,

> what is often thought of as an uneasy, precarious middle ground between full-fledged democracy and outright dictatorship is actually the most common political condition today of countries in the developing world and the post-communist world. It is not an exceptional category to be defined only in terms of its not being one thing or the other; it is a state of normality for many societies, for better or worse.[43]

From a functional/instrumental perspective, these pseudo-democratic systems actively produce a political order that tries to look like a liberal democracy in order to make domestic and international gains, without actually trying to become one.[44] This predicament is one of the main features of the democratization conundrums of the Muslim world, where the nature of political opposition generates an additional strain on the processes of democratic transition.

In the MENA region, three sets of structural issues appear to be particularly problematic. Because of the apparent weakness of civil society, scholars have been keen to stress the particular organization of state power in the (greater) Middle East. Analysts including Marsha Posusney and Eva Bellin emphasize the role played by the authoritarian elite, arguing that the strength of the coercive apparatus in the Arab world is the principal inhibitor of democracy change.[45] This line of argumentation is also invoked in conjunction with references to the notion of *asabiyya* (either regarding reconstructed tribes or clans, or regarding new military and technocratic cliques) as a key *explanan* in the politics of the (greater) Middle East.[46] Some commentators, like Akbar Ahmed, have even suggested that a notion of 'hyper-*asabiyya*' could also be used in order to understand the new security dynamics post-9/11.[47] On the more political (as opposed to securitarian) side of the argument, analysts including Volker Perthes and Ellen Lust-Okar stress how elites have managed to co-opt their opponents, as well as to exploit and manipulate the splits between opposition groups (especially the secular-Islamist divide), so that they can neutralize demands for democracy from the masses.[48] This trend is reinforced by the fact that, historically, the MENA countries are generally latecomers to the democratization process. Everywhere, autocrats learn from past mistakes, and the rise of more competitive forms of authoritarianism in relation to liberal democracy is a noticeable trend at the beginning of the twenty-first century. Unsurprisingly, efforts to liberalize and democratize the political system of Muslim countries in recent years have often been equivalent to the refinement of the euphemized, authoritarian skills of the ruling elite.[49] Finally, as Raymond Hinnebusch indicates, explanations focusing on structural state power find additional support for their case by incorporating a political economy perspective that shows how oil wealth in the contemporary international context reduces the necessity to liberalize politically.[50]

Rethinking democracy and its promotion

The problem that Islamic movements and parties create for common explanations of democratization on the southern shores of the Mediterranean is that their mobilizing potential challenges some basic assumptions about the relationship between contemporary forms of liberalism and democracy. For quite some time, analysts on the 'clash' side of the debate have maintained that all the discrete cases of opposition between Islamist views and 'western' liberal or democratic views are only the surface manifestations of a deeper and all-inclusive, illiberal and undemocratic worldview. This is a view that has been well conveyed to policy circles, despite its obvious problems of over-generalization. Opponents of the 'clash' primarily point out that there exists a more benign alternative, and emphasize the impact of the more 'democratic' and 'liberal' forms of political Islam.[51] Yet, what is commonly missing from these analyses are detailed considerations of what conceptual compromises are needed for a meaningful dialogue between opposition and government (both domestically and internationally). This void may help to explain, to some degree, the current lack of options for (liberal) democracy promotion at the policy level. The lack of a cogent conceptual framework for assessing the role of Islamists in the Mediterranean, and for engaging adequately with them, is stressed by most of the contributors to this special issue as one of the key flaws of the EU approach(es) to the region.

Because of this impoverished conceptual perspective, it is usually the case that any deviation from the liberal democratic model in the Muslim context is perceived to favour the emergence of what Fareed Zakaria calls 'illiberal democracies'.[52] An alternative to the illiberal democracy scenario is to talk about 'grey areas' of democracy, thereby suggesting the partial convergence of Islamist and liberal-democratic political agendas. This is a policy approach that is well developed in connection to US democracy promotion, with scholars including Nathan Brown, Amr Hamzawy and Marina Ottaway providing sophisticated analyses of these processes. For them, a key difficulty in the region is that the ethos of political and civil society needs to be reformed alongside the institutional setting.[53] Yet, their notion of convergence is generally viewed as a prelude to the full acceptance of existing liberal democratic models of governance, without much discussion of the flaws of these models. This is the kind of incrementalist scenario that is also most favoured by the EU when it comes to democracy promotion on the southern shores of the Mediterranean.

What remains understated in these analyses of the 'grey zone' is that the clarity which has been achieved in established liberal democracies is not merely a process of Rawlsian or Habermasian enlightenment, where legally backed, discursive processes ensure that an acceptable consensus on individual rights and collective duties is reached. It is also a more pragmatic assessment of the ability of political entrepreneurs to deliver material and ideological goods in an attractive and sustainable fashion. The choices of Palestinian voters regarding Fatah and Hamas in the 2006 parliamentary elections provided a clear illustration of that point. For all their merits, the above-mentioned analyses of democratization do not reflect upon the alternative political realities that Islamist movements are constructing, both ideologically and socially, and how far these models constitute locally viable and acceptable versions of 'democracy'.[54] Clearly, the construction of an alternative pro-democratic project is not a straightforward process. Charles Hirschkind's study of discursive interactions between Islamists and non-Islamists in Egypt illustrates the coercive undertone of apparently communicative dialogues.[55] In addition, as I indicated elsewhere, it may also be the case that, while Islamist players may welcome political liberalization as leading one step closer to their preferred model of democracy, once they reach the tipping point beyond which 'their' democracy is no longer compatible with the liberal-democratic standard currently promoted by the international community, then they may themselves settle for pseudo-democratic governance.[56] Yet, even when Islamists propose discourses and practices which are not opposed to liberal-democratic perspectives, the international community may still fail to recognize such an opportunity, as the EU's lack of involvement with key Islamic movements in the Mediterranean region illustrates today.[57]

Conclusion

As the postcolonial literature emphasizes, it is conceptually hazardous to equate democratization with secularization and westernization. Talal Asad stresses that modernity is a set of interlinked projects for the institutionalization of principles such as constitutionalism, moral autonomy, democracy, human rights, civil equality, industry, consumerism, a free market, and secularism.[58] This idea of modernity encapsulates what western policy-makers and public opinion usually understand by a modern democracy. In practice, democratization may entail curtailing some of the prerogatives of the demos for the benefit of a liberal constitutional ideal. The kind of democratic order that had become the norm at the end of the twentieth century proposes a democracy that is designed to place restraints on majority rule, with the view to protect very specific individual rights and civil liberties.[59] In most parts of the Muslim world, though, the process of democratic reinvention and institutionalization of 'a-liberal' Islamic practices is harnessed to the diffusion of a specific ethos that portrays them as virtuous components of a political project.

Islamist approaches blur the distinction between the public and the private, which is central to the functioning of contemporary liberal democratic institutions and introduce a more positive definition of liberty, which is couched in terms of religious law.[60] This observation does not imply that one should view a 'state versus church' power struggle as the sole, or even the main, bone of contention in Muslim politics when it comes to democratization in the region. As Alfred Stepan noted, 'the "lesson" from Western Europe, therefore, lies not in the need for a "wall of separation" between church and state, but in the constant political construction and reconstruction of the "twin tolerations".'[61] The ongoing reconfiguration of the secular-religious divide is bound to involve periods of crisis and confrontations. In this context, the bottom-up Islamic democratic construction of these ideological and institutional arrangements poses problems for traditional interpretations of democratization and democracy promotion, which are built on western, liberal perspectives.

To understand the new trends in democratization studies in the MENA region, there is a need to look beyond the functionalist explanations that currently dominate the field. The collapse of much of modernization theory, particularly in relation to secularization, which underpinned linear accounts of democratic transitions over the last two decades, has left a vacuum in the contemporary explanatory frameworks of democratization (or its lack thereof) in the Muslim world in general, and the MENA region in particular. Overall, the weakness of 'civil society'-based explanations opened the way for analyses based on structural factors, such as the role of security apparatuses and oil revenues, which form the backbone of accounts of the slow pace of political change in the region. Internationally, democratization processes continue to be viewed mainly as a dependent variable in a 'realist' geostrategic balance of power, with oil being a key *explanan*. Domestically, these processes are viewed mainly as a functional adaptation of Islamist movements to state repression and as their tactical adoption of a democratic discursive repertoire. Both sets of narratives are predicated upon a fairly static political order and fail fully to consider the process of democratization as an engine of change in domestic and international processes; hence the limited (and shrinking) interest in democracy promotion. As the historical trends in scholarship indicate, this situation is partly caused by the polarization of the debates about the direction of political change in the region. The contributors to this volume illustrate that there are many more aspects of democratization in the Mediterranean that need to be taken into consideration in order to have a more meaningful understanding of the contemporary political transformation – one that can truly inform policy-making.

Notes

1. Mitchell, *The Society of the Muslim Brothers*.
2. See for example Salamé, *Democracy without Democrats?*; Ayubi, *Political Islam*; Zubaida, *Islam, the People and the State*; Arjomand, *From Nationalism to Revolutionary Islam*.
3. See Diamond and Plattner, *The Global Resurgence of Democracy*; Esposito and Voll, *Islam and Democracy*.
4. Fish, 'Islam and Authoritarianism'; Tessler, 'Islam and Democracy in the Middle East'.
5. Eickelman and Piscatori, *Muslim Politics*.
6. For an interesting postcolonial perspective on this theme, see Sayyid, *A Fundamental Fear*.
7. Halpern, *The Politics of Social Change in the Middle East and North Africa*.
8. Halpern, 'Middle Eastern Studies', 111.
9. See Binder, *The Ideological Revolution in the Middle East*; Rustow, 'Turkey: The Modernity of Tradition'.
10. Kedourie, *Democracy and Arab Political Culture*; Lewis, *The Political Language of Islam*.
11. Bill and Leiden, *Politics in the Middle East*, 133.
12. Ibid.
13. Hudson, *Arab Politics*.
14. In the modern context *asabiyya* is a solidarity group founded on personal allegiances that derives directly or indirectly from clan-based or tribal solidarity networks and that displays a distinct 'group-spirit' or *esprit-de-corps*. See Khoury and Kostiner, *Tribes and State Formation in the Middle East*; Roy, 'Patronage and Solidarity Groups: Survival or Reformation'.
15. Lerner, *The Passing of Traditional Society in the Middle East*.
16. Abu-Lughod, 'Retreat from the Secular Path?'.
17. For an early (and not altogether committed) illustration of this trend see Binder, *Islamic Liberalism*.
18. This is despite many attempts to introduce more fully regional specialisms in the larger social science debates. See for example, Tessler, Nachtwey, and Banda, *Area Studies and Social Science*.
19. Huntington, 'Will More Countries Become Democratic'; Huntington, *The Third Wave*.
20. In his 1984 article, the only Islamic studies specialist that Huntington refers to in order to back his argument that Islamic political culture is an obstacle to democratic principles is the orientalist and political activist Daniel Pipes.
21. For a trenchant critique see Sadowski, 'The New Orientalism and the Democracy Debate'.
22. See Casanova, *Public Religions in the Modern World*.
23. Compare Huntington, 'The Clash of Civilizations?' with Huntington, *The Third Wave*.
24. Karatnycky, 'The 2001 Freedom House Survey'.
25. This is not to say that notions of 'political culture' cannot be deployed usefully in the region – particularly to provide accounts of political change that avoid various forms of socio-economic determinism. See Hudson, 'The Political Culture Approach to Arab Democratization'.
26. See Perthes, 'America's "Greater Middle East" and Europe', and compare Bilgin, 'Whose "Middle East"?'
27. See Adler et al., *The Convergence of Civilizations*; Pace, *The Politics of Regional Identity*.

28. See Emerson and Youngs, *Political Islam and European Foreign Policy.*
29. Halliday, 'The Politics of Islam'.
30. O'Donnell and Schmitter, *Transitions from Authoritarian Rule.*
31. Roy, *The Failure of Political Islam*; Kepel, *The Revenge of God.* Both Kepel and Roy would later add a corrective to their earlier narratives on the development of Islamism.
32. Lewis, *The Emergence of Modern Turkey*; Lewis, *The Political Language of Islam.*
33. On Turkey see, Yavuz, *Islamic Political Identity in Turkey.* More generally see Terence Ball, James Farr, and Russell L. Hanson, *Political Innovation and Conceptual Change.*
34. See for example the online outputs of the Pew Global Attitudes Project, http://pewglobal.org and World Values Survey, http://www.worldvaluessurvey.org. See also Tessler, 'Islam and Democracy in the Middle East'; Fattah, *Democratic Values in the Muslim World.*
35. Gellner, *Conditions of Liberty.*
36. Norton, *Civil Society in the Middle East.*
37. See Hawthorne, 'Middle Eastern Democracy'; Eickelman and Salvatore, 'The Public Sphere and Muslim Identities'.
38. O'Donnell, *Counterpoints.*
39. Yom, 'Civil Society and Democratization'.
40. Hefner, *Civil Islam.*
41. See Adler et al., *The Convergence of Civilizations.*
42. See Volpi, 'Pseudo-Democracy in the Muslim World'.
43. Carothers, *Critical Mission*, 164.
44. Diamond, 'Thinking about Hybrid Regimes', 24.
45. Posusney, 'Enduring Authoritarianism'; Bellin, 'The Robustness of Authoritarianism in the Middle East'.
46. See Roy, 'Patronage and Solidarity Groups'; Collins, 'The Political Role of Clans in Central Asia'.
47. Ahmed, *Islam under Siege.*
48. Perthes, *Arab Elites;* Lust-Okar, *Structuring Conflict in the Arab World.*
49. Brumberg, 'The Trap of Liberalized Autocracy'; Volpi, 'Algeria's Pseudo-Democratic Politics'.
50. Hinnebusch, 'Authoritarian Persistence, Democratization Theory and the Middle East'.
51. Salvatore and Eickelman, *Public Islam and the Common Good*; Esposito and Voll, *Islam and Democracy.*
52. Zakaria, *The Future of Freedom.*
53. See Brown, Hamzawy, and Ottaway, 'Islamist Movements and the Democratic Process in the Arab World'.
54. For some interesting recent works doing just that, see Yavuz, *Islamic Political Identity in Turkey*; Mahmood, *Politics of Piety.*
55. Hirschkind, 'Civic Virtue and Religious Reason'.
56. See Volpi, 'Pseudo-Democracy in the Muslim World'.
57. This situation evidently contributes to fostering of a mutual lack of recognition. See Emerson and Youngs, *Political Islam and European Foreign Policy.*
58. Asad, *Formations of the Secular.*
59. See Tully, *Strange Multiplicity.*
60. The case of Shi'a governance in Iraq might prove to be an interesting case in point. See Gleave, 'Conceptions of Authority in Iraqi Shi'ism'; Cole, 'The Ayatollahs and Democracy in Iraq'.
61. Stepan, 'Religion, Democracy and the "Twin Tolerations"', 42.

Bibliography

Abu-Lughod, Ibrahim. 'Retreat from the Secular Path? Islamic Dilemmas of Arab Politics'. *The Review of Politics* 28 (1966): 447–76.

Adler, Emanuel, Beverly Crawford, Federica Bicchi, A. Raffaella Del Sarto, eds. *The Convergence of Civilizations: Constructing a Mediterranean Region*, Toronto: University of Toronto Press, 2006.

Ahmed, Akbar. *Islam under Siege: Living Dangerously in a Post-Honor World*. Cambridge: Polity Press, 2003.

Arjomand, Said Amir, ed. *From Nationalism to Revolutionary Islam*, Albany: State University of New York Press, 1985.

Asad, Talal. *Formations of the Secular: Christianity, Islam, Modernity*. Stanford: Stanford University Press, 2003.

Ayubi, Nazih. *Political Islam: Religion and Politics in the Arab World*. London: Routledge, 1991.

Ball, Terence, James Farr, and Russell L. Hanson, eds. *Political Innovation and Conceptual Change*, Cambridge: Cambridge University Press, 1989.

Bellin, Eva. 'The Robustness of Authoritarianism in the Middle East: Exceptionalism in Comparative Perspective'. *Comparative Politics* 36 (2004): 139–57.

Bilgin, Pinar. 'Whose "Middle East"? Geopolitical Inventions and Practices of Security'. *International Relations* 18 (2004): 25–41.

Bill, James, and Leiden Carl. *Politics in the Middle East*. 2nd ed. Boston: Little, Brown, 1984.

Binder, Leonard. *The Ideological Revolution in the Middle East*. Chicago: University of Chicago Press, 1964.

Binder, Leonard. *Islamic Liberalism: A Critique of Developmental Ideologies*. Chicago: University of Chicago Press, 1988.

Brown, Nathan, Amr Hamzawy, and S. Marina Ottaway. 'Islamist Movements and the Democratic Process in the Arab World: Exploring Gray Zones'. *Carnegie Paper*, 67 March 2006.

Brumberg, Daniel. 'The Trap of Liberalized Autocracy'. *Journal of Democracy* 13 (2002): 46–68.

Carothers, Thomas. *Critical Mission: Essays on Democracy Promotion*. Washington, DC: Carnegie Endowment for International Peace, 2004.

Casanova, José. *Public Religions in the Modern World*. Chicago: University of Chicago Press, 1994.

Cole, Juan. 'The Ayatollahs and Democracy in Iraq'. *ISIM Paper* 7 (2006).

Collins, Kathleen. 'The Political Role of Clans in Central Asia'. *Comparative Politics* 35 (2003): 171–90.

Diamond, Larry. 'Thinking about Hybrid Regimes'. *Journal of Democracy* 13 (2002): 21–35.

Diamond, Larry, and Marc F. Plattner, eds. *The Global Resurgence of Democracy*, Baltimore: Johns Hopkins University Press, 1996.

Eickelman, Dale F., and Piscatori James. *Muslim Politics*. Princeton: Princeton University Press, 2004.

Eickelman, Dale F., and Salvatore Armando. 'The Public Sphere and Muslim Identities'. *Archives Européennes de Sociologie* 43 (2002): 92–115.

Emerson, Michael, and Richard Youngs, eds. *Political Islam and European Foreign Policy: Perspectives from Muslim Democrats of The Mediterranean*, Brussels: Centre for European Policy Studies, 2007.

Esposito, John L., and John O. Voll. *Islam and Democracy*. Oxford: Oxford University Press, 1996.

Fattah, Moataz A. *Democratic Values in the Muslim World*. Boulder: Lynne Rienner, 2006.

Fish, M. Steven. 'Islam and Authoritarianism'. *World Politics* 55 (2002): 4–37.

Gellner, Ernest. *Conditions of Liberty: Civil Society and its Rivals*. London: Hamish Hamilton, 1994.

Gleave, Robert. 'Conceptions of Authority in Iraqi Shi'ism'. *Theory Culture and Society* 24 (2007): 59–78.

Halliday, Fred. 'The Politics of Islam: A Second Look'. *British Journal of Political Science* 25 (1995): 399–417.

Halpern, Manfred. 'Middle Eastern Studies: A Review of the State of the Field with a Few Examples'. *World Politics* 15 (1962): 108–22.

Halpern, Manfred. *The Politics of Social Change in the Middle East and North Africa*. Princeton: Princeton University Press, 1963.

Hawthorne, Amy. 'Middle Eastern Democracy: Is Civil Society the Answer?'. *Carnegie Paper* no. 44. March (2004).

Hefner, Robert W. *Civil Islam: Muslims and Democratization in Indonesia*. Princeton: Princeton University Press, 2000.

Hinnebusch, Raymond. 'Authoritarian Persistence, Democratization Theory and the Middle East: An Overview and Critique'. *Democratization* 13 (2006): 373–95.

Hirschkind, Charles. 'Civic Virtue and Religious Reason: An Islamic Counterpublic'. *Cultural Anthropology* 16 (2001): 3–34.

Hudson, Michael C. *Arab Politics: The Search for Legitimacy*. New Haven: Yale University Press, 1977.

Hudson, Michael C. 'The Political Culture Approach to Arab Democratization: The Case for Bringing It Back, Carefully'. *Political Liberalization and Democratization in the Arab World: Theoretical Perspectives*, ed. Korany Bahgat, Rex Brynen, and Paul Noble, 61–76. Boulder: Lynne Rienner, 1995.

Huntington, Samuel P. 'The Clash of Civilizations?'. *Foreign Affairs* 72 (1993): 22–49.

Huntington, Samuel P. *The Third Wave: Democratization in the Late Twentieth Century*. Norman: University of Oklahoma Press, 1991.

Huntington, Samuel P. 'Will More Countries Become Democratic'. *Political Science Quarterly* 99 (1984): 193–218.

Karatnycky, Adrian. 'The 2001 Freedom House Survey: Muslim Countries and the Democracy Gap'. *Journal of Democracy* 13 (2002): 99–112.

Kedourie, Elie. *Democracy and Arab Political Culture*. Washington, DC: Washington Institute for Near East Policy, 1992.

Kepel, Gilles. *The Revenge of God: Resurgence of Islam, Christianity and Judaism in the Modern World*, trans. A. Braley. Cambridge: Polity Press, 1993.

Khoury, Philip S., and Joseph Kostiner, eds. *Tribes and State Formation in the Middle East*, Berkeley: University of California Press, 1990.

Lerner, Daniel. *The Passing of Traditional Society in the Middle East*. New York: Free Press, 1958.

Lewis, Bernard. *The Emergence of Modern Turkey*. Oxford: Oxford University Press, 1968.

Lewis, Bernard. *The Political Language of Islam*. Chicago: Chicago University Press, 1988.

Lust-Okar, Ellen. *Structuring Conflict in the Arab World: Incumbents, Opponents, and Institutions*. Cambridge: Cambridge University Press, 2007.

Mahmood, Saba. *Politics of Piety: The Islamic Revival and the Feminist Subject*. Princeton, NJ: Princeton University Press, 2005.

Mitchell, Richard P. *The Society of the Muslim Brothers*. Oxford: Oxford University Press, 1969.

Norton, Augustus R. *Civil Society in the Middle East*. Leiden: Brill, 1995–1996.

O'Donnell, Guillermo. *Counterpoints: Selected Essays on Authoritarianism and Democratization*. Notre Dame, IN: University of Notre Dame Press, 1999.

O'Donnell, Guillermo, and Philippe C. Schmitter. *Transitions from Authoritarian Rule: Tentative Conclusions about Uncertain Democracies.* Baltimore: Johns Hopkins University Press, 1986.

Pace, Michelle. *The Politics of Regional Identity: Meddling with the Mediterranean.* London: Routledge, 2006.

Perthes, Volker, ed. 'America's "Greater Middle East" and Europe: Key Issues for Dialogue'. *Middle East Policy* 11 (2004): 85–97.

Perthes, Volker. *Arab Elites: Negotiating the Politics of Change*, ed. Volker Perthes. Boulder, CO: Lynne Rienner, 2004.

Posusney, Marsha Pripstein. 'Enduring Authoritarianism: Middle East Lessons for Comparative Theory'. *Comparative Politics* 36 (2004): 127–38.

Roy, Olivier. *The Failure of Political Islam*, trans. C. Volk. Cambridge, MA: Harvard University Press, 1996.

Roy, Olivier. 'Patronage and Solidarity Groups: Survival or Reformation'. *Democracy Without Democrats? The Renewal of Politics in the Muslim World*, ed. G. Salamé, 270–81. London: I.B. Tauris, 1994.

Rustow, Dankwart A. 'Turkey: The Modernity of Tradition'. *Political Culture and Political Development*, ed. L.W. Pye and S. Verba, 171–98. Princeton: Princeton University Press, 1965.

Sadowski, Yahya. 'The New Orientalism and the Democracy Debate'. *Middle East Report* 183 (July–August 1993): 14–21.

Salamé, Ghassan, ed. *Democracy without Democrats? The Renewal of Politics in the Muslim World*, London: IB Tauris, 1994.

Salvatore, Armando, and Dale F. Eickelman, eds. *Public Islam and the Common Good*, Leiden: Brill, 2006.

Sayyid, B.S. *A Fundamental Fear: Eurocentrism and the Emergence of Islamism.* London: Zed Books, 2003.

Stepan, Alfred. 'Religion, Democracy and the "Twin Tolerations"'. *Journal of Democracy* 11 (2000): 37–57.

Tessler, Mark. 'Islam and Democracy in the Middle East: The Impact of Religious Orientations on Attitudes Toward Democracy in Four Arab Countries'. *Comparative Politics* 34 (2002): 337–54.

Tessler, Mark A., Jodi Nachtwey, and Anne Banda, eds. *Area Studies and Social Science: Strategies for Understanding Middle East Politics*, Bloomington: Indiana University Press, 1999.

Tully, James. *Strange Multiplicity: Constitutionalism in an Age of Diversity.* Cambridge: Cambridge University Press, 1995.

Volpi, Frédéric. 'Algeria's Pseudo-Democratic Politics: Lessons for Democratization in the Middle East'. *Democratization* 13 (2006): 442–55.

Volpi, Frédéric. 'Pseudo-Democracy in the Muslim world'. *Third World Quarterly* 25 (2004): 1061–78.

Yavuz, M. Hakan. *Islamic Political Identity in Turkey.* New York: Oxford University Press, 2003.

Yom, Sean L. 'Civil Society and Democratization'. *Middle East Review of International Affairs* 9 (2005): 14–33.

Zakaria, Fareed. *The Future of Freedom: Illiberal Democracy at Home and Abroad.* New York: WW Norton, 2003.

Zubaida, Sami. *Islam, the People and the State: Essays on Political Ideas and Movements in the Middle East.* London: Routledge, 1989.

Religion and Democratization in Africa

JEFF HAYNES

Two main issues form the focus of attention in this study. The first is the relationship of senior religious figures to the state in Africa and the role of the former in the region's democratization in the 1990s. The second is the political importance of 'popular' religions in Africa. The overall aim is to examine the relationship of religion and politics in Africa in the context of democratization, to: (1) establish the nature of the links between senior religious figures and state elites in Africa, (2) make some preliminary observations about the political nature of popular religions in the region, and (3) comment on the overall impact of religious actors on Africa's democratization.

Introduction

Africa[1] in the 1980s and 1990s experienced something it had not seen for decades: widespread popular calls for democratization, part of a wider package of demands for more and better economic and human rights. There followed regime change in a number of African countries, including Benin, Cape Verde, the Central African Republic, Ethiopia, Madagascar, Niger, São Tomé, Sierra Leone and Zambia. Elsewhere, however, authoritarian rulers demonstrated ability, at least temporarily, to stay put either by winning elections (Ghana, Burkina Faso) or by simply refusing to budge (Togo, Kenya, Zaire).

Demands for democratization had both domestic and external roots. Domestically, demands for reform reflected an awakening – or reawakening – of an often long-dormant political voice for various civil society groups, with trade-union officials, higher-education students, businesspeople, civil servants and religious – mostly Christian – figures initially leading and coordinating popular demands for reform.[2] Professional politicians later made such demands integral parts of their programmes for election. The widespread expectation was that popular efforts would force long-entrenched, often venal governments from office. Democratically elected regimes would take power, with new leaders tackling with energy, resourcefulness and

Jeff Haynes is Professor in the Department of Law, Governance and International Relations, London Metropolitan University, UK.

imagination pressing political, social and economic problems. Previously ignored political constituencies would be heard, human rights would be observed, including the precious freedom to criticize governments without fear of incarceration. A second factor was that Africa's democratization was the 'road map' for political change preferred by key external actors: western governments who provided Africa with the bulk of its foreign aid. In sum, recent demands for democratization in Africa are best explained through the interaction of domestic and international factors, with the former of most importance.

Religious figures, notably Christian leaders, added their voices to the clamour for change in Africa in the 1980s and 1990s. Leading Catholics were frequently involved in national conferences on the political way forward in a number of French-speaking countries, including Congo-Brazzaville, Togo, Mali, Niger, Gabon, Zaire (now Democratic Republic of Congo) and Chad. The outcome in Congo-Brazzaville was the democratic election of a new government, although the political situation remained tense. In Togo, Chad, Gabon and Zaire, on the other hand, such conferences did not lead, in the short term, either to new constitutions or democratically elected governments. In Zaire and Togo, led respectively by Presidents Mobutu and Eyadema, the outcome was stalemate, as opposition forces were too weak to unseat them.[3] In Chad, a Christian–Muslim polarization meant that the political situation remained volatile. In Gabon, Omar Bongo retained power for a while, despite the registration of 13 political parties and a powerful, although unsuccessful challenge, from an opposition leader, Paul Mba-Abesole (a Catholic priest) and his movement, *Le Rassemblement de Boucherons* (National Society of Woodcutters). In mostly Muslim Niger and Mali, however, new political leaders and democratically elected governments emerged. In sum, involvement of Catholic leaders in national democracy conferences reflected the fact that the Catholic Church was often one of only a few national institutions that had managed to keep a degree of corporate independence from the state.

The aim of this account is to examine the relationship of religion and politics in Africa in the context of democratization. Two main issues form its focus. The first is the relationship of senior religious figures to the state in Africa and the role of the former in the region's recent attempts to democratize. The second is to examine the political importance of 'popular' religions – that is, religions not legitimized by a close relationship between their leaders and those of the state, but instead with bottom up structures rooted in grassroots concerns. The first task is to establish the nature of the links between senior religious figures and state elites in Africa. The second is to make some preliminary observations about the political nature of popular religions in Africa and their varying relationships to democracy.

State and Religion in Comparative Perspective in Africa

In Africa as elsewhere, leaders of religious bodies – whether Christian or Muslim – are social products of the societies from which they come. As individuals, they may be theoretically and intellectually convinced of the benefits of democracy, understanding that concept in both structural (appropriate political institutions, including independent legislature and judiciary) and normative ('real', pluralistic, competition, worthwhile civic freedoms) terms. Yet they also have to go about their daily business in an environment characterized by state heavy handedness, the threat or expectation of military involvement in politics, shortages of economic resources, venality, corruption, and suspicion or worse between ethnic and/or religious groups. As a result, it seems plausible to surmise that their personal opinions regarding the theoretical desirability of democracy are often, and often necessarily, at least partially moulded by a pursuit of individualistic material concerns. In short, I am suggesting that many religious leaders in Africa will have both individual, as well as institutional, economic interests and concerns in terms, for example, of improving their church's 'market share', perhaps by seeking restrictions on their chief rivals.

Since Africa's independence from colonial rule, church and state developed mutually supportive relationships in many regional countries. The role of Christian churches vis-à-vis government in Africa, as elsewhere, is in theory a simple, and clear one, well expressed in the following:

> the limits of the state's sphere of action are set by the definition of 'temporal', that is, those activities of civilization that arise in the 'earthly' city … The church in no way limits the state's rights church and state complement one another, each by working in its proper realm.[4]

However, churches often found themselves on the horns of a dilemma: to what extent should they dare to criticize their increasingly authoritarian governments – even when they clearly abused power in ways that Christian morality would find unacceptable? Two distinct, mutually exclusive, options presented themselves: (1) to speak out and expect to be criticized by rulers for doing so, or (2) publicly keep quiet – but seek to change government policy by persuasion behind the scenes.

However, there was also a third option. As the extremely cordial relations between Catholic church leaders and the Mobutu regime in Zaire (now Democratic Republic of Congo) illustrates, it was in both the interests of both Church and state for there to be social and political stability, even if it required authoritarian rule to achieve it. The cordial relationship is well illustrated in a 1965 declaration from the then Archbishop of Kinshasa, Joseph Malula. Addressing President Mobutu personally, he stated that 'the Church recognizes your authority, because authority comes from God. We will loyally apply the laws you establish. You can count on us in your work of restoring the peace toward which all so ardently aspire'.[5] True to Malula's word, until the early 1990s, the Catholic hierarchy in Zaire was consistently unwilling to engage the regime in direct public confrontation. It was only after an unprecedented show of public displeasure – significantly involving young priests and nuns – that the Catholic hierarchy was galvanized publicly to oppose Mobutu's authoritarian rule.

It is claimed that senior Catholic figures were bought off by material inducements, quite apart from the fact that the institutional role of the Church was believed to be supportive of almost *any* temporal regime, including Mobutu's authoritarian rule. As the quotation from Malula indicates, God was believed to confer absolute authority on ruling governments. Understandably, Malula was anxious to continue the good working relationship with the state, to build on the mutually supportive arrangement which had typified the colonial period. Then, according to Schatzberg, 'occasional differences [between Catholic and colonial authorities were] minimal in comparison to the numerous issues on which church and state worked in concert'.[6]

More generally, for church leaders in Africa, silence in the face of poor and/or corrupt government following independence reflected a number of concerns: they themselves may have benefited materially from the status quo; many were inherently conservative and believed that governments, however bad, were exercising authority ordained by God, and, finally, such leaders often recognized that their church's corporate position in a country was in part dependent upon state acquiescence or support. In Zaire, as Boyle illustrates, the value of cooperation with civil authorities for church leaders 'leads (them) to employ... indirect modes of communication and influence in their relationship with society and the political regime'.[7] This is the idea of the 'two realms' of church and state, where the former may attempt to influence the latter by persuasion but has no other means at its disposal if it wishes to retain its privileged position. In other words, normally the church hierarchy can be no more than an interlocutor between state and society. As the trajectory of Mobutu's rule only too clearly showed, those who gain a reputation for outspoken criticism were very likely to find themselves incarcerated – or worse.[8] Such a position may also have been related to the fact that senior Christian figures were well treated personally by Mobutu. For example, 'Cardinal Malula lived in a mansion that the President gave him [in 1974]... in 1978 or so the President gave a Mercedes to every bishop, Protestant or Catholic'. The result was that Catholicism, in partnership with the powerful, independent Kimbanguist church, 'assumed some of the functions of an ideology in the service of the dominant class'.[9]

A further factor – apart from concerns with stability and the fears of repercussions of openly challenging regimes – is that some Christian leaders were personally closely associated with ruling regimes, sometimes to the extent of holding political appointments. For example, in Lesotho in the early 1970s, 'the post-independence government of Chief Leabua Jonathan and the National Party was predominantly Catholic in support and conservative in policy', enjoying the support of South Africa's apartheid regime.[10]

The position was similar in Togo. There, the ruling party, *Le Rassemblement du Peuple Togolais* (RPT), had a hegemonic position analagous to that of the dominant parties in Zaire and Lesotho. The Catholic church – with about a third of Togo's people – dominated spiritually. Together, Catholic and secular elites in the RPT dominated politically and spiritually, maintaining a strong grip on society.[11] A further example comes from Rwanda where, until 1985, the Catholic archbishop of Kigali was on the central committee of the single party, the *Mouvement Révolutionnaire National pour le Développment.* In addition, Bishop Matale's membership of the commission for instituting a one-party state in the 1970s in Zambia was also a clear manifestation of a close relationship between state and church.[12]

This is not to suggest that all senior Christian figures enjoy cosy relationships with ruling regimes. For example, the Catholic Archbishop of Monrovia, Michael Francis, is a strong and outspoken advocate of human rights and social justice in Liberia. Since the mid-1970s, he has consistently critiqued Liberia's socio-political and moral situation, underlining what he sees as three forms of corruption: 'social corruption' ('unjust imprisonment, detention without charge or trial, inhuman and degrading prison conditions'), 'professional corruption' (when government personnel abuse their positions to make money or 'employ individuals because they are of the same family, or tribe or are girlfriends'), and 'personal corruption' ('the all-pervasive sexual immorality of the country'). Over time, a number of Catholic priests in Liberia followed Francis's critical lead. But while he personally escaped governmental reprisals, other, more junior figures, were less fortunate, with many suffering harassment by the state's security services.[13]

Given the mutually supportive relationships between many senior church figures and states, how can we account for involvement of Christian leaders in Africa's recent democratization? Some analysts regard the leaders of the mainline (as distinct from the independent) churches as highly significant actors in this context. Leading Christians are said to have practically dragged unwilling, undemocratic governments towards the dreaded ballot box. Such figures are said to have led pro-democracy agitation not only because they were democrats personally (as a result of their Christianity), but also because their 'flocks' had collectively experienced diminishing benefits from non-democratic rule: poor government, bad economic policies, and unworkable ideological programmes.[14] In short, Africa's democratization is perceived to be a result of: (1) Christian leaders' tenacity, clear-sightedness, and lack of fear of the consequences of their actions, and (2) such figures' burning sense of outrage on behalf of their followers.

Proponents of the 'Christians as necessarily democrats' argument also point to interaction of international and domestic factors to explain how Christian leaders have been prominent in pro-democracy campaigns in several parts of the world. For example, Diamond notes how: 'religious institutions, especially the Catholic Church, have been prominent in the movements of a great many countries – notably, Brazil, Chile, El Salvador, Nicaragua, the Philippines, South Korea, Poland, Haiti, South Africa, and most recently Kenya – to oppose, denounce, frustrate and remove authoritarian regimes'.[15]

For Peel, Christian institutional independence and integrity in relation to state power is an essential facet of the post-colonial African structure of power relations.[16] Because, in the main, most expressions of the world religions tended to be identified with the main interest groups, whether ethnic or class, they were available in a diffuse form as a mediating element, relatively neutral ground, in social and political conflict. Religious institutions were therefore generally accorded respect by the political elite. Peel's argument locates both Christian and Muslim religious institutions as interlocutors between state and society, respected bodies whose leaders' own personal desires and preferences are subsumed in their concern to disinterestedly mediate between citizens and government.

In reality such institutions are usually class actors in partnership with the ruling regime. As a result, it is aberrant for official religious institutions to confront the state other than in rather formulaic fashion. Democratic initiatives may be little more than successful strategies of Gramscian-style 'passive revolution'. Leaders of mainline religions (both Christian or Muslim) often enjoy close relationships with state figures, and are often staunchly supportive of the status quo. This is because, as we have noted in the context of Christian religious leaders, such people may be bound to the state in a mutual project to maintain hegemonic domination over society. Islam illustrates this point.

It is often suggested that Muslims are less impressed by the claims of liberal democracy than Christians.[17] (However, two of seven African countries holding national democratization conferences in the early 1990s, Mali and Niger, were both strongly Muslim countries.) Islam is often regarded – especially by some Western analysts[18] – as an authoritarian, even totalitarian, religion. Islamists, in particular, are seen to try to impose their 'fundamentalist' visions on society as a putative means of purifying society via the imposition of Sharia law.

Three issues contextualize a discussion of the role of Islam in Africa. The first is that there are a number of versions of Islam extant in the region. Many Africans belong to Sufi brotherhoods; in addition, many ethnic groups, especially in West and East Africa, converted historically to Islam en masse; some of them will also be members of Sufi brotherhoods so the latter may also have an ethnic dimension. Orthodox conceptions of Islam – nearly always Sunni in Africa – are the province of the religious elite, the *ulama*, religio-legal scholars. Thus, 'Islam' in Africa is in fact a multifaceted term covering various Muslim interpretations of the faith.

Overall, Islamic Africa can be divided into three distinct categories, corresponding to extant social, cultural and historical divisions. On the one hand, there is the dominant socio-political and cultural position of Islam found in the emirates of northern Nigeria, the lamidates of northern Cameroun and the sheikdoms of northern Chad. Not only are religious and political power typically fused in the hands of a few individuals but there is also a parallel class structure.[19] On the other hand, there are the areas where Sufi brotherhoods predominate – generally in West and East Africa, and especially in Senegal, the Gambia, Niger, Mali, Guinea, Kenya and Tanzania. Moreover, in a number of African states, Muslims, fragmented by ethnic and regional concerns, are politically marginalized as a minority bloc. This is the situation in, *inter alia*, Ghana, Togo, Benin, and Côte d'Ivoire.

The second factor is that 'fundamentalist' Islam is rare, though not unknown, in Africa below the Sahara. This is because Sufi Islam, the faith of many African Muslims, is often a target for fundamentalists – found both within the *ulama* and their secular allies – because it is regarded as a primitive or degraded form of Islam which must be reformed or 'purified'. Such 'fundamentalist' interpretations of Islam are of political importance in Sudan (where it is the ruling ideology and key issue fuelling the three decades-long civil war) and in parts of northern Nigeria, where inter-religious conflict – leading to hundreds of deaths of Muslims and Christians since the early 2000s – are important political issues.

Third, there is ambivalence in the way that many Muslims regard the concept of liberal democracy itself. Many Muslims are said to oppose Western interpretations of democracy, where sovereignty is said to reside with the people, because it is seen as a secularized system negating God's own sovereignty. Members of the *ulama* will usually be strong supporters of the status quo. This is not least because it allows them to be integrally involved in the running of the affairs of Muslims in their state via control of national Muslim organizations. Thus a partnership with state-level politicians is crucial.

Religious Leaders and the State in Africa

Political leaders will seek to achieve or maintain domination over society by developing an ideology of their own legitimacy, justifying the status quo, through a pursuit of an often putative 'national unity'. Bolstering and underlying 'national unity' concerns is a hegemonic thrust, 'which drives the state and the self-proclaimed dominant social groups to seek to control and to shape civil society'.[20] Class concerns in Africa (best understood in a Weberian rather than an analytically less useful Marxist sense) coalesce, dominate and override all other issues, except sometimes ethnic or religious divisions. Political officials may well also be merchants and businessmen: how else to make a profit in a context of very low remuneration for employment? Because religious actors suffer from the same economic problems, many attempt to use their network of contacts to advance their own self-interest.[21] This gives them an important political role in the same way that businesspeople strive to develop contacts with political elites for mutual benefit.

Those who make it to the top of ecclesiastical structures are selectively recruited according to educational attainments and perhaps ethnic affinity, gradually socialized into the world of the political and social elites, and rewarded materially for their loyalty to the struggle to maintain the political status quo. What develops is a kind of hegemonic coalition with secular political leaders. The central goal is the maintenance of order and the continuation of elite control. Only occasionally do circumstances combine in such a way that religious leaders find themselves propelled to the forefront of popular opposition to state power. The issue here is the relationship of the sacred to the temporal. In the Christian conception the two realms of God and Caesar provide a theoretically clear-cut division of labour: religion is concerned with the spiritual aspects of life, politics with material concerns. Thus, for Christian leaders there is no necessity to propound on clearly political issues – provided the latter do not have a serious impact upon the ability of the former to practise and propound their religion. That is, provided that religious worship is tolerated by the state, democracy per se may not be that relevant to an expression of a belief in God or in the ability of the followers of a religion to worship. Many religious professionals no doubt believe that during their daily work they are performing God's mission to the best of their ability. They will be as certain as possible that their vocation is morally right, essential for the spiritual health of their countrymen and women. There may be occasional doubts of a 'technical' character, that is, they 'may doubt whether a particular action in operation or contemplation most expediently advances (their) larger life purposes, about which (they) can never be in any doubt'.[22] In other words, religious leaders' long-term goals are clear, short-term expediency while regrettable is not of profound importance in relation to the overriding objective of achieving God's kingdom on earth. The implication is that God ultimately ordains all political and social authority on earth.

The separation of church and state in western Europe created a pattern of behaviour in which Christianity's division from secular power became increasingly central to sovereignty issues. The sacred–temporal division was bolstered by the rise of secular nation states in the nineteenth century in Europe. During colonialism, western-European notions of statehood and sovereignty were transplanted to Africa. Among them were those ideas relating to Christianity's role in relation to the state, even though they derived from western Europe's particular socio-cultural background and history.

The Roman Catholic Church provides the best example of a religious organization whose mundane institutional structure has been created to most expeditiously allow God's representative – the Pope – to rule in a singular fashion. The role of the Catholic Church in Africa is of some importance both because of the large numbers of Africans who are baptized Catholics – around 120 million people, or one-fifth of Africa's population – and because the Church is the only religious institution which is a self-financing transnational organization. Historically, however, the Church has often been regarded as 'conservative, corporatist, and hostile to liberal democracy'.[24]

It is usually only when rulers appear to be governing in a manner seemingly at odds with God's law that Christian – including Catholic – hierarchies see fit to make their disquiet public.[25] For example, in Zaire, a memorandum from the Conference of Roman Catholic Bishops to President Mobutu in March 1990 criticized the political system from the point of view of its structure which, it claimed, was against reason and natural law. Zaire, the bishops argued, had a 'hybrid' political system that juxtaposed a 'liberalism', offering significant rewards to a small minority, with a regime philosophy of 'totalitarianism', which sought to gather all power to itself. Significantly, the memorandum suggested ways to reform the existing system rather than suggest the creation of a new one according to different philosophical principles. Mobutu himself was regarded as a misled national saviour, rather than as the main impediment to national progress.[26] In other words, the thrust of the bishops' memorandum was reformist in aim, rather than radical or revolutionary. Yet, despite the emollient tone and reasonable language employed, of the claimed 6,128 memoranda received by the government on the issue of the political way forward for Zaire, it refused to consider the bishops' memorandum. This was because Mobutu feared endorsing the right of religious leaders to offer political advice.[27]

It follows from this that Catholic (and, by extension, other mainline) religious leaders will sometimes openly criticize temporal rulers if they appear to be departing too radically from the path of reason and law. It does not imply that they will have an alternative programme to offer, but rather that once public opinion on an issue appears to be moving steadily in a certain direction, then Christian leaders might well add their weight to it. This also implies that Christian leaders may acquiesce in regime policies for as long as there is insufficient public opinion against them, especially when the claimed justification for authoritarian rule is national unity. Furthermore, religious leaders may well personally be beneficiaries of a close relationship with the state. Under these circumstances there is normally little temptation to protest too long or too loud unless supported by public opinion.

Post-colonial norms of state–church interaction in Africa are still to some degree contextualized by the imperial past, although the extent of this influence will differ from place to place. Because the mission churches were so closely linked to their post-colonial African successors in the minds of some contemporary rulers Christian fundamentalist churches, often regarded as a dangerous American imports by insecure regimes, are perceived with such suspicion. The response of some African governments, suspicious of the motivations and aims of Christian churches, has been to seek to control their numbers. For example, in Zaire, only three churches were allowed officially to operate until the early 1990s, not only in line with the state policy of *'authenticité'*, but also to control them and keep their leaders in thrall to Mobutu.[28]

In Kenya, on the other hand, the government of Jomo Kenyatta (1963–1978) used a different tactic: it sought to diminish the social importance of the Anglican church by encouraging the numbers of independent African churches to proliferate so that the Anglican voice would be but one among many. Further to encourage independent church leaders' support, state jobs, including Cabinet positions, were on offer.[29] The uncharacteristic willingness of the Anglican church in Kenya to tangle with the government is explained by the fact that during colonial times the overwhelmingly European congregation at Nairobi's Anglican cathedral was described as 'the colonial power at prayer'.[30] After independence the tradition of 'voice' rather than silence remained, at least for a while. Later, in Kenya, as in Uganda during the rule of Idi Amin Dada in Uganda in the 1970s, 'churches found themselves dragged against their will, into becoming foci of opposition'.[31]

Christian churches in Africa have often been unwilling to pronounce on thorny political issues, although the situation in South Africa is different. During the apartheid era (1948–1994), the white-dominated state looked to a main religious ally, the Dutch Reformed Church (NGK), for religious justification for its policy of 'separate development'. Over time, however, things began to change – in response to both internal and external developments – with other non-Afrikaner churches feeling increasingly emboldened to challenge apartheid on both religious and moral grounds. By the mid-1980s, the South African Council of Churches had come under black leadership, the ecumenical vanguard for radical 'Black theology'. Its best-known – and probably most influential expression – was the 'Kairos document'.[32] The importance of Christian opposition to white minority rule was clear by the end of the 1980s: premises of leading church organizations were fire-bombed by right-wing groups.[33] In short, with the exception of the NGK, Christian anti-apartheid institutional opposition – especially from the Roman Catholic, Anglican and Evangelical Lutheran churches – was influential in pressuring the de Klerk government to democratize.[34]

I have argued in this section that it is relatively unusual – although by no means impossible, as the example of South Africa indicates – for mainline Christian churches to express political opposition to authoritarian regimes in Africa, for a number of reasons. Apart from the idea that secular rulers may be believed to be divinely sanctioned and thus beyond mundane attack, there are also other considerations. There may be the belief that former Christian mission churches still to some extent compromised by the colonial past. In addition, religious agents may be uncomfortably vulnerable to the state's power of control. The result of these factors may well be that cooperation with authoritarian states may well seem the best policy for religious organizations to adopt and maintain.

Hegemony and Power in Africa

It is sometimes suggested that a Gramscian notion of hegemony is highly relevant to conceptions of power in Africa.[35] This involves the creation and institutionalization of a pattern of group activity in a state with a concomitant espousal of an idealized framework that strives to present itself as 'common sense'. The concept of hegemony also helps to explain how various characteristics – such as, culture, social formation and political institutions, involving individuals and corporate bodies – fit together into an overall concept of power. It also enables us to locate within a useful analytical framework, the interrelationships between state and civil society, the elite–counter-elite dichotomy, and the division between those with and those without adequate resources to prosper.

Central to an analysis of a Grasmcian conception of hegemony is the nature of power itself. In the African context, it may be insufficient to see power conventionally: the ability of one group or individual to gain the acquiescence or, at least, quiescence, of another because of the fear of the consequences of non-compliance. Power may be better thought of as a two-faceted, sometimes contradictory force. In Cox's expression 'power is a centaur, part man, part beast, a combination of force and consent'.[36] This is the crux of Gramsci's concept of hegemony: the iron fist fills the velvet glove; the former is uncovered only when deemed necessary. There is an exemplary enforcement potential, force underlies the power structure; the strong can (and will) crush the weak when necessary; and the latter know this. Yet, the use of force to gain compliance will be the last, or at least not the first, option. Indeed, force wielded by the dominant against the subordinate will not be necessary (or only very rarely) if that domination is seen as legitimate, even necessary. In other words, force will not be resorted to as long as subordinate people perceive elite domination as right and proper, or at least tolerable. Subordinates will be more inclined to view their position with relative equanimity as long as the dominant elites seek to rule by at least a modicum of consent, rather than by absolutist or dictatorial means. Ruling elites must, therefore, be concerned with the form as much as the content of its rule. Might alone cannot routinely be effective; it must be tempered with a practical concern to keep social relations relatively trouble free, a concern to rule by law as far as possible must be evident. Above all, rulers must express leadership by allusion to general, rather than specific, interests, such as 'national unity' or 'national self-determination'. Often – historically, in western European contexts – the development of (more or less) popular institutions is seen as the key for the success of a hegemonic strategy. This is because institutions help to coalesce diverse interests within a single body, giving rise to consensus and to a universalization of policy over time. Many ordinary people perceive that power relations are as they should be when the state achieves its objectives without dissent. That is, it is only 'right' that politicians and state officials rule authoritatively, that is their role.

Those involved in the quest for hegemony seek to create what Williams calls a 'unified moral order', where 'a certain way of life and thought is dominant, in which one concept of reality is diffused throughout society'.[37] In much of Africa, the 'moral order' is one where, notwithstanding increasingly ineffective appeals to 'national unity', individuals do their utmost to advance personal interests, as well as those of family and other favoured groups.

In order to locate the notion of hegemony in a form conducive to analysis, it is necessary to explain what the state amounts to in Africa. The state is best understood as the sum of two theoretically separate, yet in practice interlinked, developments. First, it is a rapacious *structure* of interlinked interests (often involving creation and perpetuation of clientelistic relationships), where 'public institutions (are) colonized and emasculated'.[38] Second, it is a hegemonic *process* whereby elites continually pursue power. Forrest suggests that 'state rulers are defined by and obtain their power and resources on the basis of their officeholding'.[39] The same form of structure-process can be applied to orthodox religious institutions. Leading figures within them will join together in a theocratic 'class' which seeks to advance their personal, as well their institution's, position in relation to competitors. The crux of the matter for temporal as for religious leaders is that public office brings private profit, creating in the process a class structure which develops on the basis of a social differentiation rooted in the practicalities of wealth accumulation, rather than in relation to the productive process (See examples earlier relating to Zaire, Togo, Rwanda and Lesotho). As a result, hegemonic striving unites individuals and groups, including some religious actors, within power structures at the national level. Certainly, some of the accrued wealth trickles down to those outside the state parameters, assured by the conglomeration of clientelistic, familial and kin relationships. Thus, the 'state' is not merely the sum of its official institutional parts, and it does not seem clear that democratization has altered things significantly in this regard. Instead, there is a partial interpenetration of the African state and society, with clientelist ties often cementing the system.

Religious institutions and figures are by no means exempt. To see why this should be the case, we need to understand how many ordinary Africans believe that the success of a religion is reflected in the wealth and status of leaders: how else would it be clear that God smiles on them? This was part of the reason why, during the colonial era, many Africans converted either to Christianity or to Islam. To many the idea of a supreme God was already culturally acceptable, as the weakness of the old gods was demonstrated conclusively by their inability to see off the new one.[40] Various – educational and welfare – benefits might well accrue to the converts who 'signed up' for the alien religion, sundering ties with the old one.

It is often noted how politics in Africa is characterized by the importance of patrimonial and clientelist relationships.[41] 'The big man, small boy syndrome' dominates political, social and economic individual relationships. Many who have an official capacity to exploit will do so as a means of personal benefit. This intermingling of public and private concerns is by no means unusual to or, of course, only found in African contexts. The patrimonial notion of power and the position of the individual in relation to the community coalesce in an understanding that power, whether spiritual, political or economic, may bring profit. Consequently, individuals may seek to develop mutually beneficial relationships with both subordinates and superiors. In political competition, cultivation of networks of reciprocity is a *sine qua non* for aspirant politicians, as well as for incumbent power holder. Those who fail to maintain networks of relationships will likely to fall prey to shifts of politics, and find themselves ousted from the positions which gave them power in the first place. Because religious institutions have to survive in an environment of resource shortages, their structural characteristics and the types of interaction between individuals may well parallel or replicate those in the secular realm. In addition, as already discussed, there may be interaction between religious and secular elites for mutual benefits.

Much of this is relevant for both Christian and Muslim religious contexts, including Islamic sub-systemic patrimonial systems that thrive in certain areas. In the northern Nigerian emirates, the northern Camerounian lamidates, and in the tribal sheikdoms of northern Chad, socio-religious culture melds both Islam and Arabic systems of patrimonial domination, in ways that resemble social structures found in parts of North Africa and the Middle East.[42] In Senegal there is a different arrangement, where Sufi *marabouts* often have important political and economic positions, first developed under French colonial rule. The leader of the most important brotherhood, the Muridiyya, does not hold an official state post, yet is regarded as especially politically powerful. This is because he holds power over his disciples, primarily found among the economically significant Wolof, who grow most of the country's major export crop, groundnuts.[43]

Senegal's high proportion of Muslims (around 90 per cent of the total population) is unusual in Africa. More often, there is a high degree of regional religious heterogeneity. Thinkers since Aristotle have taken it for granted that religious homogeneity is a prerequisite, a condition for political stability. Certainly, in Africa the relationship between state and religious leaders is often be complicated by the fact there are many religious organizations. If one set of religious figures can (or, at least, promise to) provide their followers' compliance to the rule of the current regime – as Muridiyya *marabouts* long managed to do in Senegal – then it will be of great importance for the state to reach a deal with them. Yet, the situation does not have to be characterized by the favouring of but one religion over others. Governments may well establish a working relationship with the most important religions (typically, Islam, the Roman Catholic Church, the leading Protestant church and perhaps an independent Christian church), and thereby create a degree of hegemony founded on limited religious diversity and maximal elite cooperation. In this kind of arrangement there is no necessity for overt religious competition that might undermine the collectively advantageous arrangement.

Being a de facto member of the state framework often gives senior religious leaders opportunity to amass personal wealth, in just the same way as other leaders of important societal groups, such as senior trade union officials, leaders of professional bodies, top civil servants, and ethnic leaders. There are no doubt some senior religious figures who wholeheartedly devote themselves to the spiritual health and welfare of their followers without developing additional sources of remuneration; nevertheless many others do.

Networks of reciprocity involve religious organizations in Africa in three ways. First, as already suggested, religious leaders will normally, but not invariably, co-operate with state power for both material and spiritual advantages. Threats may be issued; rewards may be offered and received. The aim either way is to ensure compliance with state objectives of control. Second, churches have been greatly influenced by what Gifford refers to as the 'Big Man model'.[44] Just as in secular contexts, senior and middle-ranking religious figures, while no doubt personally convinced of the spiritual efficacy of the religion which they embrace, may in addition understand their job primarily as a means to enhanced well being. Family members and ethnic allies may be rewarded with jobs. Profits can accrue to religious big men from their worldly business interests. In Togo, for example, some Catholic prelates are referred to as 'autoritaro-prébendier' (authoritarian-prebendalist).[45] On the other hand, the position of more lowly priests may be on the decline. There is a serious decline in applications to African Roman Catholic seminaries related to the perception that the priesthood's social and economic position is seriously diminished compared to the past.[46]

Third, leaders of African religious organizations can profit from relationships with foreign, especially western, non-governmental organisations (NGOs). Western NGOs, often mindful of state corruption, with financial resources disappearing into private pockets, often prefer to deal with religious organizations deemed to use money in more constructive ways, as well as being relatively independent of state control. Foreign donors, including those with no formal links with religious organizations, such as USAID, may pump money into church organizations because they are believed to be more honest and accountable in disbursing funds than governments. Nevertheless, some reports suggest that such favoured recipients have, on occasion, utilized foreign funds for their own personal purposes.[47]

This section has argued that leaders of mainline religious organizations often occupy important roles as interlocutors between state officials and their followers, helping the former to rule without too many overt challenges. To maintain their influential positions it is of course necessary for leaders of the mainline religions to retain their followers; as far as possible, to prevent defections to competitor religions and to bring religious 'dissidents' under their control. It is for this reason very important for them to head off religious challenges to their position. In recent times, leaders of mainstream Muslim and Christian bodies have found themselves threatened by a remarkable increase in unofficial sects and churches. The next section shifts the emphasis to the second focus of this account: popular religious groups in Africa and their impact upon state-society relationships, including democracy.

Challenging Hegemony: African Popular Religions and Democracy

For many ordinary Africans, 'politics' is something to be kept at arm's length as far as possible. It is something rather unsavoury, connoting the often dubious goings on between elite groups. Yet, on the other hand, it is undeniable that many ordinary people took to the streets in the 1980s and 1990s to demand democracy.

The dividing lines between politics and other social actions is clear cut within the social sciences, leading us to assume that reality may be neatly divided. But it is often not easy to put 'messy' reality into such discrete pigeonholes. For example, accounts of African politics often find it difficult clearly to pigeonhole individuals in relation to their class, because the once regularly employed Marxist categorization often seemed of little use in many African contexts. In the same way the relationship of religion and politics from a lower class perspective is usually dealt with by seeking to explain popular religious movements by pointing to apparently 'hidden' political objectives.[48] Yet this approach is problematic. Not least of the problems is that, as elsewhere, it is difficult to be sure where 'religion' ends and 'politics' begins in Africa. For example, during the colonial period, 'religious' movements were often also concerned both with anti-colonial goals and socio-cultural reform.[49] The point is that it is not analytically necessary to ascertain whether a religious or a political or a social objective is paramount. It is useful to understand movements as often involving a combination of motivations that defy easy, and precise, categorization. Spiritual and material concerns interact within very fluid boundaries in a context where many Africans relate to religion as a means of solving a number of personal problems, some of which will be material issues.

As noted earlier, in order to perpetuate hegemony successfully it is necessary for the dominant stratum to maintain a more or less consensual moral order with the status of 'common sense'. Subordinate classes accept such a moral order, according to materialist analysis, out of a 'false consciousness'. This allows the ruling elite to rule through consent rather than relying too heavily upon coercion. Yet, this should not be taken too far in the African context, where hegemony is rarely achieved on the basis of social and popular consent alone; coercion is always a highly useful option for the authorities to maintain social control. The false-consciousness argument is not a convincing explanation as to why subordinate class Africans obey the authorities (when they do, which is by no means all of the time); obeisance is undoubtedly as often due in part to a well-founded fear of the consequences of not toeing the line. Because of the fear of the consequences as well as the social divisions extant in most African societies, it is usually difficult to see unified political actions undertaken by subordinate classes in pursuit of their class interests. It is by no means clear whether subordinate class Africans perceive their interests to be best fulfilled by class action rather than by 'plugging in' to the networks of reciprocity and by creating popular vehicles of mobilization, including religious ones.

A 'popular religion' can be defined as a community expression of a group desire to achieve a religious satisfaction not forthcoming from extant mainline religious organizations. Both Marx and Weber stress how the 'contingent nature of the relationship between the content of an ideology and the social position of the group who are its 'carriers' is of fundamental importance when seeking to understand the social role of ideology.[50] What this suggests in relation to dominant religious traditions in Africa is that their leaders will be concerned with perpetuating and promulgating their religious vision (which is also an ideology of domination) so as to strengthen and bolster both social and theological positions.

Virtually every African country has a fair number, sometimes a very great quantity, of religious faiths and sects, often characterized by a mixture of Islam, Christianity and indigenous religions; often mainline Christian churches compete with Protestant fundamentalist and independent churches. Popular – usually Sufi – Islam competes with the orthodoxy championed by the *ulama*. Both sets of popular religions are alternative sources of orthodoxy because every religious believer contends that his or her religion is actually one in which their own conception of orthodoxy is paramount.

Bayart contends that in Africa popular religions are the ordinary person's way of cocking a snook at authority.[51] Mbembe argues that 'the current explosion of religious revivalism in Africa is another ruse by the common man to create a counter-ideology and alternative political space in response to the totalitarian ambitions of African dictators'.[52] Thus, popular religions may be potent and overt symbols of political opposition. However, this is not to claim that all popular religions are by definition politically oriented, forms of anti-establishment political mobilization in religious garb. Spiritual benefits are almost certainly commonly regarded as highly important in accounting for an individual's religious choice. It may also be important how the state *perceives* a popular religion's aims. For example, in central Africa British colonial authorities regarded the Watchtower sect as a politically revolutionary movement masquerading as a religious group.[53]

In the post-colonial era orthodox Islam has done its best to dominate its (popular) Sufi rival because the latter is often viewed as being opposed to the religious and social status quo. The wider point is that in Africa, states often appear to have trouble trying to dominate popular religious sects, to ensure that they operate according to the official rules laid down in the context of the state's hegemonic politico-administrative framework.[54] Apparently substantive manifestations of anti-regime opposition must be taken seriously. The ramifications of this are clear, and obvious: regimes must do all they can to reduce challenges to a minimum; one effective way is to bring real or imagined dissidents into the state nexus. If this is not possible, they must be neutralized.

As already argued, religion is a force that may have significant political implications for both ruler and ruled alike. Within Christianity there is a multiplicity of conceptions concealed behind an often spurious religious unity which, for example, may seek to establish the efficacy of liberation theology amongst all 'third-world' Catholics regardless of differences in culture, tradition, history and political structures. Within every supposedly universal religion there is a multiformity of forms of religious belief corresponding to the class or strata in focus. Gramsci identifies a 'Catholicism of the petit bourgeoisie and of city workers, a women's Catholicism, an intellectual's Catholicism equally varied and disconnected'.[55] This is not to argue that there is one religious orthodoxy that somehow mutates according to social or class context, but rather that there are many different 'Catholicisms' of which the hegemonic, orthodox version is but one. The same goes for Protestantism, which does not even claim to have the same uniformity and universality as Catholicism. Within Islam there are several extant conceptions corresponding to socio-cultural contexts:

- culturally dominant, strongly patrimonial Islam of northern Nigeria, northern Chad and northern Cameroon. This is an Islam inextricably linked to notions of social hierarchy and political power;
- Sufi Islam of the *marabouts*, itself is divided into 'pure' and 'corrupt' forms;
- Islam of discrete ethnic groups often carrying much cultural and racial baggage;
- 'fundamentalist' Islam (or, Islamism) often championed by radical higher education students (who may wish to recreate Iran or Saudi Arabia's theological perfections).

These categorizations by no means exhaust all the extant types of popular religious belief among Africans. The main point, then, is that various forms of popular religion relate to the perceptions, ethics and conventions of various groups divided by occupation, class or gender, and expressed through religious terminology. In Africa, reflecting an often bleakly unpromising economic and political reality, popular religions often express themselves in the apparent hopelessness, the lack of expectations of the mass of the people, where religious faith is regarded as the key to this worldly material favour. As Kabongo puts it: 'Africa at prayer looks for a miracle, it is a daily appeal for the ultimate solution to illness, poverty, and misery. That is Africa of the night, of Saturdays and Sundays. Africa of the week and of the day "manages", and corrupt and corrupting individuals die between the two worlds, struggling to survive' (my translation).[56]

While there may be merit in the argument that religion offers a variety of, mainly spiritual benefits, it is also possible to claim that popular religion is basically materialist, quite distinct from the more idealistic speculations of Weber's 'genteel intellectuals'.[57] A materialist conception of popular religion relates to particular forms of ordering and organizing religious communities. Fundamentalist sects challenge the orthodox religions both intellectually and materially. Such is the concern with the haemorrhaging of followers, that the mainline Christian churches in Africa make two lines of attack.

On the one hand, the fundamentalist churches are accused of being little (if anything) more than American Trojan horses, while at the same time the orthodox churches rush to incorporate evangelical elements (glossolalia, faith healing, copious biblical allusions) into their services. The fact that millions of Africans – in common with many others in Latin America, East Asia, and the Pacific Rim – have converted to fundamentalist Christianity over the last decade or so suggests strongly that such people find something of value there they do not in the mainline churches. At the same time, the dominance of some fundamentalist churches by wealthy foreign (especially North American) pastors, helps to confirm the association between their religion and personal prosperity. This is because they offer a vision of western consumerist success that serves as a powerful inducement for less materially successful people, an appeal over and above their purported spiritual benefits.

Despite leaders' claims to political indifference, the political significance of the fundamentalist Christian churches is manifested in a number of ways. Followers often have no problem in endorsing their westernized leaders' aversion to socialism. Quite apart from the fact that to many socialism defines itself as a negation of the very existence of God, further it is born of a first-hand experience with various types of 'African socialism', which for many people is associated with bureaucratization, elitist power concentration, waste and ideological inflexibility.

To many fundamentalist Christians in Africa, religion is concerned with social issues in the context of the creation of a counter-culture involving a communal sharing of fears, ills, jobs, hopes and material success. Earthly misfortune is a result of lack of faith; God will reward true believers. Adherents believe that people's redemption is in their own hands (or rather in both God's and the individual's hands), and that expectations that government could or should supply all or even most of people's needs and deal with their problems is misplaced. African fundamentalist Christians do not usually seek to form political vehicles for their social and economic aspirations; they believe in the biblical idea that political leaders should rule, senior religious figures should stick to spiritual matters. What this implies is that followers often do not involve themselves in the cut and thrust of political competition; but it does not mean that when a clearly political issue arises with significant connotations the fundamentalist Christian community necessarily remains silent. For example, fundamentalist Christians in Nigeria are a significant political voice, especially over the issue of Sharia law in some northern states.

Contrary to some accounts, however, it should not be assumed that such people will necessarily be strongly in favour of democracy. Huntington quotes approvingly projected figures of Christianity's growth in Africa from some 236 million believers in 1985 to 400 million early in the twenty-first century.[58] He appears to assume that this will necessarily be instrumental in forcing demands for democratization onto political agendas, although he argues correctly that most extant democracies are countries with significant proportions of Christians. Another interpretation, however, is that many such Christians follow apolitical or politically conservative sects with either no interest in democracy per se or they are believers in 'strong', that is, author-itarian, earthly government, difficult to rouse to political voice – except when their religion seems to be under attack. Overall, however, the political consequences of the spread of Christian fundamentalism – including Pente-costalism – appear unclear, with few, if any, differences, between political attitudes of various kinds of African Christians.

We have already noted that fundamentalist Islamic groups are rare in sub-Saharan Africa. Why? The region's numerous popular Muslim groups seek to follow their own Islamic orthodoxies which almost invariably will run counter to the purist, reforming versions of Islam forwarded by the often arabicized elites of the *ulama*. Running contrary to the purist trend are the desires of ordinary Muslims, confronted in their religion both by the demands of the modern nation-state for national unity as well as by the Muslim elite for them to follow the 'true' Muslim path of orthodoxy. Unlike popular Christian sects, popular Muslim groups, especially in urban areas, often function as de facto conduits of opposition and of anti-regime solidarity. This underlines how the state and the *ulama* do not have the monopoly of religio-social organiz-ation between them. As Fossaert notes: 'men-in-society [sic] are organized in and by the state, but they are also organized in families, in village commu-nities, in provinces, in workplaces, in factories in which the state is not always the proprietor, in trade unions, in parties and in associations and in other ways which the state does not necessarily control' (my translation).[59]

This fails to mention religious organizations of popular focus, but at that level, Islam is an important expression of community; at local level it is an 'anti-structure' expressing what Turner refers to as 'the powers of the weak;' in its own way, a counter-society.[60] In urban surroundings, manifes-tations of Muslim community, often outside of the state's control, include Muslim associations (such as the Hamadiyya Shadhiliyya of urban Egypt), Sufi brotherhoods and community mosques. The basic framework of worship in Islam – small groups of men meeting to pray five times a day and to study the *Quran* together in the central mosque on Fridays – often miti-gates against factionalism, at least at the community level. Islamic obser-vances, such as Friday prayers, the annual fast (Ramadan), and the *hajj*, are public manifestations of faith, part and parcel of Muslim community life. Membership of Sufi brotherhoods in Africa adds a contextualising cultural dimension to the universal religious solidarities. Sufi traditions are of mys-tique routes to communion with God, involving religion-derived song and dance meetings and the worship of local Muslim saints. The Sufi brotherhoods provide an additional source of identity in towns and cities, while the Muslim obligation to provide *zakat* (alms) is a fruitful source of patron–client relationships.[61]

What this amounts to is that Muslim civil society is not the product of universalizing Muslim cultural currents. In Africa, conceptions of Islam are often moulded by many cultural situations – including ethnicity – that adapt the orthodoxies of the Arabist Islamic conception for local use. Consequently, popular Islamic organizations can – and often do – carry political potentialities, making states both suspicious and wary of them. The state seeks to dislocate Islamic resentment by controlling and defusing it. That is, the state 'must "put its nose" into the life of the Muslim community'.[62] However, African states have often been unsuccessful when trying to mobilizing Muslim communities via a secular discourse focused on national unity.

In conclusion, popular Islamic modes may be subversive to the interests of both religious and political elites. Three types should be noted: (1) women's groups, (2) millenarian sects and (3) ethnic-religious vehicles of opposition. First, there is the Islam of the associations of Muslim women, sometimes described as 'apolitical'.[63] However, such organizations, delivering practical help for Muslim females and, in many cases, a wider orientation to change the position of women, work to improve the position of female Muslims in various ways. Such objectives are actually highly political at the level of gender politics, working as they do towards forms of women's liberation. Growing numbers of female Muslims find employment in the modern sector – as, for example, teachers and secretaries – as a direct result of the spread of education. Second, there are the millenarian sects, such as that associated with the Cameroonian Muhammad Murwa, active in Kano in the late 1970s. Third, there are ethno-religious groups utilizing Islam as a cultural referrent to focus community anger at perceived political and economic marginalization. Examples include Balukta in Tanzania and the Islamic Party of Kenya.[64]

Conclusion

Africa is a culturally and religiously diverse, politically complex, region of over 40 countries. The background to Africa's democratic transitions in the 1990s was an array of apparently unpropitious structural characteristics which, many observers believe, make it unlikely that many African countries will be able to consolidate democracy. On the other hand, impetus for reform was widespread – the result of a combination of domestic and international factors linked to the region's endemic economic and political problems. Fundamental reforms of state structures and institutions were widely deemed necessary, both at home and abroad, to correct things.

Many African democratic transitions began with popular agitation against unelected leaders which gradually developed into demands for multi-party elections and democratic governments. But, protest-led, reformist-oriented, actions, often led by religious, especially Christian leaders, 'did not necessarily lay a firm foundation for the subsequent institutionalisation of democratic regimes'.[65] We examined the role of leaders of mainline Christian – especially, Catholic churches – as well as those of national Muslim organizations and other important Muslim actors, including popular Islam. We saw that senior religious figures typically forged close relationships with the state, which tended to make them ambivalent towards the concept of fundamental political change.

Overall, the trajectory of Africa's democratization has been, on balance, disappointing. It is clear that in the context of generally inauspicious political and economic factors, religious actors have not been able to help advance democracy beyond a stage often characterized by cosmetic rather than substantial changes.

NOTES

1. 'Africa' in this paper refers to Sub-Saharan Africa.
2. M. Bratton and N. van der Walle, 'Towards Governance in Africa Popular Demands and State Responses', in G. Hyden and M. Bratton (eds), *Governance and Politics in Africa* (London: Lynne Rienner, 1997), p.32.
3. Mobutu was eventually ousted in May 1997, and died soon after in exile in Morocco.
4. 'Documents pour l'action', No.8 (March–April 1962), pp.99–100, translated and quoted in P. Boyle, 'Beyond Self-Protection to Prophecy The Catholic Church and Political Change in Zaire', *Africa Today*, Vol.39 (1992), p.52.
5. Malula quoted in Boyle (note 4) p.49.
6. M. Schatzberg, *The Dialectics of Oppression in Zaire* (Bloomington, IN: Indiana University Press, 1988), p.117.
7. Boyle (note 4) p.51.
8. Schatzberg (note 6) pp.30–51.
9. W. MacGaffey, 'Religion, Class and Social Pluralism in Zaire', *The Canadian Journal of African Studies*, Vol.24, No.2 (1990), pp.261–2.
10. A. Hastings, *A History of African Christianity, 1950–75* (Cambridge: Cambridge University Press, 1979), p.189.
11. C. Toulabor, 'Temoignage sur le Diocese de Lomé', *Politique Africaine*, No.43 (1991), pp.123–5.
12. Hastings (note 10) p.188.
13. P. Gifford, *Christianity and Politics in Doe's Liberia* (Cambridge: Cambridge University Press, 1993), pp.73–83.
14. L. Diamond, 'The Globalization of Democracy', in R. Slater, B. Schutz and S. Dorr (eds), *Global Transformation and the Third World* (Boulder, CO and London: Lynne Rienner, 1993), pp.21–70; R. Joseph, 'The Christian Churches and Democracy in Contemporary Africa' in J. Witte, Jr (ed), *Christianity and Democracy in Global Context* (Boulder, CO: Westview, 1993), pp.231–47.
15. Diamond (note 14) p.49
16. J.D.Y. Peel, 'An Africanist Revisits *Magic and the Millennium*', in E. Barker, J. Beckford and K. Dobbelaere (eds), *Secularisation, Rationalism and Sectarianism* (Oxford: Clarendon Press, 1993), p.162.

17. S. Huntington, *The Third Wave. Democratization in the Late Twentieth Century* (Norman, OK, University of Oklahoma Press, 1991).
18. See, for example, F. Fukuyama, *The End of History and the Last Man* (Harmondsworth, UK: Penguin), p.236.
19. J.-F. Bayart, *The State in Africa* (London: Longman, 1993), p.189.
20. J.-F. Bayart, 'Civil Society in Africa', in P. Chabal (ed), *Political Domination in Africa* (Cambridge: Cambridge University Press, 1986), p.112.
21. Gifford (note 13).
22. F. Northedge, *The International Political System* (London: Faber, 1976), p.58.
23. H. Johnston and J. Figa, 'The Church and Political Opposition', *Journal for the Scientific Study of Religion*, Vol.27, No.1 (1988), pp.32–3.
24. Diamond (note 14) p.24.
25. H. Williams, *International Relations in Political Theory* (Milton Keynes: Open University Press, 1992), p.36.
26. F. Soudan, 'Zaire Les Evêques Accusent', *Jeune Afrique*, 9 April 1990, pp.2–5.
27. Lawyers Committee for Human Rights, *Zaire. Repression as Policy* (New York: Lawyers Committee for Human Rights, 1990), p.23.
28. Schatzberg (note 6).
29. T. Ranger and O. Vaughan, 'Postscript' in T. Ranger and O. Vaughan (eds), *Legitimacy and the State in Twentieth Century Africa* (Basingstoke: Macmillan, 1993), pp.255–61.
30. J. Lonsdale, 'The Emerging Pattern of Church and State Co-operation in Kenya', in E. Fashole-Luke, R. Gray and A. Hastings (eds), *Christianity in Independent Africa* (London: Rex Collings, 1978), pp.121–39.
31. L. Pirouet, 'Religion in Uganda under Amin', *Journal of Religion in Africa*, Vol.11, No.1 (1980), p.15.
32. J. Haynes, *Religion and Politics in Africa* (London: Zed, 1996), pp.90–92.
33. I. Harris, S. Mews, P. Morris and J. Shepherd, *Contemporary Religions: A World Guide* (London: Longman, 1992), p.466.
34. Huntington (note 17) pp.113–14.
35. D. Laitin, *Hegemony and Culture. Politics and Religious Change Among the Yoruba* (Chicago, IL: Chicago University Press, 1986); P. Chabal, *Power in Africa: An Essay in Political Interpretation* (London: Macmillan, 1992); Schatzberg (note 6).
36. R. Cox, 'Social Forces, States and World Orders Beyond International Relations Theory', in H. Williams, M. Wright and T. Evans (eds), *International Relations and Political Theory* (Milton Keynes: Open University Press, 1993), p.286.
37. G. Williams, '*Egemonia* in the Thought of Antonio Gramsci', *Journal of the History of Ideas* (October–December 1960), p.587, quoted in J. Femia, 'Hegemony and Consciousness in the Thought of Antonio Gramsci', *Political Studies*, Vol.23, No.1 (1975), pp.30–31.
38. R. Bates, 'The Politics of Economic Policy Reform A Review Article', *Journal of African Economies*, Vol.2, No.3 (1993), p.419.
39. J. Forrest, 'The Quest for State "Hardness" in Africa', *Comparative Politics*, Vol.20, No.4 (1988), p.439.
40. R. Horton, *Patterns of Thought in Africa and the West* (Cambridge: Cambridge University Press, 1993).
41. See, for example, Joseph (note 14); Bayart (note 19); Chabal (note 35).
42. V. Le Vine, 'African Patrimonial Regimes in Comparative Perspective', *Journal of Modern African Studies*, Vol.18, No.4 (1980), pp.663–4.
43. R. Fatton, *The Making of a Liberal Democracy. Senegal's Passive Revolution, 1975–1985* (Boulder: Lynne Rienner, 1987), p.100.
44. Gifford (note 13) p.310.
45. C. Toulabor (note 11) p.123.
46. R. Luneau, *Laisse Aller mon Peuple! Eglises Africaines au-delà des Modeles?* (Paris: Karthala, 1987).
47. Gifford (note 13) pp.311–12.

48. See, for example, R. Buijtenhuijs, 'Dini Ya Msambwa Rural Rebellion or Counter-society?', in Wim van Binsbergen and Michael Schoffeleers (eds), *Theoretical Explorations in African Religion* (London: KPI, 1985), pp.322–42.
49. T. Ranger, 'Religious Movements and Politics in Sub-Saharan Africa', *African Studies Review*, Vol.39, No.2 (1986), pp.1–70.
50. A. Giddens, *Capitalism and Modern Social Theory* (Cambridge: Cambridge University Press, 1971), pp.211–12.
51. Bayart (note 19) pp.256–8.
52. A. Mbembe, *Afriques Indociles. Christianisme, Pouvoir et Etat en Societé Postcoloniale* (Paris: Karthala, 1988), p.96.
53. K. Fields, *Revival and Rebellion in Colonial Central Africa* (Princeton, NJ: Princeton University Press, 1985).
54. Forrest (note 39) p.428.
55. A. Gramsci, *Selections from the Prison Notebooks*, edited by Q. Hoare and G. Smith (London: Lawrence and Wishart, 1971), pp.419–20.
56. I. Kabongo, 'Derourante Afrique ou la Syncope d'un Discours', *Revue Canadienne des Études Africaines*, Vol.18, No.1 (1982), p.18.
57. Giddens (note 50) p.211.
58. Huntington (note 17) p.281.
59. R. Fossaert, *La Societé. Volume 5, Les Etats* (Paris: Le Seuil, 1978), p.149.
60. V. Turner, *The Ritual Process. Structure and Anti-Structure* (Ithaca, NY: Cornell University Press, 1969).
61. J. Paden, *Religion and Political Culture in Kano* (Berkeley, CA: University of California Press, 1973).
62. C. Coulon, *Les Musulmans et le Pouvoir en Afrique Noire* (Paris: Karthala, 1983), p.50.
63. M. Piel, *African Urban Society* (Chichester: John Wiley, 1984), p.199.
64. Haynes (note 32) pp.163–4, 188–91.
65. Bratton and van de Walle (note 22) p.278.

Bullets over ballots: Islamist groups, the state and electoral violence in Egypt and Morocco

Hendrik Kraetzschmar[a] and Francesco Cavatorta[b]

[a]*Arabic and Middle Eastern Studies, University of Leeds, UK;* [b]*School of Law and Government, Dublin City University, Dublin, Ireland*

This article is concerned with state-sponsored electoral violence in liberalized autocracies. The first section of the paper identifies a number of variables that can help explain the decision calculus of authoritarian incumbents to deploy force against strong electoral challengers. The second section then examines these propositions with reference to Egypt and Morocco. Drawing on recent parliamentary elections in both countries the article questions why, despite facing the challenge of political Islam, the two regimes differed so markedly in their willingness to manipulate the polls by recourse to violence. Whilst the Egyptian authorities decided to abrogate all pretence of peaceful elections in favour of violent repression against the Muslim Brotherhood candidates and sympathizers, no such tactics were deployed by the ruling elite in Morocco. We suggest that three principal factors influenced the regimes' response to this electoral challenge: (1) the centrality of the elected institution to authoritarian survival; (2) the availability of alternative electioneering tools; and (3) the anticipated response of the international community. The article concludes by suggesting that in order to understand better when and how states deploy violence in elections, we need to focus on a more complex set of factors rather than simply on the electoral potency of key opposition challengers or the authoritarian nature of the state.

Introduction

The phenomenon of violence in elections is one of many paradoxes with which political scientists have to grapple. Whilst theoretically the notions of elections and violence seem incompatible, in practice they often go hand in hand. Multiparty elections epitomise efforts at managing political conflict by non-violent means, and are commonly regarded as the ultimate remedy for conflict in society. Yet reality is often multifaceted, with outbursts of violence accompanying elections at various stages of the process, either in the lead-up to, during or in the aftermath of polling day.

The phenomenon itself is as old as the electoral principle. It was as much a feature of elections in ancient Rome, the Victorian era, and nineteenth-century America, as it sadly remains in modern times.[1] Acts of violence causing death and destruction have in the past marred elections in countries across continents and different political systems, and continue to do so. And yet the phenomenon has evoked limited scholarly interest. As Rapoport and Weinberg remark, despite a plethora of research on political violence, there is a paucity of comparative studies on its 'little brother', electoral violence.[2] The only analyses at hand are those by Rapoport and Weinberg themselves and a number of studies addressing the issue of electoral violence in conflict and transitional settings.[3] Even less is available when it comes to the phenomenon of state-sponsored electoral violence. A few case studies apart, no academic work exists which broadly explores the question of when and why states resort to coercion in elections.[4]

In keeping with the theme of the special issue, this article examines the third area of research spelled out by Schwarzmantel in his introductory contribution: 'violence as a challenge to democracy'. According to Schwarzmantel this challenge carries two dimensions. As far as liberal democracies are concerned the challenge of violent politics emanates primarily from social movements seeking better inclusion and recognition within the polity, whilst in non-democracies or in liberalizing countries where uncertainty over the process is high it is often the regime itself which resorts to violence as a means of securing authoritarian survival.

Focusing on the later scenario, this article explores state sponsorship of political violence in elections with a specific focus on the Arab world where we can observe, paradoxically, both the persistence of authoritarianism and a significant increase in electoral contests. The article puts forward a number of variables that can help explain why and when authoritarian incumbents deploy violent electioneering tactics as a means of 'carving the democratic heart out of the electoral contest'.[5] Essentially, we suggest that one ought to look beyond the nature of authoritarianism and the electoral potency of opposition challengers to understand the conditions under which states are likely to resort to such tactics. Three factors are identified that may explain state sponsorship of electoral violence. First, we focus on the institutional framework in a given country and consider the centrality and effective policy-making powers of the elected institutions for authoritarian elites. How important is the institution for which elections are held? Second, we explore the availability of alternative electioneering devices falling short of the resort to force, and how the regime employs such alternatives to manage the election process. Finally, we emphasize that domestic decision-making takes into account the anticipated response of the international community to the use of electoral fraud in general and of electoral violence in particular.

This theoretical framework is then examined in the context of recent parliamentary elections in Egypt (2005) and Morocco (2007). The two cases lend themselves to an exploratory analysis of state-sponsored election violence for a number of reasons. To begin with, they are both authoritarian countries with a liberalizing agenda and can be defined as 'liberalized autocracies'.[6] Second, they are representative of the political dynamics in many countries across the Arab world where existing regimes are somehow able to survive despite the lack of popular legitimacy and the presence of a strong Islamist opposition. Third, the two countries, like many others in the region, have increasingly taken elections seriously over the last decade because of both domestic and international pressures for reform. Finally, the two countries are paradigmatic of the two types of regime we find in the region. Morocco represents the political and institutional dynamics that we find in Arab monarchies where rulers are unelected and where legitimacy can be characterized as 'traditional'. Egypt exemplifies the manner in which politics takes place in authoritarian republics where 'strong' presidents are elected and have to deal with specific electoral constraints. This allows for an examination of how electoral contests occur in the two countries and how authoritarian incumbents respond to strong challengers at the ballot box.

Electoral potency, threat perceptions, and state-sponsored violence in authoritarian elections

This article adopts a simplified decision-theoretic approach to the study of state-sponsored violence in authoritarian elections. It assumes that authoritarian incumbents are rational actors whose principal objective is to remain in power and whose decision to resort to, tolerate or refrain from violence against political opponents is a strategic choice amongst many to ensure regime survival. State-sponsored violence is thus neither irrational nor indiscriminate, but constitutes a course of action that is deliberate and usually targeted at opposition forces perceived as posing a most serious threat to authoritarian incumbency.

We define *electoral violence* as acts or threats of coercion, intimidation or physical harm perpetrated to affect the process and/or outcome of an election. The instigators of such violence can include both state actors (police, secret services, armed forces) and non-state actors (e.g. political parties and guerrilla, rebel or paramilitary groups). Where the former is involved we are dealing with so-called *state-sponsored electoral violence*. This is a form of political violence instigated either directly by the state authorities or by regime proxies, such as militias, ruling parties, regime-hired troublemakers, and so forth. Following Gartner and Regan[7] we have included regime proxies in our definition of state-sponsored violence based on the assumption that the central authorities hold significant sway over these agents and their actions.

With few exceptions, it appears that most instances of state-sponsored electoral violence occur in non-democratic regimes.[8] Illustrative cases in point are the coercive tactics recently employed by authoritarian incumbents in elections in Zimbabwe (2008) and Ethiopia (2000).[9] For these regimes, as for any electoral autocracy, authoritarian survival in a liberalized environment is of paramount concern, and resorting to violence in elections constitutes one of several illegitimate strategies to secure this survival at the ballot box. Alongside ballot fraud and vote buying, brute force, or the failure to prevent it, is often used by the authorities and/or their proxies to distort the electoral competition in favour of regime-supportive forces and to quell any post-election outburst of popular anger at the rigging of the election result, as happened for instance in the aftermath of the 2009 presidential poll in Iran. Acts of regime-perpetrated electoral violence can take various forms, ranging from targeted killings of prominent opposition figures, the physical disruption of opposition rallies, the beating and/or arbitrary arrest of opposition candidates and sympathizers, to coercive measures aimed at preventing voters from casting their ballots.

When deployed by authoritarian incumbents, the overall objectives and targets of state-sponsored violence in elections are thus relatively easy to discern. Usually the overriding aim is to neutralize key electoral challengers and the targets of such violence are those opposition forces perceived as posing the greatest threat to the electoral status quo. What is more difficult to determine however, and of interest here, is the decision-calculus that drives authoritarian elites to use force as an electioneering tool in the first place, particularly as it is the regime itself that has decided on holding multiparty elections. Is it possible to predict a state's propensity to resort to violence in elections? If so, when and how do authoritarian incumbents determine that the benefits of deploying force outweigh both the loss of domestic legitimacy that invariably goes hand in hand with this repressive strategy, and the possible ire of the international community?

For authoritarian rulers the very notion of opposition is suspect and treated as a potential or real threat to regime survival. Obviously, the degree to which autocrats tolerate political opposition is contingent on the nature of authoritarianism (closed vs. competitive autocracies) and the types of demands articulated by their opponents.[10] Pliant and weak opposition parties, for instance, which are allowed to garner a limited number of seats in parliament in return for their acquiescence in the existing order, pose no serious electoral challenge to incumbent regimes and are thus essentially non-threatening. In fact, some scholars have argued that, where allowed to operate, these opposition forces help sustain a veneer of democratic governance within inherently autocratic structures and as such prolong rather than endanger regime survival.[11] The situation may change dramatically, however, wherever the electoral potency of the opposition is enhanced, that is where non-regime forces show any real sign of grassroots support, organizational capacity, and/or willingness to challenge the boundaries of acceptable dissent. In these circumstances then, authoritarian incumbents are faced with real challengers at the ballot box.

At first glance it therefore appears that electoral potency features critically in the decision-calculus of autocrats to use force against challengers in elections. And indeed, with the electoral equilibrium under threat, authoritarian governments may be tempted to deploy repressive means to sustain the electoral status quo. Yet electoral potency on its own cannot explain the choice of violence. One could, for instance, conceive of a strong opposition being allowed to do well in elections simply because the institution for which parties are competing is constitutionally relatively powerless. Equally, one could think of the role that political parties actually play in any political system, contrasting regimes reliant on a ruling party to ones based on unelected decision-makers such as monarchs. These regimes may inevitably view electoral competition and its challenges very differently and thus diverge in their readiness to resort to force during an election.

It is thus apparent that other important factors must be considered in order to fully understand the decision-making rationale of authoritarian incumbents in resorting to violence in elections. As mentioned earlier, we propose three variables that may help explain when electoral potency turns into an electoral threat which, from the regime's point of view, warrants violent repression. The first variable to examine is the centrality for authoritarian survival of the institution for which parties and candidates are competing. Authoritarian rulers have to identify the importance of the institution and decide whether losing power within it would undermine significantly their legitimacy and ability to rule unhindered. It becomes therefore important to determine where the particular institution is located in terms of its constitutional relevance. Accordingly, in a political system where the executive and legislative powers are elected and mutually inter-dependent, the stakes of electoral competition are quite high because the authoritarian incumbent could conceivably have much to lose if a strong opposition were to take advantage of even limited openings. This has been the case for instance in Algeria in 1990 when the Islamic Salvation Front (known by its French acronym, FIS) won the legislative elections. The number of seats it won would have made it possible for the party to change the constitution. The Algerian parliament was therefore a very significant institution and its 'loss' to the Islamists was countered with significant violence. Conversely, in the context of a political system where the main executive institution is beyond electoral politics, as in executive monarchies, electoral competition for the legislature might not constitute a significant challenge to the authoritarian incumbent because formal legitimacy derives from other sources. Thus, a monarch might be more willing and even encourage effective pluralism.[12] The Jordanian elections reflect this logic, as supreme executive powers are in the hands of the monarch, who uses parties in parliament to selectively support his policies.

The second factor to examine concerns the nature of the electoral contest itself and the tools available to incumbents to influence its outcome. Elections in authoritarian systems have the overarching objective of fostering regime legitimacy, but they can be either threatening or legitimizing.[13] Threatening elections mean that authoritarian incumbents have been forced to open up the political system defensively due to either domestic or external pressures or both, and the electoral competition becomes therefore a potentially dangerous test of popularity. The ruling elite in this case is very aware of the potentially snowballing effects of such elections if it does not deliver results that make survival possible, and is willing to influence the outcome with all the means at its disposal, including violence.

On the contrary, legitimizing elections serve the purpose of demonstrating the existence of political pluralism, and whilst incumbents also attempt to control the results, such results do not have the same significance. First, the regime's legitimacy rests elsewhere and, second, it is precisely by allowing a degree of effective pluralism that incumbents derive both domestic and international benefits. In this case the instrument of violence would be damaging to the survival of the regime because it would indicate that the other tools to remain in power are no longer effective.

The third and final factor has to do with the international response which authoritarian elites must anticipate when deploying force against political opponents. For authoritarian regimes the recourse to violence as an electioneering tool not only carries domestic risks, but can also incur significant external costs. These costs can range from moral condemnation to the withdrawal of vital economic and military aid, the suspension of bilateral/multilateral trade agreements or the imposition of economic and/or political sanctions.[14]

No liberalizing regime that breaches the norms of electoral good governance is likely to escape some form of international condemnation. In the past, Western governments have on numerous occasions issued statements reminding the regimes in question of their commitment to free and fair elections. The real issue, therefore, is not so much whether offending regimes will be reprimanded, but whether key Western allies are prepared to impose negative sanctions in order to pressure authoritarian incumbents to improve their rights record in elections. Two factors may play into the decision of whether and when Western governments are prepared to do so. First, it may depend on whether or not regime repression is perceived as a democratization-threatening or a democratization-saving exercise. If it is the latter, then some form of repression against political opponents, including the use of force, may be tolerated and would not damage the overall democratizing legitimacy of authoritarian incumbents. Second, Western governments may also shy away from deploying negative sanctions against regimes considered 'pivotal states' in a geo-strategic sense.[15] Here again, authoritarian stability and the survival of a pro-Western government may outweigh any concern for democratic reforms, particularly if such reforms would benefit forces perceived as inherently anti-Western. In both scenarios then, the external costs of violent repression are likely to be short-term and limited, and unlikely to damage the rulers' overall credentials as democratising regimes or their strategic partnership with the West.

Regime violence in Egypt's 2005 parliamentary elections

Egypt last went to the polls in autumn 2005 to elect a new president and lower house of parliament. The months leading to the polls were marked by an air of measured optimism that the voting experience would be qualitatively different from past elections. Whilst no-one assumed that Mubarak would lose the presidency or the ruling National Democratic Party (NDP) its stranglehold over the legislature, developments in and outside the country nonetheless suggested that this time around there would be no 'election business as usual'. Confronted with an emboldened reform movement at home and a US administration eager to see Egypt take a lead in regional democratization efforts, the regime found itself under unprecedented pressure to organize clean and peaceful elections.[16]

At first, this pressure appeared to be having the desired effect. In February 2005 Mubarak unexpectedly announced a reform of the presidential election law, opening the presidency for the first time in the country's history to multi-candidate contestation. The elections themselves, which took place on 7 September, were hailed by the international community as a significant step towards democracy and seen as evidence that Mubarak was committed to cleaner elections. Observers lauded the calm and overall openness that prevailed throughout the campaigning period and on polling day itself, and commented positively on the fact that opposition candidates were allowed to campaign relatively unhindered.[17]

Little over a month later, the parliamentary election campaign seemed to kick off to a similarly encouraging start. Yet again the regime appeared more relaxed about opposition activism than in the past, granting it an exceptional margin of freedom during the campaigning period. Even the Muslim Brotherhood, long vilified by the government, enjoyed unprecedented freedom during the campaign, with the group's candidates and cadres being allowed to canvass their message relatively openly and without the usual government interference and intimidation.[18] It thus appeared that the upcoming poll would run peacefully and that the new legislature would be more pluralist than its predecessors.

This was not to be, however. Far from passing peacefully, Egypt bore witness to an election that was marred by the most serious outbreak of political violence since the 1995 parliamentary poll. By the time the polling stations closed on 9 December 2005, the elections had cost 11 lives and left over 500 people wounded in scores of violent clashes.[19] According to observers on the ground, most of the violence took place in rounds two and three of the voting and involved in a vast majority of instances the Egyptian security forces and NDP-hired troublemakers on the one side and Brotherhood candidates and their supporters on the other.[20] In fact, the ferocity with which this violence pitted the regime and its proxies against the Islamist opposition constituted a sad hallmark of the 2005 parliamentary elections. Whilst not immune to regime interference, none of the other opposition parties contesting the elections were party to, or the target of, the scores of clashes that occurred between regime and Islamists.[21]

This raises the question of how to explain the sudden and unexpected outburst of political violence in the later phases of the 2005 parliamentary elections. To be sure, election-related violence is not uncommon in Egypt, and by comparison the 2005 parliamentary poll was not even the most bloody. What is so remarkable about these elections and in need of explanation, however, is the fact that the violence broke out so late in the election process and that it stood in sharp contrast to the relative quiet and openness that had prevailed during the campaigning period.

Table 1. Casualties of electoral violence, 1995–2005.

Parliamentary elections	Deaths	Injured
1995	80	1500
2000	10	64
2005	11–13	500

Sources: Thabet, 'Egyptian Parliamentary Elections', 19; Egyptian Organisation for Human Rights, *Future Parliamentary Victims*.

As far as state involvement is concerned, we posit that the use of force by the security services and NDP troublemakers was calculated and targeted against the opposition group posing the gravest electoral threat to ruling party candidates. For the regime this threat emanated from the Muslim Brotherhood (MB), which, by virtue of its exceptionally strong showing at the ballot box,[22] endangered the NDP's stranglehold over the legislature, which constitutes a key pillar to authoritarian survival. Another important factor was that from the regime's point of view the use of force against the MB was deemed both necessary and viable. It seemed necessary because so late in the election process the regime had run out of alternatives to turn the situation around and manufacture an NDP landslide. It was considered viable, because in this particular instance Cairo's domestic threat perceptions coincided with American security concerns over rising 'Islamist extremism' in the region, which meant that Egypt was unlikely to come under fire from Washington over the deployment of repressive force against the Brotherhood and its sympathizers.

It is widely recognized that the Muslim Brotherhood constitutes by far the most potent political threat to the regime.[23] For Mubarak the MB has long lost its utility as a bulwark against leftist forces, and is nowadays regarded as a serious menace to the regime. Not only is the group greater than other opposition parties in its resource capacity (both human and financial), organizational reach, and ability to muster grassroots support, but also in the assertiveness with which it challenges the secular foundations of the Egyptian regime and its pro-Western foreign policy.[24] Perilously close to the red lines of 'acceptable opposition behaviour', the Muslim Brotherhood is thus susceptible to regime repression.[25]

Whilst a total crackdown on the group has never been on the cards – primarily because this would drive the Islamists underground and cut off millions of Egyptian citizens from vital social services provided by the group – the authorities have always made it clear that serious MB forays into national politics would not be tolerated. The regime remains fiercely opposed to the notion of a legalized Muslim Brotherhood party and, although in past elections it did allow MB members to stand as independents, it has taken great care to contain their electoral potency.[26] In the legislative elections of 1995 and 2000, for instance, the group was subjected to a systematic and unrelenting clampdown on its candidates and supporters. As a consequence of this and other forms of regime-perpetuated electoral malpractice, the group has had little success in translating its support on the Egyptian street into a meaningful presence in parliament. In 1995 the MB won just one, and in 2000, 17 of the 444 elective assembly seats.[27]

However, with the authorities showing greater leniency towards the Brotherhood in the 2005 parliamentary election campaign, the group's electoral fortunes improved dramatically. Early signs that MB candidates were benefiting en masse from less government interference transpired in the first round of voting, by the end of which the group had captured 34 of the 164 available seats.[28] For the MB this was a remarkable success, given that 67% of its candidates had won their electoral contests and that so early on in the polling process the group had already doubled the number of its representatives in the Egyptian legislature.

The regime, meanwhile, must have read these first-round results with some alarm. Not only had the NDP fared relatively poorly, capturing 'just' 112 of all available seats,[29] but there was a real danger that similar Brotherhood inroads in the rounds to come would cost the ruling party its two-thirds majority in parliament. As will be discussed below, this considerable majority has been critical to the survival of the Mubarak regime ever since the turn to multiparty politics.[30] The danger of losing this majority then turned into a realistic prospect in the second round of voting, which still left the NDP 108 seats short of the 303 mandates needed. To defend its hegemonic position in the legislature, the NDP thus needed to capture at least 80% of the remaining seats in the final round of voting, a percentage it had fallen far short of in rounds one and two. As documented in Table 2, in the first round of voting the NDP won 68% and in the second round just 58% of all elective seats. The Brotherhood, by contrast, appeared to be on track to win a historic number of mandates, capturing a further 42 seats in the second phase of the polls. With the electoral tide turning against the NDP, and time running out, the regime thus felt compelled to revert to a well-tested strategy of violent repression in order to block any further Brotherhood inroads and secure election victory.[31] Discounting the damage this sudden outburst of violence has done to the reform credentials of the Egyptian regime, it appears to have aided the NDP in securing the 303 mandates needed to retain its two-thirds majority in parliament.

Table 2. NDP & MB inroads by voting phases (I–III).

	NDP gains		MB gains		
	Candidates	Seats	Candidates	Seats	Total no. of seats
Phase I	(112) 68%	(112)[1] 68%	(51) 67%	(34) 21%	164
Phase II	(83) 58%	(83) 58%	(60) 70%	(42) 29%	144
Phase III	(110) 81%	(110) 81%	(49) 24%	(12) 9%	136
Total	(305) 69%	(305) 69%	(160) 55%	(88) 20%	444[2]

Data sourced from: Konrad Adenauer Foundation, *Die Aegyptischen Parlamentswahlen 2005*.
Notes: [1] Including NDP Independents. [2] Includes only directly elected seats.

The determination of the Egyptian authorities to defend by all means necessary the NDP's two-thirds majority in 2005 underscores the high stakes nature of legislative elections in presidential autocracies. In Egypt, parliament is constitutionally endowed with significant legislative and oversight powers which, if left unchecked, can seriously endanger the foundations of authoritarian rule. To prevent this from happening, and to ensure parliament remains de facto subservient to the political executive, the regime relies on the NDP and its capacity to win two-thirds majorities at the ballot box. With this majority secured, Mubarak was able in the past to control the plenary debates and committee work in parliament and ensure that the opposition lacked the numerical strength to obstruct the passage of critical government legislation or to push through liberalizing reforms, censor cabinet ministers or impeach the president.[32] Crucially also, over the past three decades it has allowed Mubarak to govern by emergency rule, which must be granted and periodically renewed by the lower house of parliament with a two-thirds majority.[33] Whilst the constitutional powers of the presidency are vast, these emergency provisions have endowed Mubarak with important additional tools to regulate and control political life without appearing illegal. Emergency powers allow the president to govern by decree, suspend basic civil liberties, censor the press, and detain regime critics without trial, all for the 'good' of safeguarding national security and public order.[34] In practice, of course, the regime has deployed most of these powers to tackle domestic opponents, including most prominently the Muslim Brotherhood.[35] Critical to authoritarian survival, the capacity to govern by emergency rule was thus to be defended at all costs, if needed by resort to illegitimate vote-gaining strategies.

As for the question of why the regime resorted to violence, the decision must be interpreted as a measure of last resort, conditioned by the absence of viable alternatives to manufacture desired election outcomes so late in the voting process and the minimal external costs this repressive strategy appeared to inflict on the Mubarak administration. As far as the former is concerned, it is likely that the unavailability of *tawzir* (ballot fraud) critically shaped the regime's decision calculus to relinquish its commitment to peaceful elections. Ballot fraud, or ballot-box stuffing, is not only common in authoritarian elections, but where available, constitutes a most effective tool to correct unexpected and/or undesired opposition inroads until very late in the election process. In the event, however, the presence of judicial supervision rendered it very difficult, if not impossible, for the Egyptian authorities to resort to this illegitimate electioneering device. Full judicial supervision had been introduced by the regime in 2000, following a Supreme Constitutional Court (SCC) ruling that declared unconstitutional the practice of staffing ballot stations with government employees.[36] With both the casting and counting of ballots outside its direct control, the regime in 2005 seemed starved of options to 'correct' the results in favour of the ruling party.

The regime thus found itself caught between a rock and a hard place. Letting the election run its course could cost the NDP its two-thirds majority and land it with a potent opposition bloc in parliament. Resorting to dirty electioneering tactics to 'correct' the election results, including the use of force, on the other hand, would further undermine the regime's legitimacy at home and tarnish Mubarak's carefully rebuilt image as a reform-minded leader abroad. In the end, the regime opted for what it must have perceived as the lesser of two dangers to authoritarian survival, cracking down harshly on the MB, its candidates and sympathizers.

This decision was paired with the knowledge that a violent clampdown on the MB would not carry any negative repercussions for Cairo's close strategic relation with the USA. For although the Bush administration had singled out Egypt as a vanguard in renewed efforts to push for democratization in the region, it was apparent that Washington did not wish to see the Mubarak regime replaced by an Islamist-led government that openly opposed peace with Israel and objected to Cairo's close relations with the US.[37] For the Bush administration democratic alternance was not desirable at any cost and certainly not when it threatened to jeopardize Cairo's position as a pro-Western status quo power, a key arbitrator in the Middle East peace process and a vital ally in the global fight against Islamist terrorism.[38]

A clear indication of this caveat to US democracy promotion in Egypt can be found in the pronouncements made by Bush administration officials during the 2005 parliamentary elections. Indeed, despite the apparent heavy-handedness of the Egyptian security forces against the MB in the second and third rounds of voting, the US State Department showed little willingness to condemn the violence publicly, let alone exert any normative or material pressure on Mubarak to comply with his promise of 'free elections'.[39] Instead, US officials reiterated the view that Mubarak was committed to the pursuit of peaceful elections and that Washington had no reason to question this commitment.[40] What is more, what State Department officials said sounded remarkably similar to the official position taken by the Egyptian leadership. Explicit reference to the Brotherhood was avoided and its impressive showing at the ballot box essentially overlooked. For Washington, as for Cairo, it was not the group that had participated and won a significant number of seats in parliament – given that they were outlawed as a political party – but independent candidates with no party or ideological affiliation.[41]

Because the US and Egypt saw eye to eye on the threat posed by the Brotherhood, the Mubarak regime rightly assumed that Washington would impose few external costs on any efforts to contain the group's electoral inroads. Indeed, beyond limited condemnations of its election management (something the regime could weather) the Bush administration never signalled that it would review its annual economic and military aid to Egypt, let alone impose sanctions in response to the evident manipulation of the parliamentary poll. For the US, turning a blind eye to Egypt's heavy-handedness was thus seen as the 'lesser of two evils' in comparison to the prospect of a significantly emboldened Islamist group in parliament.

In summary, the state's recourse to violence against the MB in the later phases of the 2005 parliamentary poll highlights a number of important facts about the current state of Egyptian politics. First, it underscores the doubtful commitment of the Mubarak regime to clean elections and more broadly to the pursuit of democratic reforms. Indeed, it illustrates yet again that pledges of reform will remain just that when critical pillars of authoritarian survival are under attack. Second, it reveals the potency of the Muslim Brotherhood as a serious electoral challenger to the regime, and the regime's apparent incapability to tackle its electoral ascendancy by political means. Finally, it illustrates that as long as the political threat emanates from forces hostile to the US and to close US–Egyptian relations, Washington is unlikely to pursue its democracy promotion agenda more aggressively in the Arab world.[42] If anything, the new Obama administration is likely to reduce even further the pressure of democratization on Arab allies, given the president's belief in refraining from heavily interfering in the domestic politics in the region.

Regime manipulation without violence: Morocco's 2007 parliamentary election

Two years after Egypt, on 7 September 2007, Moroccans went to the poll to elect a new lower house of parliament. There was a significant degree of expectation both domestically and internationally about these elections for two important reasons. First, the elections were meant to confirm the steady progress towards democratization that the Kingdom had been making for at least a decade, with the King himself presenting them as a watershed. Second, most analysts had predicted that the Islamist Justice and Development Party (PJD) would top the polls and there was considerable curiosity as to how the King and the *Makhzen*, which represents an informal governing alliance between the monarch, his advisers, selected businessmen, high-ranking bureaucrats, and tribal chiefs operating as the unelected and unaccountable decision-maker in the country beyond the control of the elected government, would deal with this scenario. Whilst it should be kept in mind that the PJD is generally considered not to be antagonistic to the monarchy, a very high electoral score might have emboldened those within the party eager to display a much more forceful opposition to the current policies. In any case, it should be underlined that since its entry into electoral politics, the PJD has never joined governing coalitions, maintaining therefore a degree of distance from both the monarchy and the other political parties.

On a superficial level, the same domestic and international constraints that applied to the Egyptian case were also present in Morocco. The international community expected the elections to demonstrate that external support for the monarchy was well founded because King Mohammed VI was indeed moving the country towards democracy. Domestically, the elections were lauded as the culmination of a process of socio-political change that had seen the King push for a progressive liberal reform of the family code, the expansion of a range of civil liberties, and the creation of a reconciliation commission to investigate past human rights abuses.[43] The Kingdom would finally move towards substantial political reforms, the missing element so far in Mohammed VI's liberalizing agenda.

The strategy of including Islamist groups into the political and institutional game had been a 'risk' that King Mohammed VI's predecessor, Hassan II, had been willing to undertake in order to avoid the 'Algerian scenario', and he proceeded to include the PJD in the parliamentary scene. Mohammed VI continued his father's policy towards the PJD and the party ran in a limited number of constituencies in 2002 showing considerable strength.[44] In 2007 the PJD was allowed to run in all constituencies and it was tipped as the inevitable frontrunner. Indeed, most observers and the leaders of the other parties expected it to win a clear plurality of both votes and seats, and members of the PJD itself were confident of topping the polls, claiming that they were 'able to obtain 70 seats'.[45] Obviously, there was no question of the PJD winning an absolute majority of the 325 seats in parliament, but even the PJD's winning the largest share of seats would have caused considerable domestic and international anxiety.

The election campaign officially started only two weeks before polling day and it displayed a very interesting feature: the strong involvement of the state in trying to boost participation without openly taking sides with any of the parties in competition. The mobilization of the electorate included 'commercials urging youth to fulfil their national and social duty' and travelling caravans in the countryside to increase voter turnout.[46] This demonstrates that the King and the *Makhzen* had a great interest in the success of the parliamentary poll because it would reinforce the positive external perception of the regime. It is also for this reason that the state apparatus refrained from meddling with the electoral process, thus turning the election into what Storm describes as the 'most competitive, free and fair in the country's history'.[47] The positive sanctions obtained from the international community and from independent monitors also confirm the view that the 2007 elections were indeed a watershed for Morocco in terms of freedom and fairness.[48]

The proactive role played by the authorities to ensure the elections would pass off peacefully and the absence of any interference in the electoral process by the state contrast sharply with the Egyptian experience in 2005, although there was significant gerrymandering and toleration of a degree of vote-buying. Mohammed VI considers elections an important legitimising exercise, but a predicted landslide by the PJD was a significant risk as it could expose the weakness of the regime. How then does one explain the King's gamble of holding reasonably free and fair elections in the face of the expected victory of an Islamist party, which had traditionally sat in opposition and had been held as morally responsible for the wave of terrorism experienced by Morocco in 2003 and 2004? Upon closer inspection, it emerges that the anticipated landslide victory of the PJD, which ultimately did not materialize, was not perceived as overly problematic for the King and his advisers for a number of reasons.

First of all, legislative elections in Morocco are not very meaningful because they do not fundamentally shift the balance between elected representatives and the Palace. As mentioned previously, this is not the case in Egypt where the legislature and the executive have a mutually sustaining relationship. Whilst Denoeux posits that the Moroccan legislature is not as toothless as the literature argues and that it 'is making growing contributions to political representation and executive branch oversight',[49] there is no doubt that without far-reaching constitutional reforms the executive powers of the King severely limit the chamber's influence in the political system.[50] For instance, the King is responsible for appointing the prime minister, but he does not have to choose the leader of the party topping the poll for this post. More significantly, the King appoints the most important ministers, including Interior and Foreign Affairs. These and other constitutional prerogatives make elected officials unable to affect significantly the policy-making process because most of the input for policy comes directly from the palace or indirectly from ministers appointed by the King.[51]

Second, Moroccan elections, including those of 2007, are carefully managed by the Palace. While it is true that the 2007 contest represented the freest and fairest ones in the Kingdom's history, such elections are not immune from interference. Thus, the Palace was able to gerrymander the electoral districts, favouring the overrepresentation of the countryside, in order to ensure that the parties loyal to the monarch (*les parties du Roi*) did well. Also, vote-buying was largely tolerated. These two instruments were sufficient in many ways in 2007 to manipulate the outcome of the elections before they even took place. In addition to these direct tools of interference, there are other traits of the Moroccan political system that reinforce the ability of the Palace to tolerate and even encourage the participation of potentially threatening parties. For example, as Storm convincingly demonstrates, 'not since the first Moroccan parliamentary elections in 1963 ... has a political party been able to obtain more than 15% of the valid votes cast',[52] indicating that the fragmentation of the Moroccan party system prevents parties from reaching high individual scores. The Moroccan polity is characterized by a tradition of multiparty politics with a number of significant cleavages. In the absence of either overt coercion or widespread electoral fraud, the 2007 elections simply reflected divisions within Moroccan society and the peculiarity of the electoral system which encourages fragmentation. This sharply contrasts with the Egyptian party system, where the dominant party functions as a transmission belt between the presidency and society. In Morocco, political parties are technically independent from the executive monarchy, suffering from what Willis terms 'the illusion of significance'.[53] They operate in a context where the King relies on the wider *Makhzen* to consolidate his power.

Another important factor allowing the Palace to be 'relaxed' about the electoral process is that political Islam in Morocco is not represented primarily by the PJD and therefore both its participation in the electoral process and its score should be analysed in this context. Political Islam in Morocco is varied with at least three broad trends represented.[54] There is the participatory moderate trend of the PJD, which has accepted the primacy of the King in the political process and therefore 'does politics' within the limits set by the monarch. There is also the modern *salafi* trend linked to international violent Islamist networks. Finally there is the radical, but peaceful trend represented by the Justice and Charity Group (*al Adl*). Being the most popular Islamist movement in Morocco, al-Adl is semi-legal and refuses to participate in institutional politics because it would mean legitimizing the King as Commander of the Faithful, which runs against the conviction of the Group that the monarch has no such religious legitimacy.[55] This means that 'the popularity of the fundamental opposition rhetoric of Justice and Charity among Islamist constituencies has kept the PJD from mobilising wide segments of the disenfranchised population'.[56] The fragmentation of the Islamist camp is an asset for the regime and its 'divide and rule' strategies.[57] This makes the PJD radically different in terms of threat perception to the MB in Egypt.

Finally, the role of elections in Morocco is to provide a spectacle for international consumption; they are not meant to be meaningful expressions of the will of the people. Morocco has thrived since independence by being perceived as a pluralist polity. The international dimension of the legitimacy of the Moroccan regime should not be underestimated and Moroccan monarchs have traditionally been responsive to the expectations of the international community. Whilst a significant degree of authoritarianism was tolerated during the Cold War as Morocco was an ally of Western countries, the international political transformations of the early 1990s and social changes within Morocco required a change in the legitimizing discourse of the monarchy. The solution was found in the adoption of the language of democratization, whereby, under the prudent guidance of the monarchy, Morocco would make the transition from authoritarianism to some form of inclusive constitutional democracy underpinned by strong political parties and an active civil society. The international community encouraged and supported this top-down transition,[58] as it was in line with its new pro-democracy foreign policies. On coming to power Mohammed VI deepened the reforms that Hassan II introduced late in his reign and presented his vision for Morocco as being based on the dual and mutually reinforcing dynamics of democratization and development. Mohammed VI is in many ways no different from his father and has continued to integrate Morocco into Western economic and political structures, signing a free trade agreement with the US and deepening ties with the EU.[59] In addition, Morocco has been an important partner in the 'war on terror'. All this has been possible partly because of the appearance of a gradual democratization process taking place in the country. Even when the country was ruled with an iron fist by the monarch through the *Makhzen*, legislative mult-party elections were held and Léveau defined the country then as having a 'political system based on authoritarian pluralism'.[60] Election results were fixed in advance of the contest in order for the King to be better able to distribute power and influence a complex system of patronage that would ultimately allow him to remain in control of most policy-making power. This strategy was quite successful and Hassan II was able to survive in power and, as Howe highlighted, 'Morocco [was] generally respected by world powers as a stable constitutional monarchy engaged in the democratic process and as an Islamic voice of moderation'.[61] Morocco is perceived as an advanced 'democratizer' and this reputation cannot easily be tarnished by electoral violence. In this context, legislative elections play an important role and their smooth running, fairness and international monitoring constitute a legitimizing asset for the monarch. This is even more the case precisely because an Islamist party was allowed to run, strengthening the impression of genuine political change. Without this reputation, Morocco would not be able to extract as many benefits from the international community. Some would argue that appearing to be a 'democratizer' is not an important pre-condition for having good relations with the West and this is generally true, as the cases of neighbouring Tunisia and Algeria demonstrate. However, it is important to look at where each country stands in terms of international reputation. Morocco always thrived on presenting itself as a pluralist society with a multiparty system and obviously deviating from that would detract from its reputation. Tunisia and Algeria had a very different type of image abroad and therefore probably enjoyed more latitude when it comes to their reputation as democratizers.

The manipulation of the electoral process in 2007 did not paradoxically take place during the electoral process itself, as it had done in Egypt. Rather, such manipulation is inherent in the Moroccan political system where the constitutional role of the King, unelected and unaccountable to popular will, ensures that the elected officials have very little weight in determining policy-making. Thus, the 2007 elections can rightly be labelled free and fair, but certainly not as historic and breaking with the past as they have been presented by international scholars, external actors, and Moroccan media and politicians.[62] It follows that analysing the results and expecting on that basis to make meaningful inferences about the strength of political parties and the political views of ordinary Moroccans is misleading.[63] The only piece of data that can tell us something about the electoral process is turnout, a shocking 37% in 2007. This sharply contrasted with the efforts by the state, the political parties, and the King himself to encourage participation after the already very low turnout figure of 51.6% in the 2002 legislative elections. In addition to poor turnout, one-fifth of the votes cast were invalid, further reducing the percentage of Moroccans who actually participated in such 'historic elections'. The disaffection of voters towards the political system as a whole indicates that electoral contests do not represent an arena for meaningful confrontation and debate, thereby decreasing significantly the necessity for the regime to employ violence to fix their outcome. Paradoxically, abstention seems beneficial to the monarchy because it delegitimizes the political parties rather than the monarch, as voters opt out of the system leaving the King in his unquestioned position of supreme power over all other political actors.

In conclusion, the absence of violence and of interference in the electoral process do not constitute signs of democratization, but simply indicate that the manipulation strategy of the regime sees elections as central elements of international legitimacy and that they should therefore be conducted with high standards. The 2007 elections were certainly an improvement on previous contests when vote-buying and fraud occurred on a massive scale and when some parties, as was the case for the PJD in 2002, were only partially able to compete freely. However, this does not substantially modify the decision-making balance in the political system, which is heavily tilted towards the monarchy. In this context, it is therefore obvious that violence from both state authorities and from autonomous political groups would be extremely damaging for the image of Morocco and for its self-perception. On the one hand, the monarch and the security apparatus refrain from using violent coercion and, increasingly, from practices such as ballot box stuffing because this would send the signal that the country is no longer on the road to democracy. On the other hand, widespread electoral violence on the part of political movements would indicate not only that the state is not in control but, more crucially, that there is strong opposition to elections *per se*, once again presenting an image of instability that the monarchy is very keen to avoid.

Conclusion

Far from being antithetical, elections and violence are often intertwined. This is particularly the case, as one would expect, in conflict-ridden societies and liberalizing countries. It is increasingly, however, a phenomenon that is also encountered in fully fledged authoritarian regimes. Whilst there is a significant amount of scholarship dealing with the question of why authoritarian leaders even bother holding elections in the first place, this article attempts to explain under which conditions rulers employ violence once the electoral process has begun. Whilst the electoral potency of the opposition is certainly an important element in the rational calculus that rulers make when deciding to employ or refrain from the use of force in elections, there are other factors that need to be taken into account. It is necessary first of all to analyse the relative importance of the institution for which elections are called for. Second, there is the need to examine the alternatives that a regime has in order to influence the outcome of elections. Finally, in an increasingly interdependent world, one has to take into account the reactions of the international community.

The cases of the legislative elections in Egypt in 2005 and in Morocco in 2007 provide strong empirical evidence for the validity of the theoretical framework built around the three variables outlined above. Within this framework, it is quite unsurprising that the Mubarak regime decided to resort to violence to manage the 2005 legislative elections. The importance of parliament in the Egyptian institutional setting, the absence of alternatives to violence such as fraud so late in the game, and knowledge of the support of the international community and the potency of the Muslim Brotherhood combined to make the crackdown on the Muslim Brotherhood a viable and safe strategy for the regime. The use of violence was both rational and effective. The absence of electoral violence in Morocco is equally unsurprising given the weak role parliament plays in the Moroccan political system, the existence of viable alternatives to influence the outcome and the reliance of Morocco on an international image of a much stronger 'democratiser' than Egypt. Unlike in the Egyptian case, electoral violence would undermine the Moroccan regime. The paradox of it all is that the rulers of Morocco and Egypt share similar domestic and international constraints and it would be expected that they behave in a similar manner when faced with domestic challenges. This is obviously not the case and as Albrecht and Wegner highlighted in their work on Islamism in the two countries, institutions matter[64] and significantly influence choices like the use of violence during elections. The findings from Morocco and Egypt point to the necessity of looking beyond the threat of opposition potency when explaining electoral violence and they can be used to better understand how political institutions shape the responses of rulers facing similar domestic challenges.

Acknowledgements

Francesco Cavatorta wishes to acknowledge the financial support received from the Dublin City University Career Start Programme in carrying this research out. He also wishes to thank the colleagues of the Centre for Contemporary Middle East Studies at the University of Southern Denmark for their hospitality during the academic year 2008–2009.

Notes

1. Richter, 'The Role of Mob Riot'; Rapoport and Weinberg, 'Elections and Violence'.
2. Rapoport and Weinberg, 'Elections and Violence', 16–17.
3. Hoeglund, 'Electoral Violence'; Linantud, 'Whither Guns'; Snyder, *From Voting to Violence*; Wilkinson, *Votes and Violence*.
4. Tronvoll, 'Voting, Violence and Violations'; Raftopoulos, 'Zimbabwe's 2002 Presidential Election'; Kriger, 'Zanu(PF) Strategies'.
5. Schedler, 'The Menu of Manipulation', 42.
6. Brumberg, 'The Trap of Liberalised Autocracy'.
7. Gartner and Regan, 'Threat and Repression', 275.
8. Non-democracies are regimes that do not fulfil the minimum requirements of electoral democracy, as defined by Schumpeter (1947) and Przeworski (2000). Typically such regimes either (1) do not hold competitive legislative/executive elections altogether, (2) hold non-competitive single party elections only, or (3) allow for limited multiparty contestation, yet under conditions that are neither free and fair nor allow for the possibility of power alternation. See Przeworski, et al., *Democracy and Development*, 28–9; Schumpeter, *Capitalism, Socialism and Democracy*, 269.
9. See also Friedrich Ebert Stiftung, *Political and Electoral Violence*; Human Rights Watch, *Bullets for Each of You*.
10. Diamond, 'Elections without Democracy'.
11. Zartman, 'Opposition as Support'; Albrecht, 'How Can Opposition Support Authoritarianism'?.
12. Albrecht and Wegner, 'Autocrats and Islamists'.
13. Davenport, 'From Ballots to Bullets', 521.
14. Gartner and Regan, 'Threat and Repression', 277.
15. Chase, Hill, and Kennedy, 'Pivotal States'; Trisko, 'Coping with the Islamist Threat'.
16. Hamzawy and Brown, 'Can Egypt's Elections Produce', 2–3.
17. See for instance the United States Congressional Research Service, *Egypt: 2005 Presidential and Parliamentary Elections*.
18. Abaza, 'Political Islam', 14. In contrast to past elections, for instance, not a single Brotherhood candidate or supporter was arrested during the election campaign. See Howaidy, 'The MB Conundrum'.

19. Some accounts put the figure at 13 election-related deaths. See United States Congressional Research Service, *Egypt: 2005 Presidential and Parliamentary Elections*.
20. Due to a shortage of judges to supervise the polling stations, the government in 2000 decided to spread the voting process over three phases. In the 2005 elections the three rounds of voting were held between 9 November and 9 December.
21. A detailed account of the violence marring the voting process during the 2005 parliamentary elections can be found in a number of monitoring reports. See for instance, Egyptian Association for Supporting Democratic Development, *Press Releases 1–3* and Egyptian Organisation for Human Rights, *2005 Parliamentary Elections Initial Report: Third Phase Round One*.
22. The MB won an unprecedented 88 seats in 2005, which amounts to nearly 20% of all elective seats in the legislature. See also Table 2 in this article.
23. Albrecht and Wegner, 'Autocrats and Islamists'.
24. Rutherford, *Egypt after Mubarak*.
25. Gartner and Regan, 'Threat and Repression', 275–6; Davenport, 'Multi-Dimensional Threat Perception'.
26. Langohr, 'An Exit from Arab Autocracy', 117. Officially, the Muslim Brotherhood is a banned Islamist organization.
27. Makram-Ebeid, 'Egypt's 1995 Elections' and 'Egypt's 2000 Parliamentary Elections'. Since 1990, parliamentary elections in Egypt are held on the basis of a majority run-off system in 222 two-member constituencies.
28. As in past elections, in 2005 the MB focussed its campaigning efforts on brotherhood strongholds. It also refrained from placing candidates against government heavyweights as a measure of appeasement. Observers have noted that because the MB targeted primarily 'safe' constituency seats, the 2005 results may not reflect the actual electoral support the group carries in the entire country. See Ezzat, 'Marriages of Convenience'.
29. These included 44 so-called NDP independents, which after having failed to secure their party's nomination, had opted to contest the elections outside the formal NDP umbrella.
30. Egypt abrogated the one-party system in favour of limited multiparty elections in 1979.
31. State-sponsored violence apart, in rounds two and three of the elections the security forces arrested over 1000 MB cadre and sympathizers, closed polling stations prematurely, and prevented voters from casting their ballot. See Sullivan, 'Will the Muslim Brotherhood Run in 2010?'
32. A detailed analysis of the powers of the Egyptian legislature can be found in Baaklini, Denoeux, and Springborg, *Legislative Politics in the Arab World* and El-Mikawy, *The Building of Consensus*, 97–125.
33. Egypt was governed under emergency rule between 1967 and 1980, and has been again since the assassination of Sadat in 1981. Emergency legislation was last renewed by parliament for a two-year period in 2008.
34. Singerman, 'The Politics of Emergency Rule', 29–30.
35. Wolff, 'Constraints on the Promotion', 104.
36. Makram-Ebeid, 'Egypt's 2000 Parliamentary Elections'; Langohr, 'Cracks in Egypt's Electoral Engineering'.
37. See US State Department, *Daily Press Briefing by Sean McCormack* (8 September 2005).
38. Jordan and Pauly, 'The Centrality of Egypt'.
39. Kohstall, 'Reform Pirouettes', 33.
40. See US State Department, *Daily Press Briefing by Sean McCormack* (30 November 2005).
41. Ibid.
42. Durac, 'The Impact of External Actors'.

43. Storm, 'Testing Morocco', 38.
44. Willis, 'Morocco's Islamists'.
45. Storm, 'Testing Morocco', 41.
46. Ben-Layashi, 'Morocco's 2007 Elections', 72.
47. Storm, 'The Parliamentary Election', 359.
48. See for instance the US State Department, *Daily Press Briefing by Sean McCormack* (10 September 2007).
49. Denoeux and Desfosses, 'Rethinking the Moroccan Parliament', 79.
50. See Omar Benchorou, 'Les pouvoirs constitutionels du Roi', *Le Journal Hebdomadaire*, 23 April 2005.
51. Amar, *Mohammed VI*.
52. Storm, 'The Parliamentary Election'.
53. Willis, 'Political Parties in the Maghrib'.
54. Laskier, 'A Difficult Inheritance'.
55. Beau and Graciet, *Quand le Maroc Sera Islamiste*; Zeghal, *Les Islamistes Marocains*.
56. Hamzawy, 'The 2007 Moroccan Parliamentary Elections', 4.
57. Cavatorta, 'More than Repression'.
58. Ottaway and Riley, 'Morocco'.
59. On US–Morocco relations see White, 'Free Trade as a Strategic Instrument'. On EU–Morocco relations, see Cavatorta et al. 'EU External Policy-making'.
60. Léveau, 'Morocco at the Crossroads', 95.
61. Howe, 'Fresh Start', 59.
62. See, for instance, the declaration by Marina Ottaway, Middle East Program director at the Washington-based Carnegie Endowment for International Peace: 'these elections are historic for Morocco – and the international community – since there's a good chance that an Islamist party will emerge as the single most important party'. Ottaway, cited in Jacinto, 'Elections Put Moroccan Women at the Crossroads'. See also how the EU validated the elections as both transparent and aimed at strengthening the process of democratization. The statement (in French) is available at http://europa.eu/rapid/pressReleasesAction.do?reference=MEMO/08/211&format=HTML&aged=0&language=EN&guiLanguage=en (accessed 20 November 2009).
63. See Burgat,'Les élections législatives marocaines du vendredi 7 septembre 2007 ou le jouet cassé'.
64. Albrecht and Wegner, 'Autocrats and Islamists'.

Notes on contributors

Hendrik Kraetzschmar is Lecturer in Middle East politcs at the University of Leeds. He holds a PhD in comparative politics from the London School of Economics and Political Science and has also taught at the American University in Cairo. His current research focuses on the nature of electoral and party politics in the Middle East and North Africa.

Francesco Cavatorta is Senior Lecturer in International Relations and Middle East Politics at the School of Law and Government, Dublin City University. He holds a PhD in political science from Trinity College Dublin. His current research focuses on civil society activism in the middle East and North Africa.

Bibliography

Abaza, Khairi. 'Political Islam and Regime Survival'. *Policy Focus* 51 (2006): 1–24.
Albrecht, Holger. 'How Can Opposition Support Authoritarianism: Lessons from Egypt'. *Democratization* 12, no. 3 (2005): 378–97.

Albrecht, Holger, and Eva Wegner. 'Autocrats and Islamists: Contenders and Containment in Egypt and Morocco'. *The Journal of North African Studies* 11, no. 2 (2006): 123–41.

Amar, Ali. *Mohammed VI. Le Grand Malentendu.* Paris: Calmann-Lévy, 2009.

Baaklini, Abdo, Guilain Denoeux, and Robert Springborg, eds. *Legislative Politics in the Arab World: The Resurgence of Democratic Institutions.* Boulder, CO: Lynne Rienner Publishers, 1999.

Beau, Nicolas, and Catherine Graciet. *Quand le Maroc Sera Islamiste.* Paris: La Découverte, 2006.

Ben-Layashi, Samir. 'Morocco's 2007 Elections: A Social Reading'. *Middle East Review of International Affairs* 11, no. 4 (2007): 72–8.

Brumberg, Daniel. 'The Trap of Liberalised Autocracy'. *Journal of Democracy* 13, no. 4 (2002): 56–68.

Burgat, Francois. 'Les élections législatives marocaines du vendredi 7 septembre 2007 ou le jouet cassé'. *Mensuel de l'Université,* 1 December 2007. http://www.lemensuel.net/ 2007/12/01/les-elections-legislatives-marocaines-du-vendredi-7-septembre-2007-ou-le-jouet-casse (accessed 22 April 2009).

Cavatorta, Francesco. 'More than Repression; Strategies of Regime Survival: The Significance of *Divide et Impera* in Morocco'. *Journal of Contemporary African Studies* 25, no. 2 (2007): 187–203.

Cavatorta, Francesco, Raj Chari, Sylvia Kritzinger, and Arantza Gomez. 'EU External Policy-Making and the Case of Morocco: Realistically Dealing with Authoritarianism?' *European Foreign Affairs Review* 13 (2008): 357–76.

Chase, Robert S., Emily B. Hill, and Paul Kennedy. 'Pivotal States and US Strategy'. *Foreign Affairs,* January/February 1996: 33–51.

Davenport, Christian. 'From Ballots to Bullets: An Empirical Assessment of How National Elections Influence State Uses of Political Repression'. *Electoral Studies* 16, no. 4 (1997): 517–40.

Davenport, Christian. 'Multi-Dimensional Threat Perception and State Repression: An Inquiry into Why States Apply Negative Sanctions'. *American Journal of Political Science* 39, no. 3 (1995): 683–713.

Denoeux, Guilain P. 'Corruption in Morocco: Old Forces, New Dynamics and a Way Forward'. *Middle East Policy* 14, no. 4 (2007): 134–51.

Denoeux, Guilain P., and Helen Desfosses. 'Rethinking the Moroccan Parliament: The Kingdom's Legislative Development Imperative'. *Journal of North African Studies* 12, no. 1 (2007): 79–108.

Diamond, Larry. 'Elections Without Democracy: Thinking about Hybrid Regimes'. *Journal of Democracy* 13, no. 2 (2002): 21–35.

Durac, Vincent. 'The Impact of External Actors on the Distribution of Power in the Middle East: the Case of Egypt'. *The Journal of North African Studies* 14, no. 1 (2009): 75–90.

Egyptian Association for Supporting Democratic Development. *Press Releases 1–3.* Cairo, 26 November 2005. http://www.ndi.org/libraryquicksearch?op0=%3D& filter0=egypt (accessed 25 February 2009).

Egyptian Organisation for Human Rights. *2005 Parliamentary Elections Initial Report: Third Phase Round One.* Cairo, 1 December 2005. http://www.eohr.org/report/ (accessed 27 February 2009).

Egyptian Organisation for Human Rights. *Future Parliamentary Victims: EOHR's Report on Fact-Finding Mission to Monitor Results for 2005 Future Parliamentary Victims in the Governorates,* Cairo, 30 January 2006. http://www.eohr.org/report/ (accessed 27 February 2009).

El-Mikawy, Noha. *The Building of Consensus in Egypt's Transition Process.* Cairo: The American University in Cairo Press, 1999.

Ezzat, Dina. 'Marriages of Convenience'. *Al-Ahram Weekly*, 29 December 2005–4 January 2006.

Ebert Stiftung, Friedrich. *Political and Electoral Violence in East Africa*. Working Papers on Conflict Management, no. 2 (2001). http://library.fes.de/pdf-files/bueros/kenia/01398.pdf (accessed 14 May 2009)

Gartner, Scott Sigmund, and Patrick M. Regan. 'Threat and Repression: The Non-Linear Relationship between Government and Opposition'. *Journal of Peace Research* 33, no. 3 (1996): 273–87.

Hamzawy, Amr. 'The 2007 Moroccan Parliamentary Elections: Results and Implications'. *Carnegie Endowment for International Peace*, 11 September 2007. http://www.carnegieendowment.org/files/moroccan_parliamentary_elections_final.pdf (accessed 12 June 2009).

Hamzawy, Amr, and Nathan J. Brown. 'Can Egypt's Troubled Elections Produce a More Democratic Future'. *Carnegie Endowment for International Peace*, December 2005. http://www.mafhoum.com/press9/262S24.pdf (accessed 12 June 2009).

Hoeglund, Kristine. 'Electoral Violence in Conflict-Ridden Societies: Concepts, Causes and Consequences'. *Terrorism and Political Violence* 21, no. 3 (2009): 412–27.

Howaidy, Amira. 'The MB Conundrum'. *Al-Ahram Weekly*, 10–16 November 2005.

Howe, Marvine. 'Fresh Start for Morocco'. *Middle East Policy* 8, no. 2 (2001): 59–67.

Human Rights Watch. *Bullets for Each of You–State-Sponsored Violence since Zimbabwe's March 29 Elections*, June 2008. http://www.hrw.org/en/reports/2008 (accessed 14 May 2009).

Jacinto, Leela. 'Elections Put Moroccan Women at the Crossroads'. Association for Women's Rights in Development, 18 June 2007. http://www.awid.org/eng/Issues-and-Analysis/Library/Elections-Put-Moroccan-Women-at-Crossroads/(language)/eng-GB (accessed 19 November 2009)

Jordan, B.J., and Robert J. Pauly Jr. 'The Centrality of Egypt to the Future of the Greater Middle East'. In *Strategic Interests in the Middle East: Opposition or Support for US Foreign Policy*, ed. Jack Covarrubias and Tom Lansford, 157–70. Burlington, VT: Ashgate, 2007.

Kohstall, Florian. 'Reform Pirouettes: Foreign Democracy Promotion and the Politics of Adjustment in Egypt'. *Internationale Politik und Gesellschaft* 3 (2006): 32–45.

Konrad Adenauer Foundation. *Die Aegyptischen Parlamentswahlen 2005: III. Wahlgang*, 22 December 2005. http://www.kas.de/proj/home/pub/18/1/year-2005/dokument_id-7763/index.html (accessed 12 April 2009).

Kriger, Norma. 'Zanu(PF) Strategies in General Elections, 1980–2000: Discourse and Coercion'. *African Affairs* 104, no. 414 (2005): 1–34.

Langohr, Vicky. 'Cracks in Egypt's Electoral Engineering: The 2000 Vote'. *Middle East Report*, November 2000. http://www.merip.org/mero/mero110700.html, (accessed 26 September 2009).

Langohr, Vicky. 'An Exit from Arab Autocracy'. *Journal of Democracy* 13, no. 3 (2002): 116–22.

Laskier, Michael M. 'A Difficult Inheritance: Moroccan Society under King Mohammed VI'. *Middle East Review of International Affairs* 7, no. 3 (2003): 1–20.

Léveau, Remi. 'Morocco at the Crossroads'. *Mediterranean Politics* 2, no. 2 (1997): 95–113.

Linantud, John L. 'Whither Guns, Goons and Gold? The Decline of Factional Electoral Volence in the Philippines'. *Contemporary East Asia Studies* 20, no. 3 (1998): 298–318.

Makram-Ebeid, Mona. 'Egypt's 1995 Elections: One Step Forward, Two Steps Back?' *Middle East Policy* 4, no. 3 (1996): 119–36.

Makram-Ebeid, Mona. 'Egypt's 2000 Parliamentary Elections'. *Middle East Policy* 8, no. 2 (2001): 32–44.

Ottaway, Marina, and Meredith Riley. 'Morocco: From Top-Down Reform to Democratic Transition'. *Carnegie Papers* 71 (2006): 3–20.

Przeworski, Adam, *et al*. *Democracy and Development: Political Institutions and Well-Being in the World, 1950–1990*. Cambridge: Cambridge University Press, 2000.

Raftopoulos, Brian. 'Briefing: Zimbabwe's 2002 Presidential Election'. *African Affairs* 101 (2002): 413–26.

Rapoport, David C., and Leonard Weinberg. 'Elections and Violence'. *Terrorism and Political Violence* 12, no. 3 (2000): 15–50.

Richter, Donald. 'The Role of Mob Riot in Victorian Elections, 1865–1885'. *Victorian Studies* 15, no. 1 (1971): 19–28.

Rutherford, Bruce K. *Egypt after Mubarak: Liberalism, Islam and Democracy in the Arab World*. Princeton, NJ: Princeton University Press, 2008.

Schedler, Andreas. 'The Menu of Manipulation'. *Journal of Democracy* 13, no. 2 (2002): 36–50.

Schumpeter, Joseph. *Capitalism, Socialism and Democracy*. London: Allen and Unwin, 1947.

Singerman, Diane. 'The Politics of Emergency Rule in Egypt'. *Current History* 101, no. 651 (2002): 29–35.

Snyder, Jack. *From Voting to Violence: Democratisation and Nationalist Conflict*. New York: Norton, 2000.

Storm, Lise. 'The Parliamentary Election in Morocco, September 2007'. *Electoral Studies* 27 (2008): 359–64.

Storm, Lise. 'Testing Morocco: The Parliamentary Elections of September 2007'. *Journal of North African Studies* 13, no. 1 (2008): 37–54.

Sullivan, Denis. 'Will the Muslim Brotherhood Run in 2010?' *Arab Reform Bulletin,* May 2009. http://www.carnegieendowment.org/arb/?fa=show&article=23057 (accessed 8 May 2009).

Thabet, Hala G. 'Egyptian Parliamentary Elections: Between Democratization and Autocracy'. *African Development* 31, no. 3 (2006): 11–24.

Trisko, Jessica N. 'Coping with the Islamist Threat: Analysing Repression in Kazakhstan, Kyrgyzstan and Uzbekistan'. *Central Asian Survey* 24, no. 2 (2005): 373–89.

Tronvoll, Kjetil. 'Voting, Violence and Violations: Peasant Voices on the Flawed Elections in Hadiya, Southern Ethiopia'. *Modern African Studies* 39, no. 4 (2001): 697–716.

United States Congressional Research Service. *Egypt: 2005 Presidential and Parliamentary Elections*. Washington, DC, 15 January 2006. http://fpc.state.gov/c18192.htm (accessed 3 March 2009).

US State Department. *Daily Press Briefing by Sean McCormack*. Washington, DC, 8 September 2005. http://2001-2009.state.gov/r/pa/prs/dpb/2005/52801.htm accessed 20 February 2009.

US State Department. *Daily Press Briefing by Sean McCormack*. Washington, DC, 30 November 2005. http://2001-2009.state.gov/r/pa/prs/dpb/2005/57483.htm, (accessed 20 February 2009).

US State Department. *Daily Press Briefing by Sean McCormack*. Washington, DC, 10 September 2007. Reprinted by African Press Organization, http://appablog. wordpress.com/2007/09/10/parliamentary-elections-in-morocco/ (accessed 23 April 2009).

White, Gregory. 'Free Trade as a Strategic Instrument in the War on Terror? The 2004 US–Moroccan Free Trade Agreement'. *Middle East Journal* 59, no. 4 (2005): 597–616.

Wilkinson, Steven I. *Votes and Violence: Electoral Competition and Ethnic Riots in India*. Cambridge: Cambridge University Press, 2004.

Willis, Michael J. 'Morocco's Islamists and the Legislative Elections of 2002: The Strange Case of the Party that Did Not Want to Win'. *Mediterranean Politics* 9, no. 1 (2004): 53–81.

Willis, Michael J. 'Political Parties in the Maghrib: Ideology and Identification. A Suggested Typology'. *The Journal of North African Studies* 7, no. 3 (2002): 1–28.

Wolff, Sarah. 'Constraints on the Promotion of the Rule of Law in Egypt: Insights from the 2005 Judges' Revolt'. *Democratization* 16, no. 10 (2009): 100–18.

Zartman, William. 'Opposition as Support of the State'. In *The Arab State*, ed. Giacomo Luciani. Berkeley, CA: University of California Press, 1990.

Zeghal, Malika. *Les Islamistes Marocains*. Paris: La Decouverte, 2005.

Islamic reformation discourses: popular sovereignty and religious secularisation in Iran

Naser Ghobadzadeh and Lily Zubaidah Rahim

Department of Government and International Relations, University of Sydney, Sydney, Australia

Disputes over the outcome of the June 2009 presidential election in Iran rapidly developed into a contest about the legitimacy of the Islamic state. Far from being a dispute between religious and non-religious forces, the main protagonists in the conflict represented divergent articulations of state–religion relations within an Islamic context. In contrast to the authoritarian legitimisation of an Islamic state, the Islamic reformation discourse is based on secular-democratic articulations of state–religion relations. This article focuses on the ideas of four leading Iranian religious scholars who advocate a secular-democratic conceptualisation of state authority. Disputing the religious validity of divine sovereignty, they promote the principle of popular sovereignty based on Islamic sources and methods. This reformist conceptualisation is rooted in the notion that Islam and the secular-democratic state are complementary.

An ascendant paradigm

Religious resurgence in the closing decades of the twentieth century challenged the veracity of the global secularisation thesis popularised by Herbert Spencer, Karl Marx, Max Weber and Emile Durkheim. In particular, the emergence of political Islam has strongly contradicted this perspective. Related to the rise of political Islam is the hostile attitude towards secularism in much of the Muslim world, which we refer to as the 'Islamism- secularism conflict'. In many countries, religious forces have succeeded in mobilising the Muslim masses to resist secularisation processes initially undertaken by the colonial West and maintained by post-colonial authoritarian states. But, as Pippa Norris and Ronald Inglehart suggest, it may be premature to desert the secularisation perspective entirely.[1] A review of political Islam's achievements, specifically its nuanced relationship with secularism, may shed new light on the debate. By re-examining the divine versus popular sovereignty dichotomy, this paper argues that a passive secularism[2] is emerging from the lived experience of political Islam in post-revolutionary Iran. In this model, the relationship between religion and secularism is not antithetical. Religious sources can stimulate democratic secularism, whereby the separation of religion from the institutions of the state, rather than the separation of religion from politics is promoted. This conceptualisation is premised on a complementary relationship between Islam and democratic secularism. It is worth noting that whereas western secularisation was rooted in the Christian-religious reformation, in the Islamic world secularisation was promoted prior to the advent of religious reformation.[3] Instructively, the current re-conceptualisation of democratic secularism in Iran is inspired by religious reformation discourses postulated by religious intellectuals engaged in jurisprudential–theological debates.

Drawing attention to the religious features of the early secularisation processes in the West, Nader Hashemi reminds us that John Locke employed religious methods and sources to promote the separation of church and state. Hashemi maintains that a similar process is taking place in the contemporary Islamic world through the religious reformation discourse.[4] Just as Iranian religious scholars are currently contesting the concept of divine sovereignty, a similar discourse was debated in seventeenth century England. There is a vast corpus of literature addressing the political instability that marked the reign of Charles I of England (1625–1649), which culminated in his execution in 1649. This episode heralded the erosion of the divine right of kingship in the West. The English Glorious Revolution of 1688, followed by the French and American revolutions of the late eighteenth century, institutionalised the ideal of popular sovereignty.[5] During the French Revolution, secularism and popular sovereignty were promoted while the divine right of kings was refuted.[6] This chapter of Western political history resonates with the current situation in Iran. *Inter alia*, the religious reformation discourse and its interpretation of religious sources promote the view that popular sovereignty is not only compatible with Islamic principles but is also a form of governance suited to accommodating the core aims and spirit of Islam.

Sovereignty in the Shi'ite school: a potted history

In Islamic history, discourse based on the concept of divine versus popular sovereignty can be traced back to the Prophet Mohammad's demise in the seventh century AD. It is, in fact, the very basis of Shi'a/Sunni sectarian division. When the Prophet Mohammad died in 632 AD, two proposals emerged regarding his succession. The majority of Muslims (i.e. the Sunnis) believed that governance was not a sacred matter and that it should be decided by Muslims, whose consent (*Baya'at*) is the source of the ruler's authority. However, the minority Shi'a Muslims contended that the Muslim ruler should possess divine right and that God had appointed the Prophet's son-in-law Ali as the righteous ruler.[7] According to the main branch of Shi'ism (*Asna Ashari* or the 12 Imams), the right to govern was directly anointed by God to the 12 Imams, all of whom are descendants of Imam Ali and believed to be infallible. The 12th Imam, *Mahdi*, will supposedly return to form a just government.

In reality, none of the above 12 Imams, apart from Imam Ali,[8] could form a government based on Shi'ite theology. Since the disappearance of the 12th Imam in 941 AD (the Occultation era), de-politicised Shi'ism[9] has been the dominant ideal in the Shi'ite school. However, this was reconfigured by Ayatollah Ruhollah Mousavi Khomeini (1900–1989), who was the first in Shi'ite history to conceptualise the direct political-leading role for jurists through the doctrine of *Velayat-e Faqih* (rule of the Islamic jurist). This doctrine was implemented following the 1979 revolution.[10] Khomeini's doctrine by no means advocates the sole representation of the people. *Valy*, in the Arabic language, means Guardian or Custodian. In the literal sense, it refers to a parent or to one who is appointed to protect a ward.[11] Khomeini purported that the Prophet Mohammad and all of the 12 Shi'ite Imams possessed the divine right to be political leaders in the Islamic world.[12] Stressing the necessity of establishing an Islamic state in the occultation era, he argued that in line with the political authority of 'the infallibles',[13] learned Islamic jurists possess the divine right to lead Islamic society. He further asserted that the political authority of the jurists does not differ from that of the Prophet Mohammad:

> The idea that the governmental power of the Most Noble Messenger (s) were greater than those of the Commander of the Faithful ('a), or that those of the Commander of the Faithful ('a) were greater than those of the faqīh, is false and erroneous. ... God has conferred upon government in the present age the same powers and authority that were held by the Most Noble Messenger and the Imāms.[14]

Khomeini explicitly questions the argument that the *Valey-e Faqih*[15] should be indirectly chosen by the people's vote through the mediation of the Assembly of Experts: '*Velayat-e Faqih* is not something created by the Assembly of Experts,[16] *Valey-e Faqih* is something created by Almighty God. It is the same guardianship of the Noblest Messenger'.[17] Thus, the task of the 'Assembly of Experts is to prove the *Velayat-e Faqih* ... they want to ratify something, which is told by Almighty God'.[18] In sum, Khomeini's doctrine has served to rationalise the concept of divine sovereignty.[19]

Popular sovereignty: a democratic Shi'ite articulation

Khomeini's political thought has been the dominant discourse within the Shi'ite school since the 1970s. By contrast, the religious reformation discourse, based on progressive interpretations of religion and the state, was popularised in the early 1990s. The issue of sovereignty remains a key theme in the writings of the many scholars who subscribe to this discourse. Questioning the validity of divine sovereignty, they argue that Islam accepts the consent of subjects as the source of state authority. These scholars include Mohsen Kadivar, Ayatollah

Montazeri, Abdolkarim Soroush and Mohammad Mojtahed-Shabestari, to name but a few. They have played a pioneering role in proposing progressive ideas in their own specific areas of expertise. Recognised as a traditional religious scholar, Ayatollah Montazeri deployed progressive ideas within the community of traditional religious jurists. Similarly, while Kadivar outlines his arguments within a jurisprudential framework, he employs academic language. This approach has considerable support from within the religious educated and upper middle-classes. Soroush and Mojtahed-Shabestari base their arguments from theological and philosophical frameworks and have attracted audiences that are both religious and secular in orientation. Moreover, their influence on fellow Islamic scholars is substantial and their discourses have been employed by scholars to generate debate on religion–state relations in Iran.

The immediate impact of these scholars on the political sphere is of additional importance. Prior to the victory of reformist president Khatami in 1997, the writings of these scholars along with those of others, were published by the *Kayhan Farhangi*, *Kian* and *Salam*.[20] *Inter alia*, these writings paved the way for the emergence of a reformist movement. The current reformist 'Green Movement' is in many respects a manifestation of their scholarly thoughts. For example, large numbers gathered to attend Montazeri's funeral in Qum in December 2009, transforming it into an opportunity to protest against the Islamic state. The wide publicity surrounding Soroush's letters to Khamanei and Kadivar's letter to the head of the Assembly of Experts are other examples of their prominence in the political sphere. Finally, the ideas of these reformist scholars exemplify the internal shifts within the religious discourse in contemporary Iran. It is worth recalling that these scholars contributed to the Islamic revolution in 1979 and actively participated in the institutionalising of the Islamic state in the 1980s. Thus, their reformist perspectives represent the sentiment of many Iranians who once supported the unity of the state and religion but have come to reconsider this symbiotic relationship based on their lived experience of the Islamic Republic (IR) of Iran.

Even though these reformist scholars dispute authoritarian readings of religion in politics, and promote the principle of popular sovereignty, they employ different approaches in advocating the compatibility of Islam and secular democracy. Ayatollah Montazeri, for example, confined his argument to jurisprudence, providing a more democratic interpretation of religious sources. By contrast, Soroush argues that democracy cannot be extracted from Islam. In this article their views are categorised according to jurisprudential and non-jurisprudential approaches.

Jurisprudential approach: Kadivar and Montazeri

In line with the ruling clergy in Iran, the Quran, the *Hadith* and tradition constitute the foundation of progressive reformist re-conceptualisations of Islam. However, while religious conservatives support an authoritarian interpretation to justify the concept of divine sovereignty, reformists interpret these sources contextually. Mohsen Kadivar, a visiting Professor at Duke University, questions the jurisprudential validity of the notion of divine sovereignty. Kadivar argues that only six appointive positions are mentioned in the Quran, none of which are based on the claim of divine political authority for jurists. But like the ruling clergy, he maintains that the socio-political authority of the Prophet and infallible Imams was directly conceded by God.[21] However, Kadivar contradicts the doctrine of *Velayat-e Faqih* by questioning the extension of this socio-political authority to jurists in the occultation era. Based on his examination of the relevant *Hadiths*, Kadivar argues that jurists possess only two appointive positions: judgement and *Efta* (religious decrees).[22] As such, jurists do not possess divine political authority to lead Muslims, as was the case with the Prophet Muhammad and the 12 Shi'a Imams. He concludes that '*Velayat-e Faqih*, be it of religious or civil order, appointive or elective, absolute or conditional, lacks credible religious foundation'.[23]

Kadivar promotes a state-based popular sovereignty model on the grounds that neither the Quran nor the *Hadith* provide specific guidelines on state formation. In his view, 'Islam acknowledges that human faculties are capable of finding appropriate solutions in these fields [forms of political systems]. In other words, politics is a matter of intellect, and the ability to reason is a human trait'.[24] Arguing that numerous competing political models that do not contradict the tenets of the Shari'a can be supported, Kadivar maintains that it has been left to the people from different periods and societies to articulate the most appropriate political system.[25] He further argues that democracy is the ideal political system for the Islamic world because it is the best product of human reasoning and experience:

> [D]emocracy is the least erroneous approach to the politics of the world. (Please note that least erroneous does not mean perfect or even error free.) Democracy is a product of reason, and the fact that it was first put to use in the West does not preclude its utility in other cultures – reason extends beyond geographical boundaries. One must adopt a correct approach, regardless of who came up with the idea.[26]

The most high-ranking reformist jurist to conceptualise a democratic notion of the doctrine of *Velayat-e Faqih* was the late Ayatollah Montazeri (1922–2009), who ironically advocated inclusion of *Velayat-e Faqih* in the Constitution in 1979. Had Montazeri not challenged Khomeini in 1989, he would have been appointed the second *Valey-e Faqih* after Khomeini's death.[27] Disillusioned by the experiences of the Islamic state, Montazeri reconfigured his ideas on *Velayat-e Faqih*.[28] However, his religious position and background led Montazeri to continue supporting a direct engagement of the clergy in politics.[29] Like the ruling clergy, he did not doubt that the divine source of political authority resided with Prophet Mohammad and the 'infallible Imams'.[30] Significantly, he also supported the political leadership of jurists in the occultation era but distanced himself from the ruling clergy by questioning the doctrine of *Nasb-e Um* (generic appointment).[31] This doctrine purports that although no specific person is appointed as leader of an Islamic society, all learned Islamic jurists simultaneously possess the divine right of political authority. Proposing five possible scenarios[32] from which to choose one of the eligible jurists as head of state, he concluded that it was impossible to have a functional form of government based upon the doctrine of generic appointment.[33] Montazeri concluded: 'According to the Quranic verses and *Hadith*, only the qualifications of the sovereign can be extracted, but not more than these qualifications. This is not a basis for the appointment of jurists in the contemporary era'.[34] This actually contradicts Khomeini's doctrine of *Velayat-e Faqih* which argues that the learned Islamic jurist is specifically appointed as a divine political authority.

Contradicting the doctrine of generic appointment, he outlined the 'theory of elect' (*Nazariy-e Nakhb*) to provide religious justification for popular sovereignty and maintained that 'in contrast to the theory of appointment (*Nazariy-e Nasb*), according to which the jurists' right to govern is directly legitimised by the appointment by God, in this theory (*Nakhb*) the source of state legitimacy . . . is the people's election not divine appointment'.[35] Thus, from a jurisprudential point of view, the people's consent is required to legitimise the Islamic state during the occultation period.[36] Providing a democratic interpretation of key Quranic verses and *Hadith*, his reading of the *Shura* (consultation) verses in the Quran,[37] affirms popular sovereignty.[38] Allegiance (*baya'at*), which has a strong tradition in Islamic history and was the means by which the Prophet and Imam Ali assumed political leadership, was frequently cited by Montazeri to justify the electoral system.[39]

In the 'elective, conditional doctrine of *Velayat-e Faqih*' proposed by Montazeri, *the Valey-e Faqih* is accountable to the people and not to God and chosen for a specific term as with other political authorities.[40] Finally, the key aspect of Montazeri's political thought includes the acceptance of the concept of social contract as the source of state authority. In line with contractarianism, Montazeri saw state authority as based on a contract between subjects and the sovereign. In the 13 centuries-old history of Shi'ism, Montazeri was the first jurist to employ Islamic theology to determine state–citizen relations based on a social contract, akin to the principles espoused by Locke and Rousseau.[41] Montazeri's exact words are worth quoting:

> From a rational and religious point of view, the electing of a sovereign by the people . . . is of necessity a social contract, which is indispensible when it is developed and contracted through allegation. When elected, the sovereign is responsible for carrying out delegated tasks due to the contract's conditions and limitations. People ought to support him and obey his order unless he violates religious principles or the rules of the contract.[42]

Non-jurisprudential approach: Soroush and Mojtahed-Shabestari

Along with the jurisprudential approach, theological, philosophical and even ultra-religious reasoning have been employed by progressive reformists to question the religious justification of divine sovereignty. Scholars subscribing to this approach do not structure their arguments solely on religious sources such as the Quran and

Hadith. Basic human rights principles and modern reasoning are also employed to argue for the promotion of popular sovereignty. Abdolkarim Soroush and Moham-mad Mojtahed-Shabestari are two influential leading scholars in this regard. They advocate a form of secularism that distances divinity from the socio-political sphere. In his magnum opus, *Theoretical Constriction and Expansion of Shari'a*, Soroush conceptualises the separation of 'religion' from 'religious knowl-edge'. He states that whereas religion is a sacred, eternal and fixed phenomenon, human knowledge of religion is a worldly, intermittent and temporary phenom-enon. He further argues that as the human understanding of religion is incomplete and imperfect, no one can claim to possess a definitive understanding of religion.[43] Adding a worldly dimension to the concept of revelation, his theory of *The Expansion of Prophetic Experience* contends that revelation has been effected by the characteristics and personal history of the Prophet Mohammad. As a human being, the experience of the Prophet was accidental and the very experience of revelation in the Arabic culture and language is merely a factual phenomenon. In other words, revelation was a historically accidental occurrence rather than an essential attribute of religion.[44] Similarly, Soroush's notion of *Substantial and Accidental in Religion* maintains that the Quran reflects Arabic culture and history of the revelation era. As such, jurisprudential principles and the Shari'a are accidental dimensions of the Quran and therefore subject to revision in order to remain relevant.[45]

Having provided a brief explanation of Soroush's intellectual paradigm,[46] his postulations on the divine and popular source of state authority will now be dis-cussed. Soroush purports that governance is a non-jurisprudential and ultra-reli-gious issue.[47] Pointing to issues of the prophecy and *Imamate*,[48] which fall within the theological rather than jurisprudential realm, Soroush maintains that 'as a theory of state, the doctrine of *Velayat-e Faqih* ought to be discussed in theo-logical rather than jurisprudential terms'.[49] As the Quran and Hadiths are the main sources of reasoning in jurisprudence, this approach invites the inclusion of other sources and methods of reasoning. This explains the infrequent reference to the Quran, *Hadith* and Islamic tradition at the core of Soroush's discourse on govern-ance.[50] In questioning the religious validity of the doctrine of *Velayat-e Faqih*, he explores the concept of guardianship (*Velayat*), by focusing on two forms of guar-dianship, namely spiritual and political guardianship. Spiritual guardianship incor-porates a theosophical notion (*Irfan*), according to which there is just submission; that is, the master orders and the devotee obeys without question and without seeking any explanation. Soroush further contends that as this notion of guardian-ship is an exclusive relationship between two persons, it therefore is not applicable to the socio-political context. For Soroush, political leadership does not require submission. Imam Ali, the only Shi'ite Imam to have the opportunity to lead the Islamic world, possessed political rather than spiritual guardianship. Soroush fur-nishes a variety of examples to highlight that the political decision-making of Imam Ali and other Shi'ite infallibles were in fact criticised by their followers. In many instances, they were guided by this criticism. For Soroush, the doctrine of '*Velayat-e Faqih* does not resemble anything related to theosophical and spiritual guardianship. It is only the similarity of the term guardianship that has led some to associate and confuse this guardianship (meaning presidency and leadership) with the other notion of guardianship, which is exclusive to the 'friends of God' (*Uliya-e Allah*) and to those who are special before God'.[51]

In advocating the concept of popular sovereignty, Soroush does not base his argument on Islamic principles. He contends that in contrast to the modern world in which human beings are rights-carriers, in the religious context, human beings are essentially duty-bound subjects. Since jurisprudential regulations are based on the latter approach, they are restricted to the duties of Muslims.[52] Given that not all human rights can be derived from religious principles, it ought to be understood in non-jurisprudential terms. He insists that the key human right of overseeing the ruler does not have a religious basis. Citizens are the source of state authority owing to the secular right of subjects to demand accountability from their rulers. Their right to oversee rulers provide subjects with the right to criticise and, if necessary, dethrone rulers:

> If you have the right to oversee the government, it can easily be proved that you have the right to rule. It is insensate to tell someone that you have the right to dethrone a ruler but not the right to appoint a ruler. The right to appoint is prior to the right to dethrone.[53]

From Soroush's point of view, the two key governance questions are: (a) what values do believers expect from a government? and (b) what methods should they use to achieve these values? The second question pertains to the issue of governance techniques and thus falls into the scientific category. Soroush maintains that scientific-experimental questions are inherently non-religious:

> If we ask 'what should be done to have a successful state?' this question will be translated into questions such as how the education system should be instituted? How the country's economy should be managed? How the health and housing systems should operate? ... Each and every one of these questions is a scientific question ... If we refer these questions to religion, we are making a mistake ... these aspects of governing have a rational nature. Wise men should get together and formulate arrangements for the managerial aspects of governance.[54]

Soroush characterises the current political system in Iran as a 'jurisprudential state' (*Hukomat-e Feqhi*) and argues that jurisprudence is incapable of providing answers to all issues pertaining to governance and is subject to shortcomings. It is bounded by the limitations of time and place.[55] Soroush distinguishes between generic values, which are extra-religious, such as justice, truth, humanity and honesty, and religious values such as outlawing usury, the drinking of wine or the *Hijab* issue.[56] Soroush argues that generic values are related to the nature of governance, rather than religion: 'If a state intends to succeed, it must be just. Just governance is, of course, confirmed by religion; but, it does not earn its justice from religion'.[57] However, in terms of religious values, Soroush advocates a restricted role for government. In a religious society, the state may play an indirect role in fulfilling these sets of values. Indirect intervention by the state includes providing an appropriate material environment for the fulfilment of these values by believers. He further argues that human beings have two kinds of needs, primary needs and secondary needs, and that religious values are secondary needs. In a religious society, the state is responsible for fulfilling believers' primary needs and liberating believers from these concerns, so that 'an opportunity to think and deliberate upon their secondary needs – including spiritual faith – is provided for believers'.[58]

While the main aim of Montazeri is to present a democratic understanding of religious sources, Soroush deems these efforts as doomed to failure, maintaining that:

> We have put behind us a period in which some scholars ... have sought to extract democracy from Islam ... Abul Ala Maududi and Bazargan were looking for this conceptualisation. For example, they interpret Quranic references to consultation (Shura) as parliament; and, when there is talk about allegiance (Baya'at), they understand it as election ... We have come to a blest consensus, which proves that this is impossible and doomed to fail.[59]

Soroush controversially purports that democracy is not extractable from Islam. However, this does not necessarily distance him from those who subscribe to the idea of the compatibility between Islam and democracy. He argues that democracy is a method of governance aimed at minimising error based on the principle of popular sovereignty. But where do these principles come from? Soroush purports that 'they are not extractable from the principles of Islam, although they are not inconsistent with it either'.[60] As the ideal of popular sovereignty is achieved through rational human reasoning and because Islam does not dictate a specific form of state, there is no conflict between Islam and popular sovereignty.[61]

Mohammad Mojtahed-Shabestari is another key Muslim intellectual who refutes the concept of divine sovereignty from a theological and philosophical standpoint.[62] Like Soroush, he argues that governance should not be solely based on a religious doctrine and that Muslims 'may approach politics and governance as philosophical and scientific issues without violating the core message of the holy text and tradition'.[63] He also insists that modern political notions such as democracy, freedom and human rights should not be rationalised by the Quran and *Hadith*.[64]

Soroush and Mojtahed-Shabestari, unlike Kadivar and Montazeri, challenge the status of the Shari'a in Islam by highlighting the importance of direct individual-God relations. Mojtahed-Shabestari dismisses the need for both legal (the Shari'a) and human mediators (the clerics). More controversially, even revelation is questioned: 'the core of Islamic faith ... exists in the relationship between a human being and God, with or without revelation'.[65] Mojtahed-Shabestari proposes the concept of 'religious experience' which relegates the Shari'a to a set of regulations which have been extracted from the holy text and tradition by jurists. However, this is not the core premise of religion. Insisting on the priority of faith over the Shari'a, Mojtahed-Shabestari maintains that as every person interprets and personally experiences the revelation and message of God as an individual experience, it cannot be imposed upon others.[66] Thus, attempts to dictate the interpretation of religion impedes the individual and genuine process of experiencing religion.[67] State intervention in religion thus, 'stands in direct contradiction to the true essence and spirit of religion'.[68] As religious experience is an ongoing process, freedom of thought that is free of internal sensuality and external barriers (authoritarian rule) is necessary for genuine religious experience. Internal freedom, according to Mojtahed-Shabestari is subject to external freedom. As religious experience cannot be nurtured within an authoritarian political system, democracy is not only compatible with religion but also crucial to cultivating religious consciousness in the Muslim world.[69]

Mojtahed-Shabestari also proposes a hermeneutic approach to the Quran to counter the influence of state intervention in religion. As every person approaches the text with presuppositions, these presuppositions impact on their understanding of the text, thus making it impossible for a neutral reading. The crucial point in Mojtahed-Shabestari's approach is that the reader's presuppositions are profoundly influenced by consciousness and cognition of contemporary times. Therefore, like Soroush, Mojtahed-Shabestari concludes that no individual reading of the holy text can ever be complete because human consciousness and knowledge are always evolving.[70] Therefore, 'a distinctive aspect of God's word is its perpetual interpretative feature. No interpretation of God's word is the ultimate understanding ... there should always be an open path for new interpretations'.[71]

The distinction between vertical and horizontal relations can serve to conceptualise the tensions between religion and democracy.[72] According to Mojtahed-Shabestari, God–human relations are communicated through individual religious experience and submission and obedience is the main feature of such vertical relations. By contrast, politics and human rights are based on human–human relations. Thus, in terms of governance, consent, agreement and rational reasoning ought to be employed to regulate the inherently horizontal relations between individuals.[73]

Mojtahed-Shabestari argues that jurisprudence is an Islamic science to be observed rationally and according to context.[74] For him jurisprudential knowledge constitutes three commandments: worshiping, trading and governance. Mojtahed-Shabestari argues that jurists have traditionally maintained rationality in the realms of 'worshipping' and 'trading' but not in the area of contemporary governance. He states: 'Religious decrees are not congruent with these questions [contemporary political questions] ... thus, political jurisprudence has departed from its rational context'.[75] Mojtahed-Shabestari expands this argument in terms of the impossibility of attributing popular sovereignty to a jurisprudential context based on the Quran. Paralleling Soroush's theory of *The Expansion of Prophetic Experience*, he argues that the Quran is a human production of revelation and not *The Revelation*. In other words, the holy text grew out of the Prophet Mohammad's personal experience of revelation.[76] As the Revelation is an extension of the notion of the religous experience to the Prophet, the holy text is thus a product of the Prophet Mohammad's religious experience.[77] According to this logic, commands presented in the holy text are responses to the socio-political and cultural conditions of the revelation era, and not eternal commands. 'There are no timeless commands/prohibitions in the revelatory words because both commands/prohibitions and human beings – including the Prophet – are ephemerally existent; thus, timeless commands and prohibition are impossible'.[78] Therefore, 'if there is a Quranic verse about a specific issue, it does not mean that it should always be practiced'.[79] This conceptualisation suggest that the political features of the Quran and *Hadith* are responses to the socio-political context of the revelation. As such, many Quranic commands today are not directly relevant because the contemporary socio-political context is profoundly different. Mojtahed-Shabestari enjoins Muslims to accord priority to the eternal message underpinning the Quranic commands which is justice.

Mojtahed-Shabestari interprets the Prophet Mohammad's governance in Medina as a factual occurrence that is not integral to his prophetic mission. In the revelation era, the essence of religion (justice) was manifested in the Prophet's political leadership. However, in the contemporary era, this historical phenomenon does not provide sufficient justification for the unchallenged political authority of jurists. By contrast, the essence of religion can be more accurately represented in the contemporary era through the concept of popular sovereignty. For Mojtahed-Shabestari, popular sovereignty is worthy of support, not because it is decreed by the Quran or tradition but because it is the only plausible method of capturing the spirit and essence of Islam which is rooted in justice. As the Quran does not prescribe any timeless form of state, it is the responsibility of Muslims to articulate a political system that can capture the essence of Islam. In the contemporary world, the establishment of a democratic political system is not only appropriate but also fulfils the core principle of Islam which is based on justice.[80]

Conclusion

Although the political crisis in Iran was triggered by widespread protests challenging the outcome of the 2009 presidential election, it rapidly transformed into protests challenging the legitimacy of the Islamic state. The cry 'Where is my vote?' rapidly morphed into more far reaching slogans such as: 'Death to Dictator', 'Death to the Islamic Republic' and 'Independent, Freedom, Iranian Republic'. 'Iranian' replaced 'Islamic' in the most well-known slogan of the 1979 revolution: 'Independent, Freedom, Islamic Republic'. This discernible shift was followed by serious discussions in political and scholarly works contesting the legitimacy underpinning the unity of the state and religion. The religious feature of this contest is of tremendous importance as to date, liberals, leftists and/or nationalist have failed to pose a serious threat to the legitimacy of the IR. It has been primarily reformist Islamic discourse that has effectively challenged the legitimacy of the Islamic state.[81] This alternative articulation of religion–state relations raises the possibility of the co-existence of Islam and political secularity[82] and the growing support for an indigenous model of democratic secularism which differs from the pre-revolutionary top-down authoritarian secularisation model.

Iranian reformist religious scholars have played a significant role in promoting a democratic-secular articulation of state authority within a religious context. The religious scholars discussed above have had a profound influence leading up to of the reformist era (1997–2005) and the Green Movement (2009 onwards). Ironically, these scholars supported the establishment of the Islamic state in the 1970s and effectively contributed to the institutionalisation of the Islamic state in the 1980s. However, disillusioned by the authoritarian excesses of the Iranian Islamic state, they have re-conceptualised state–religion relations. Employing religious sources and methods, they challenge the legitimacy of the Islamic state, a shift that has led to a secular articulation of politics. This discourse strongly mirrors the early secularisation process in the West, wherein the concept of popular sovereignty was conceptualised by theorists such as Locke and Rousseau to reframe religion–state relations and contributed to the secularisation of politics. The authoritarian excesses of Iran's Islamic state have neither led to the abandonment of religion in the political sphere nor to the re-emergence of anti-religious secularism. Instead, a religious reformation discourse based on the compatibility between Islam and political secularism has generated considerable public support. As such, further research into theological debates in the political sphere and the principle of popular sovereignty will contribute to a more comprehensive understanding of the rising prominence of secular-democracy in Iran.

Acknowledgements

We thank Professor John Keane for his conceptual contribution and Professor Jeffery Haynes as well as the anonymous reviewers for their constructive comments.

Notes

1. Norris and Inglehart, *Sacred and Secular*; Norris and Inglehart, 'Uneven Secularization'.
2. We borrow this concept from Ahmet Kuru who proposes that while assertive secularism aims to exclude religion from the socio-political sphere, passive secularism incorporates the public visibility of religion. See Kuru, *Secularism and State Policies*.
3. Filali-Ansary, 'Challenge of Secularization'.
4. Hashemi, *Islam, Secularism*.
5. Bukovansky, *Legitimacy and Power*; Morgan, *Inventing the People*; Wootton, *Divine Right and Democracy*.
6. Sajo, 'Preliminaries', 628.

7. This does not mean that contemporary Sunni states are more democratic than their Shi'a counterparts. Like other religious issues, the political thought of both the Shi'a and Sunni world have evolved in various political configurations.

8. Imam Ali's governance (656–661) is considered by the Shi'a as the only legitimate rule in early Islamic history. From a historical point of view, it was the only Shi'ite state headed directly by a Shi'ite religious leader until the formation of the IR of Iran, when religious leaders took direct political control. As El Fadl writes 'Until recently neither Sunnite nor Shi'ite jurists ever assumed direct rule in the political sphere'. Abou El Fadl, Cohen, and Chasman, *Islam and the Challenge*.

9. According to this notion, Shi'ite religious leaders adopted a passive approach to the political sphere. The 'infallible Imam' was believed to be the only one who possessed the right to govern. Therefore, for most of Shi'ite history, religious leaders awaited the return of the last Imam.

10. Kadivar, 'Theories of State', 3–4.

11. Mehdi Haeri Yazdi challenges the political doctrine of *Velayat-e Faqih* by referring to the very meaning of the term. He argues that *Velayat* refers to a relationship between custodian and ward. By no means can it be applied to governmental and political issues. He maintains that 'This relationship is not possible between a person and a group of people'. See Haeri Yazdi, *Wisdom and Government*.

12. Khomeini and Algar, *Islam and Revolution*, 40.

13. In the Shi'ite school, infallibles refer to 14 specific persons including the Prophet Mohammad, his daughter Fatima and 12 Imams who are descendants of Fatima.

14. Khomeini and Algar, *Islam and Revolution*, 62.

15. *Valey-e faqih* is the religious title of the Supreme Leader. Actually, 'Supreme Leader' is the political tag for the *Valey-e Faqih*.

16. Assembly of Experts includes 86 clerics who are directly elected by the public to an eight-year term. According to the Constitution, this assembly is responsible for electing the Supreme Leader. This has been practised just once: when the founder of the IR died on 3 June 1989, the Assembly chose Khamanei as the Supreme Leader on the following day. See Ehteshami and Zweiri, 'Understanding Iran's Assembly'.

17. Khomeini, *Book of Light*, 95, 2006.

18. Khomeini, *Book of Light*, 27, 2000.

19. There is a counter-argument, which asserts that Khomeini's occasional confirmation of the centrality of the subjects' role proves his subscription to a form of dual-legitimacy. For example, see Goudarzi, Jawan, and Ahmad, 'Ayatollah Khomeini', P103–14.

20. Prior to the reformist era (1997–2005), there were several publication restrictions and these publications were the only channels available for reformists to disseminate their ideas.

21. Kadivar, 'Appointive Government'.

22. Kadivar, 'Government by Mandate', 9.

23. Kadivar, 'Velayat-e Faqih', 2002.

24. Ibid.

25. Kamrava, *Intellectual Revolution*, 165.

26. Kadivar, 'Velayat-e Faqih', 2002.

27. Montazeri was the designated successor of Khomeini. Appointed by the Assembly of Experts on 24 November 1985 and dismissed by Khomeini on 26 March 1989, he was actually the shadow *Valey-e Faqih* for more than four years.

28. Akhavi, 'Thought and Role of Ayatollah', 647.

29. Montazeri, 2000, 99–100.

30. Abdo, 'Islamic Republic', 18; Montazeri, 2000, 122–178.

31. *Nasb-e Um, as opposed to Nasb-e Khas* (specific appointment) refers to the Godly appointment of certain persons, for example, the Prophet Mohammad and the 12 Imams.
32. For a detailed discussion of these five scenarios, see Akhavi, 'Thought and Role of Ayatollah', 645–66.
33. Montazeri, 2000, 188–214.
34. Montazeri, *Perspectives*, 35–6.
35. Montazeri, *Religious State*, 24.
36. Montazeri, 2000.
37. 'And those who answer the call of their lord and establish worship, and whose affairs are a matter of counsel, and who spend of what we have bestowed on them' (Surah 48, Verse 38) (translated by Marmaduke Pickthall).
38. Montazeri, 2000, 288–90.
39. Ibid., 2000, 305–26.
40. Kadivar, 'God', 64, 69.
41. Soroush, 'Khatami's Practical Hesitation'; Soroush, 'Soroush's Speech'.
42. Montazeri, *Perspectives*, 36.
43. Kamali, 'Theory of Expansion'; Soroush, *Theoretical Constriction*; Vahdat, 'Islamic Modernity'.
44. Soroush, *Expansion of Prophetic Experience*.
45. Soroush, 'Substantial and Accidental'.
46. Discussions centring on Soroush's thought include Soroush, Sadri, and Sadri, *Reason, Freedom*; Ghamari-Tabrizi, *Islam and Dissent*; Aliabadi, 'Abdolkarim Soroush'; and Jahanbakhsh, *Islam, Democracy*.
47. Jahanbakhsh, 'Abdolkarim Soroush', 21.
48. *Imamate* is among the basic principles of Shi'ite school. The 12 Imams are believed to be appointed by God to lead Muslims. This is a fundamental distinguishing feature between Shi'a and Sunni Islam.
49. *Jurisprudence* accepts the basic principles of Islam such as monotheism, prophecy of Mohammad and the eternity of the Quran as unchallenged givens. By contrast, theology incorporates the study of god, religion and rational inquiry into the basic principles of religion. Soroush, 'Analysing the Concept', 2.
50. Mottaqi, 'Soroush's Flourishing Workbook', 48.
51. Soroush, 'Spiritual Guardianship', 20.
52. Soroush, *Reason, Freedom*; Soroush, 'Shi'a and the Challenges'.
53. Soroush, 'Analysing the Concept', 5–6.
54. Ibid., 6.
55. Soroush, 'Functions and Benefits', 2–16; Soroush, 'Minimalist and Maximalist', 2–9.
56. Soroush, 'Analysing the Concept', 6–7.
57. Ibid., 7.
58. Ibid., 10.
59. Soroush, 'Shi'a and the Challenges'.
60. Soroush, 'Democracy'.
61. Jahanbakhsh, *Islam, Democracy*; Soroush, 'Democracy'.
62. Mojtahed-Shabestari, an influential Shi'ite theologian, spent 18 years in a Qum seminary. He was appointed Manager of the Islamic Centre in Hamburg in the 1970s and, after the revolution, served as a member of parliament for four years. He decided to eschew politics after his term in parliament, opting to teach at the Faculty of Theology and Religious Studies of the University of Tehran until 2006, when he was pressured into retirement.
63. Mojtahed-Shabestari, *Some Thoughts*, 77.

64. Mojtahed-Shabestari, 'Political Tyranny'.
65. Mojtahed-Shabestari, 'Islam Is a Religion'.
66. Mortazavi and Manouchehri, 'Religious Reading'.
67. Mojtahed-Shabestari, 'Right, Duty, State'; Mojtahed-Shabestari, 'Critique of Official Reading'.
68. Kamrava, *Intellectual Revolution*, 168.
69. Mojtahed-Shabestari, *Faith and Freedom*, 34–45; Vahdat, 'Islamic Modernity', 215–216.
70. Mojtahed-Shabestari, *Hermeneutics*.
71. Mojtahed-Shabestari and Kiderlen, 'Interpretation of Quran'.
72. Hashemi, *Islam, Secularism*, 10–11.
73. Mojtahed-Shabestari, 'Human Rights'; Mortazavi and Manouchehri, 'Religious Reading'.
74. Mojtahed-Shabestari, 'Abstract and Rational', 8.
75. Ibid.
76. Mojtahed-Shabestari, 'Prophetic Reading'.
77. Initially, Mojtahed-Shabestari publicised this idea in an article 'Prophetic Reading of the World' published by *Madraseh* quarterly, which was banned following the publication of this article.
78. Mojtahed-Shabestari, 'Difficult Path'.
79. Mojtahed-Shabestari, 'Practicing a Verse'.
80. Mojtahed-Shabestari, 'Abstract and Rational'.
81. The reformist movement (1997–2005) can be characterised as another political momentum sparked by a similar religious reformation discourse against the authoritarian trend of the Islamic state.
82. Soroush develops two notions of secularism: 'political secularism' and 'philosophical secularism'. Political secularism refers to the separation of religion from the state. The legitimacy of the government should derive from the people, not from religion or divine right. And the state should be neutral with regard to religious matters. Philosophical secularism refers to a person's world view. In other words, there is neither a God nor a supernatural world. See Soroush, 'Political Secularism' and Soroush, 'Militant Secularism'.

Notes on contributors

Naser Ghobadzadeh completed his undergraduate and Master degrees in political science at Shahid Beheshti (Ex-National) University, Iran. His Master's thesis was awarded the Best Dissertation by Iranian Ministry of Science in 2003. Between 2002 and 2003, Naser worked as editor-in-chief at the foreign policy service of the Iranian Students' News Agency (ISNA). He was also the communications officer with UNDP and head of the Information Resource Centre (IRC) of UNICEF in Tehran. He is completing a PhD at the Department of Government and International Relations, University of Sydney, Australia. His book entitled *A Study of People's Divergence from Ruling System* (2002), scrutinizes value changes in Iran and its impact on the politico-religious mosaic. Working at the intersection of religion and politics, Naser's research interests include state-religion relations, Islam, secularism, Middle East and Iranian politics.

Lily Zubaidah Rahim teaches Southeast Asian Politics and Reformist Islam at the Department of Government and International Relations, University of Sydney. *The Singapore Dilemma: The Political and Educational Marginality of the Malay Community* (Oxford University Press, 1998/2001) established her as a leading researcher on socio-political developments in Singapore. Her second sole-authored book *Singapore in the Malay World: Building and Breaching Regional Bridges* (Routledge, 2009) focuses on Singapore's mercurial relations with neighbouring Malaysia and Indonesia. She is currently engaged in a global project on reformist Islam and secularism. Her multidisciplinary research interests have been published in numerous international journals and book chapters. They include an eclectic range spanning from governance in authoritarian states, democratisation, ethnicity, regionalism and political Islam. Email:mailto:lily.rahim@sydney.edu.au

Bibliography

Abdo, G. 'Re-thinking the Islamic Republic: A 'Conversation' with Ayatollah Hossein 'Ali Montazeri". *The Middle East Journal* 55, no. 1 (2001): 9–24.

Abou El Fadl, K., J. Cohen, and D. Chasman. *Islam and the Challenge of Democracy: A Boston Review Book.* Princeton, NJ: Princeton University Press, 2004.

Akhavi, S. 'The Thought and Role of Ayatollah Hossein'ali Montazeri in the Politics of Post-1979 Iran'. *Iranian Studies* 41, no. 5 (2008): 645–66.

Aliabadi, A.M. 'Abdolkarim Soroush and the Discourse of Islamic Revivalism'. PhD thesis, New School University, New York, 2005.

Bukovansky, M. *Legitimacy and Power Politics: The American and French Revolutions in International Political Culture.* Princeton, NJ: Princeton University Press, 2002.

Ehteshami, A., and M. Zweiri. 'Understanding Iran's Assembly of Experts, Policy Brief No. 1, The Centre for Iranian Studies (CIS)', Durham University, 2006, http://www.dur.ac. uk/resources/iranian.studies/Policy%20Brief%201.pdf (accessed June 20, 2010).

Filali-Ansary, A. 'The Challenge of Secularization'. *Journal of Democracy* 7, no. 2 (1996): 76–80.

Ghamari-Tabrizi, B. *Islam and Dissent in Postrevolutionary Iran: Abdolkarim Soroush, Religious Politics and Democratic Reform.* New York: I.B. Tauris, 2008.

Goudarzi, M., J. Jawan, and Z. Ahmad. 'Ayatollah Khomeini and the Foundation of Legitimacy of Power and Government'. *Canadian Social Science* 5, no. 6 (2010): 103–14.

Haeri Yazdi, M. *Hekmat va Hokumat* [Wisdom and Government]. London: Shadi, 1994.

Hashemi, N. *Islam, Secularism, and Liberal Democracy: Toward a Democratic Theory for Muslim Societies.* New York: Oxford University Press, 2009.

Jahanbakhsh, F. 'Abdolkarim Soroush: New Revival of 'Religious Sciences". *ISIM Newsletter* 8, no. 1 (2001a): 21.

Jahanbakhsh, F. *Islam, Democracy and Religious Modernism in Iran, 1953–2000: From Bazargan to Soroush.* Leiden: Brill, 2001b.

Kadivar, M. 'Nazariyeh hay-e doulat dar Figh'h-e Shi'a' [The Theories of State in the Shi'ite Jurisprudence]. *Rahbord* 2, no. 4 (1994): 1–42.

Kadivar, M. 'Hukomat-e entesabi' [Appointive Government]. *Aftab* 1, no. 2 (2000a): 8–13. http://www.kadivar.com/Index.asp?DocId=2300&AC=1&AF=1&ASB=1&AGM= 1&AL=1&DT=dtv (accessed May 12, 2010).

Kadivar, M. 'Yek Bar-e Digar Hukomat-e Velaei' [Government by Mandate Again]. *Doran-e Emrooz* 1, no. 80 (2000b): 9.

Kadivar, M. 'Velayat-e Faqih and Democracy', *The Middle East Studies Association of North America Conference*, Washington, 2002, http://www.kadivar.com/Index. asp?DocId=1&AF=1&ASB=1&AGM=1&DT=dtv (accessed April 12, 2010).

Kadivar, M. 'God and his Guardians'. *Index on Censorship* 33, no. 4 (2004): 64–71.

Kamali, H. 'The Theory of Expansion and Contraction of Religion: A Research Program for Islamic Revivalism', *drsoroush*, 1995, http://www.drsoroush.com/English/On_ DrSoroush/E-CMO-19950200-1.html (accessed April 25, 2011).

Kamrava, M. *Iran's Intellectual Revolution.* New York: Cambridge University Press, 2008.

Khomeini, R. *Sahifeh Nour* [Book of Light], vol. 10. Tehran: Moasseh Tanzim va Nashre Asare Imam, 2000.

Khomeini, R. *Sahifeh Nour* [Book of Light], vol. 6. Tehran: Moasseh Tanzim va Nashre Asare Imam, 2006.

Khomeini, R., and H. Algar. *Islam and Revolution: Writings and Declarations of Imam Khomeini*. Berkeley: Mizan Press, 1981.

Kuru, A.T. *Secularism and State Policies Toward Religion: The United States, France, and Turkey*. Cambridge: Cambridge University Press, 2009.

Mojtahed-Shabestari, M. *Hermeneutics, Ketab, Sunnat* [Hermeneutics, the Book and Tradition]. Tehran: Tarh-e No, 1996.

Mojtahed-Shabestari, M. 'Bastar-e maanavi va ughalaei-e fiqh' [Abstract and Rational Context of Jurisprudence]. *Kiyan* 9, no. 46 (1999): 5–13.

Mojtahed-Shabestari, M. 'Haq, taklif, hukomat' [Right, Duty, State]. *Aban* 1, no. 121 (2000a): 4.

Mojtahed-Shabestari, M. *Iman va Azadi* [Faith and Freedom]. Tehran: Tarh-e No, 2000b.

Mojtahed-Shabestari, M. 'Zolmat-e siasy va ameriyyat mottlaq' [Political Tyranny and Absolute Authority]. *Baztab-e Andishe* 2, no. 15 (2001): 7–13.

Mojtahed-Shabestari, M. *Naghdi Bar Gheraat-e Rasmi Az din: Bohranha, Chaleshha va rah-e hallha* [A Critique of Official Reading of Religion: Crises, Challenges and Solutions]. Tehran: Tarhe No, 2002.

Mojtahed-Shabestari, M. 'Rah-e doshvar-e Mardomsalari' [Difficult Path of Democracy]. *Aftab* 4, no. 22 (2003): 30.

Mojtahed-Shabestari, M. *Taamolati Bar Gheraat-e Ensani Az Din* [Some Thoughts on the Humanly Reading of Religion]. Tehran: Tarhe No, 2004.

Mojtahed-Shabestari, M. 'Geraat-e nabavi az jahan' [Prophetic Reading of the World]. *Madraseh* 2, no. 6 (2007a): 92–100.

Mojtahed-Shabestari, M. 'Ya hoqhogh-e basher ya hoqhoghe khoda, moghalet-e ast' [Human Rights or God's Rights; A Sophistry]. *Jamaat-e davat va eslahe Iran*, 2007b, http://www.islahweb.org/html/modules.php?op=modload&name=News&file=article&sid=665&mode=thread&order=0&thold=0 (accessed 15 June 2010).

Mojtahed-Shabestari, M. 'Amal be ayaei dar Quran hamishegi nist' [Practicing a Verse of Quran Is Not Perpetual]. In *Islam and Human Rights*, ed. S.S.-a.d. Mirdamadi, RadioZamane, 2008a, http://www.vatandar.com/attractive/shabestari.htm (accessed July 28, 2011).

Mojtahed-Shabestari, M. 'Islam Is a Religion, Not a Political Agenda', *Qantara*, 2008b, http://www.qantara.de/webcom/show_article.php/_c-478/_nr-783/i.html (accessed June 16, 2010).

Mojtahed-Shabestari, M., and E. Kiderlen. 'Kare tafsir-e Quran payan napazir ast' [Interpretation of Quran Is an Unceasing Project], *Süddeutsche Zeitung*, trans. Sit-e Farhangi-e Neeloofar, 2007, http://neeloofar.ir/thinker-/59-1388-10-19-19-52-43/442-1388-12-11-21-06-37.html (accessed June 18, 2010).

Montazeri, H. *Mabani-e Feqhi-e Hukomat-e Islami: Imamat va Rahbari* [The jurisprudential foundations of the Islamic state: Iamamat and Leadership]. Tehran: Saraei, 2000.

Montazeri, H. *Perspectives (Published Ideas and Messages of Grand Ayatollah during his House Arrest)*. Qum: The Office of Grand Ayatollah Montazeri, 2003.

Montazeri, H. *Hukomat-e dini va hughogh-e Ensanha* [Religious State and Human Rights]. Tehran: Saraei, 2008.

Morgan, E.S. *Inventing the People: The Rise of Popular Sovereignty in England and America*. New York: Norton, 1978.

Mortazavi, S.K., and A. Manouchehri. 'Gera'at-e dini-e Mojtahede-Shabestari va rabbet-e on ba araye siyasi-e vay' [Religious Reading of Mojtahed Shabestari and Its Relations with his Political Thoughts]. *Maanagera*, 2009, http://mojtahedshabestari.blogfa.com/post-27.aspx (accessed July 28, 2011).

Mottaqi, M. 'Karname karyabe Soroush' [Soroush's Flourishing Workbook]. *Aftab* 3, no. 19 (2002): 44–51.

Norris, P., and R. Inglehart. *Sacred and Secular: Religion and Politics Worldwide.* Cambridge: Cambridge University Press, 2004.

Norris, P., and R. Inglehart. 'Uneven Secularization in the United States and Western Europe', in *Democracy and the New Religious Pluralism*, ed. T.F. Banchoff, 3–53. New York: Oxford University Press, 2007.

Sajo, A. 'Preliminaries to a Concept of Constitutional Secularism'. *Int J Constitutional Law* 6, no. 3–4 (2008): 605–29.

Soroush, A. 'Khadamat va Hasanat-e Din' [The Functions and Benefits of Religion]. *Kiyan* 5, no. 27 (1994a): 2–16.

Soroush, A. *Qabz va Bast-e Teorik-e Shari'at: Nazariy-e Takamul-e Ma'refat-e Dini* [Theoretical Constriction and Expansion of Shari'a: The Theory of Evolution of Religious Knowledge]. Tehran: Serat, 1994b.

Soroush, A. 'Tahlil-e Mafhoom-e Hukomat-e Dini' [Analysing the Concept of Religious Government]. *Kiyan* 6, no. 32 (1996): 2–13.

Soroush, A. 'Din-e Agalli va Aksari' [Minimalist and Maximalist Conceptions of Religion]. *Kiyan* 8, no. 41 (1998a): 2–9.

Soroush, A. 'Velayat-e bateni va velayat-e Siasi' [Spiritual Guardianship and Political Guardianship]. *Kiyan* 8, no. 44 (1998b): 10–20.

Soroush, A. 'Zati va Arazi-e Dar Din' [Substantial and Accidental in Religion]. *Kiyan* 8, no. 42 (1998c): 4–19.

Soroush, A. 'Tazabzob-e amali-e Khatami risheh dar tazabzob-e fekri-e ishan darad' [Khatami's Practical Hesitation Is Rooted in Uncertainty in his Thoughts], *drsoroush*, 2004, http://www.drsoroush.com/Persian/News_Archive/F-NWS-13830903-Gooyanews.htm (accessed June 2, 2010).

Soroush, A. 'Political Secularism and Philosophical Secularism'. *Baztab-e Andishe* 6, no. 64 (2005a): 21–31.

Soroush, A. 'Tashayyo va Chalesh-e Mardomsalari' [Shi'a and the Challenges of Democracy], *drsoroush*, 2005b, http://www.drsoroush.com/Persian/News_Archive/P-NWS-1384-05-10-LectureInParis.html (accessed May 20, 2010).

Soroush, A. *Bast-e tajrubih-e nabavi* [The Expansion of Prophetic Experience]. Tehran: Serat, 2006.

Soroush, A. 'Militant Secularism', *drsorous*, 2007, http://www.drsoroush.com/English/On_DrSoroush/E-CMO-2007-Militant%20Secularism.html (accessed February 16, 2010).

Soroush, A. 'Democracy Is Not Extractable from Islam', *rooz*, 2010, http://www.roozonline.com/english/interview/interview/article/2010/march/17//democracy-is-not-extractable-from-islam.html (accessed April 27, 2010).

Soroush, A., M. Sadri, and A. Sadri. *Reason, Freedom, & Democracy in Islam: Essential Writings of Abdolkarim Soroush*. New York: Oxford University Press, 2000.

Vahdat, F. 'Post-revolutionary Islamic Modernity in Iran: The Intersubjective Herme Neutics of Mohamad Mojtahed Shabestari', in *Modern Muslim Intellectuals and the Quran*, ed. S. Taji-Farouki and Institute of Ismaili Studies, 193–224. New York: Oxford University Press, 2004.

Wootton, D. *Divine Right and Democracy: An Anthology of Political Writing in Stuart England*. New York: Penguin Books, 1986.

The religious experience as affecting ambivalence: the case of democratic performance evaluation in Israel

Pazit Ben-Nun-Bloom[a], Mina Zemach[b] and Asher Arian[c]

[a]Department of Political Science, Tel Aviv University, Tel Aviv, Israel; [b]Dahaf Public Opinion Research Institute, Tel Aviv, Israel; [c]Department of Political Science, The City University of New York Graduate Center, New York, USA and The Israel Democracy Institute, Jerusalem, Israel

Religiosity increases both criticism and instability in democratic performance evaluations, and accordingly decreases reliance on these assessments in the construction of political self-efficacy, trust in institutions, and patriotism. This is due to the conflicting experiences that religious citizens of democracies live through; while their personal religious environment often adheres to many undemocratic characteristics, their experience as citizens contains assorted democratic attributes. These results, from heteroskedastic maximum likelihood models using data from a 2006 representative survey among Israeli Jews, augment the exclusive focus of the literature of democratic attitudes on the strength of attitudes, and shift attention from policy attitudes to other evaluative judgements.

Democratic regimes hinge on their citizens' attitudes. Citizens' norms and traditions critically influence effective democratic governments,[1] as well as economic performance and stability in democracies.[2] Thus, it is important to identify groups with distinct patterns in their democratic attitudes.

Based on a large body of literature demonstrating a value conflict between religiosity and democracy – where religiosity is associated with tradition, conformity, and security, suppressing stimulation and self-direction,[3] and democratization encourages practically the opposite set of values[4] – religiosity was suspected of correlating with undemocratic attitudes and norms.

Indeed, the authoritarian personality theory argued that personal inclinations toward religion are connected to undemocratic leanings,[5] and other studies reported that the religious and the non-religious differ on a range of democratic attitudes.[6] In contrast, others suggested evidence that religious socialization is not utterly contradictory to democratic values.[7]

Yet, this line of research assumes that the religious and non-religious vary only in the *strength* or *direction* of their democratic attitudes. This paper's main argument and finding is, however, that they also differ in the *crystallization* of the concept of democracy, such that religiosity increases the *ambivalence* of democratic attitudes and diminishes their *stability*, and accordingly, decreases *reliance* on democratic attitudes for constructing related political positions and beliefs, such as trust in institutions, patriotism, and political efficacy. These findings serve as further evidence of the conflict between religiosity and democracy, manifest as a reduced application of democratic concepts in religious public opinion.

By allowing for religious freedom and encouraging participation and political organization, democratization in the Middle East could promote the return of religion to the public sphere.[8] It is this paper's goal to study to what extent religious citizens indeed experience ambivalence between democratic and religious values.

Ambivalence and conflicting experiences

The nature of political attitudes is much better understood today than it was two decades ago. Building on classic memory-based attitude theories, political scientists used to refer to and measure political attitudes as objects saved in memory along with the justification of their formation. Good citizens were supposed to be able to locate, retrieve and report their attitude towards an issue upon request, or else be perceived to hold 'non-attitudes' or to be 'innocent of ideology'.[9] Attitudes were supposed to be not only static and retrieved as is from 'drawers' in memory, but also unidimensional and bipolar, such that negative and positive arguments were collapsed into a single scale.[10]

In contrast with this conceptualization of political attitudes, more current literature has demonstrated that concepts are constructed when need arises – that is on the spot at the moment of judgement – constituting a dynamic process susceptible to influence by the specific context as well as individual goals and experiences.[11] Thus, people have several associations attached to an issue, and the attitude they report when asked on a survey is an estimation of the central tendency measure of their relevant distribution of considerations.[12] People are said to be ambivalent when their relevant consideration distribution for an issue consists of competing considerations – for example, feelings, beliefs, values – which they simultaneously endorse.[13]

Conceptualizing response on a survey question as a process of summing a distribution of considerations or associations draws attention to two concepts – response variability and the assumption of bipolar space – both set the ground for the study of ambivalence. First, derived from this literature is the idea that we should study not only the distribution's constructed mean but also its variability.[14] Thus, two people may have the same mean for their consideration distribution, but differ on the variance, such that their answers could be similar on average, but the larger distribution variance will lead to less predictable and more volatile responses upon repeated sampling. The distribution's variability may increase either when different considerations/associations are in conflict – that is, when a person is ambivalent, or when the certainty in the considerations is low – that is, a person is unknowledgeable or the attitude is not crystallized.[15] These two reasons for response variability differ in terms of the effect information has on them: while adding information should reduce variance due to low information, it is expected to increase the variance due to ambivalence.[16]

The type of consideration political scientists usually stress as responsible for ambivalence in judgements is internalized conflict among core values.[17] The literature on value-driven ambivalence usually builds on abstract political concepts and beliefs such as economic inequality, limited government, equal opportunity, and religion as the values underlying ambivalence. When two such values are relevant to a political issue yet 'push' the opinion in different directions, the person internalizing both values (and the public debate contrasting them) is expected to show ambivalence in his attitude on this issue. For instance, simultaneously valuing a woman's right over her body and the foetus's right to life, or internalizing the salient public debate contrasting these principles, yields ambivalence on abortion policy. Indeed, such value-driven ambivalence has been detected in a range of attitudes toward policies, such as abortion, social welfare, affirmative action, campaign finance reform and more,[18] as well as towards candidates and electoral evaluations.[19]

A second consequence of the theory of dynamic attitudes is that people may hold several thoughts on an issue at the same time, rather than a unidimensional bipolar attitude according to which they like/dislike a candidate, or agree/disagree with a policy. Indeed, psychologists often present the competing considerations underlying ambivalence as simultaneous strong positive and negative attitudes or affects.[20] This can happen, for example, when a person strongly likes several aspects of a political party's platform and at the same time strongly dislikes other aspects, or views a candidate as liberal on some issues and conservative on others.[21]

Both the political science and political psychology literature on ambivalence traditionally concentrate on ambivalence within a range of policy choices confined to highly contentious 'position' issues. Instead, this paper focuses on ambivalence in evaluations of democratic performance of the political system.

We argue that when evaluating the implementation of democratic principles (such as freedom of speech), the religious draw on their experiences both as persons subordinate to religious rules and as citizens in a democratic country. Due to inherent conflicts between religion and democracy, religious terminology and socialization offer experiences that conflict with democratic experiences like free media, freedom of speech, or gender equality.[22] Thus, the two environments provide evaluatively inconsistent beliefs concerning democratic performance.[23]

Three main hypotheses follow. First, experiencing both the non-democratic aspects of their religious world as well as the more democratic aspects of living in a democratic country, the religious person's mean evaluation of democratic performance is expected to be more *critical* than that of secular citizens, who experience the latter but not the former.

At the same time, we expect the conflicted experiences to yield a more *ambivalent* evaluation of democratic quality, since the religious person's distribution of considerations includes both democracy in action – elections, freedom of speech for minorities, etc. – and strong examples of an authoritative non-democratic environment. Thus, we expect both consequences of the conflicted experiences – more critical and more ambivalent evaluations – to increase as religiosity increases.

Thirdly, we expect that ambivalent evaluations will be less relied on for the construction of political attitudes. The literature demonstrates several effects ambivalence has on political attitudes, among which are reducing attitudes' predictability and stability,[24] decreasing attitudinal extremity, lowering confidence in judgements, improving the level of balance or accuracy in political judgements,[25] and increasing response latencies.[26] While these consequences focus on the effect ambivalence has on the structure of the attitude it manifests itself in (intra attitudinal structure), we focus on the influence ambivalence has on other relevant political attitudes (inter attitudinal structure).

Classic balance theory suggests that one strives for attitudinal consistency, that attitudes are connected to each other, and that a change to one of the attitudes in the structure may violate the consistency.[27] Thus, the inherent instability of ambivalent attitudes should decrease reliance upon them in constructing other attitudes, to avoid potential changes and inconsistencies. In our simple example, emitting an ambivalent evaluation of the level of competitiveness in one's country suggests that this evaluation will be less predictive of other political evaluations, say, of the level of social trust than would have been another type of evaluation. Conformingly, ambivalence in partisanship was, in fact, found to decrease reliance on party identification as a political cue.[28]

Democratic performance evaluations and religiosity among Israeli Jews

Evaluations of the political system in general often show strong effects for explaining democratic support.[29] Democratic Performance Evaluations (DPE), in particular, are one's attitudes toward democracy, and concern the question of 'how far democratic practices conform to democratic principles',[30] that is the public's perception of the democratic regime's functioning quality, such as the extent to which freedom of speech, equal rights or corruption exist in a country.

Similar to the prevalent division of democratic norms in terms of support for rights and liberties and support for institutions,[31] democratic functioning quality too is often divided into two major factors: institutions and rights.[32] The institutional aspect refers to the quality of functioning of institutions and implementation of behaviours that protect the rule of law by making government accountable to the people (for example, accountability, representation, participation and constraint). The legal aspect examines the implementation of respect for and protection of various basic rights (for example, civil, property, political and minority rights).

Whereas the Israeli public's evaluations of democratic performance have been regularly measured since 2003,[33] the effect of religiosity on these evaluations is under-explored to date. Even when differences in DPE among the religious and non-religious are noted, a theory explaining these empirical findings is lacking.

While the Jewish religious community in Israel is highly diverse, Jewish denominations are often divided into four groups, by their observance of the religious commandments as codified in books such as *Shulchan Aruch*,[34] and their relationship to Zionism: Ultra-orthodox (Haredi) is an umbrella term for several groups who adhere to all or most of the 613 commandments, and typically reject Zionism;[35] Orthodox Jews observe also Jewish laws but at the same time embrace Zionism; Traditional Jews typically believe in God and observe some of the commandments; Secular Jews characteristically eschew belief in God, and may embrace a small set of cultural Jewish customs and values.[36]

Researchers often agree that observance of the religious commandments is bound to be in tension with democracy, as the Halacha (Jewish religious law) promotes a set of values that directly contradicts democratic values. Thus, religion is based upon belief and transcendent truth, whereas the democratic system encourages scepticism and assumes that the validity of laws and practices is contextual. Additionally, democratic values tend toward universality and global implementation of civil rights for every person and government, whereas the religious public considers itself as entitled to more rights than others.[37] Other values in the Israeli secular culture such as individuality, hedonism, innovation, openness, achievement and competition tend to challenge traditional religion as well.

Indeed, the literature usually focuses on the effect of religiosity on endorsement of democratic norms and principles, with the widely accepted premise concerning the tension between Halacha and democratic principles.[38] Accordingly, religiosity was found to be an important variable in explaining commitment to democracy and endorsement of democratic principles in Israel as well as influencing the comparative rating of core Israeli principles, specifically democracy.[39] For instance, Peres shows that a considerable number of ultra-Orthodox Jews state their preference for a government that imposes a religious way of life, even if it is not elected democratically, while the rest of the respondents would not support an undemocratic government, even if they approve of its policies;[40] and Peres and Yuchtman-Yaar found secularism to be the most important factor in influencing tolerance and the tendency to prefer democracy over nationalism.[41]

Yet two questions are currently unanswered. First, assuming increasing religiosity decreases endorsement of democratic principles, does it also influence the manner in which the concept of democracy is conceived? Secondly, if religiosity makes difficult the sheer conceptualization of democracy, does it also reduce the application of democratic concepts in other political attitudes?

Focusing on democratic performance evaluations, various alternative hypotheses may be raised. First, unlike democratic norms and support for democratic principles, DPE is a more 'objective' evaluation, in which a person is asked to assess the level of democratic implementation in the country rather than state their preference for certain values or norms. Accordingly, one may argue that evaluating the implementation of democracy should be relatively free of one's appreciation for democracy itself: a person can evaluate the implementation of civil rights in her country whether or not they support democracy. In addition, the level of democracy implementation is typically not at the heart of debates involving different core principles and values, with one correlating to high democratic quality in the country and the other suggesting that democracy in Israel is in bad shape; consequently, a value-driven ambivalence is not being predicted for this evaluation. Another alternative hypothesis could be that religious people should report higher levels of democratic implementation, as their resistance to democracy may lead them to think the democratic implementation in the country is 'more than enough'.

In contrast to these previously suggested hypotheses, we hypothesize that religiosity increases criticism in democratic performance evaluation, as well as ambivalence toward these attitudes, as a result of exposure to different experiences. The religious way of life generally offers very little democracy. Jewish Halacha presents a set of rules – alternates to the democratic laws and norms – that determine the proper behaviour of individuals and society in all fields.[42] For instance, the Jewish orthodox person's everyday routine is subjugated to predetermined rules affecting every aspect of his life from meals, clothing, prayer times and hobbies, to interpersonal relationships, choice of partners, sexual life and child rearing. From time to time, rabbis decide on new obligatory religious rules, concerning new issues arising as part of the modern life style (for example, use of electricity, vehicles, media consumption, internet, cellular phones, etc.).

Consequently, the Jewish orthodox person in Israel experiences an undemocratic environment to a greater extent than he does a secular one. This increases as religiosity increases, as the ultra orthodox environment is more cohesive, separated from other groups, and enforces the implementation of religious rules compared to the orthodox.

Nevertheless, orthodox and ultra orthodox people experience the democratic environment as well, both through political participation (for example, they are represented in the Knesset, vote in elections, and protest in local and national matters), and by using the services of the Israeli institutions and bureaucracy (for example, the courts, educational systems, public funding, media, etc.). In addition, the salient debate about tension between democratic principles and Halacha is directly addressed by Jewish religious leaders in a range of ways. Some religious authorities advocate adapting religious life to modern values, others identify specific areas of life in which the Halacha should be the final authority for religious people, and yet others accept the implementation of democracy until the spiritual level of the people develops and the rule of the Torah replaces democracy.[43]

In short, orthodox people have both democratic and undemocratic experiences in their lives, and have a wide variance in their distribution of democratic implementation. As their religiosity increases, their undemocratic experiences further expand, and the variance in the distribution grows. At the same time, as religiosity increases, more non-democratic experiences are present which lowers their overall evaluation of the implementation of democracy.

Methods

We draw on data from the Democracy Index Project of the Israel Democracy Institute. 1016 respondents, a representative sample of Israel's adult Jewish population (18 and older), were interviewed by phone in Hebrew and Russian in February 2006. The sampling error at a 95% level of confidence was $+/-2.8$.[44]

The model

The literature suggests two main types of measures for ambivalence. One type focuses on individuals' level of ambivalence, by either directly asking the respondents about their ambivalence toward an issue or difficulty in answering a question, by counting spontaneous ambivalent comments, or by counting and weighting negative and positive comments or responses concerning the issue.[45]

While such direct measure has the advantage of yielding an ambivalence score for each respondent, it requires a certain consciousness of being ambivalent; when asked directly, a respondent needs to know he is ambivalent on the issue, when asked about negative and positive considerations one needs to be aware of the considerations responsible for his ambivalence and accurately represent them, which assumes both ability and motivation.

The second type of measurement, which we will rely on in this article, infers ambivalence from the estimation of error variance in maximum likelihood models.[46] By defining a variance equation in such models, we can test hypotheses about variables which increase or decrease the error variance – that is, the instability – in the dependent variable. Thus, when the sign on a coefficient in the variance equation is positive, there is a positive relationship between the error variance in the dependent variable (that is, ambivalence) and the independent variable. In contrast, when the sign is negative, the variance in the dependent variable decreases (that is, ambivalence decreases) with an increase in the explanatory variable.

Accordingly, two types of models are needed to examine our argument concerning the threefold effect of religiosity on DPE. First is a heteroskedastic Maximum Likelihood (MLE) model with DPE as the dependent variable and religiosity as an explanatory variable both in the mean equation (to examine if religious holds more critical DPE) and in the variance equation (to examine if religious holds more ambivalent DPE). Second is a set of models in which the power of DPE as an explanatory variable for various political attitudes is compared across different levels of religiosity, to examine the hypothesis that an increase in religiosity reduces the effectiveness of DPE as an explanatory variable.

Some control variables are used in our models, as one may argue that people who differ on the level of religiosity also differ on a variety of other characteristics explaining any differences revealed in DPE. Such characteristics may include level of political knowledge, economic status, education, age, political identification, perception of democracy as a desirable regime for Israel, and the gender of the participants, such that the religious are presumably less politically sophisticated, less wealthy, less educated, younger on average, less liberal, and less convinced of democracy as a desirable regime for Israel. Also, immigrants from the former USSR, who are generally less religious, are expected to show lower DPE, as Arian, Philippov, and Knafelman report that many immigrants from the former Soviet Union are dissatisfied with Israeli democracy, and have very low political efficacy and less democratic attitudes compared to the general public.[47] To control for these alternative explanations, all variables above are integrated in the models when examining the mean equation.

Some variables may be predicted to influence the error variance in the attitude, since they are expected to affect the cognitive capacity or the existence of relevant contextual knowledge about the democratic performance of Israel. First, young adults may have a less crystallized DPE, both because it is a highly abstract concept and since they have less experience with institutions.[48] In the same manner, political sophistication and education may reduce stochastic variance since they imply greater contextual knowledge and also may be a proxy for cognitive capacity (which is presumably related to a measure of years of schooling). Finally, immigrants from the former Soviet Union may be less informed about the democratic performance (DP) in Israel and at the same time less familiar with democratic political culture, thus show more noise in their DPE. As all these variables may be related to religiosity, they will be integrated in the variance equation as controls.

The primary model of DPE in this paper, then, has two main parts: religiosity and another set of variables expected to influence the evaluation of DP, and also to influence the stochastic component of the DP evaluation. To test the ambivalence hypothesis, the heteroskedastic component of the model must be examined directly, and we will rely on a heteroskedastic Maximum Likelihood Estimate for our linear regression model. Although the DPE is non-negative, it is fairly continuous with mean .503, median .515, and its percentiles suggest a bell-curve shape; thus, a normal function is defined for the model. Being more robust to various functional forms, an Ordinary Least Squares (OLS) regression will be used to assess the robustness of the findings. Since the variance is non-negative, we define an exponential equation to constrain it accordingly. The mean equation is specified as a function of religiosity, finding democracy to be desirable for Israel, political identification, political knowledge, economic status, education, age, being an immigrant from the former USSR, and gender. The variance equation is specified as a function of religiosity, political knowledge, education, age (specified differently than in the mean equation) and being an immigrant from the former USSR.

Measures

Democratic performance evaluation is a multi-dimensional concept that often calls for tradeoffs across its components, which makes its measurement particularly challenging. In this paper, DPE comprises evaluations of ten facets of democratic quality: four evaluations of the institutional aspect (representativeness, accountability, governmental integrity, stability); five evaluations of the legal aspect (equal rights, the rule of law, equality before the law, freedom of speech, religious freedom); and overall satisfaction with democratic quality. Measures were constructed for the three individual dimensions, as well as for a joint scale. The joint DPE scale was found to be reliable ($\alpha = 0.713$). The mean value on this scale was 0.503, with a standard error of 0.150.

The other measures used in the analysis, as well as some descriptive statistics, are shown in Table A1 in the appendix. All measures were coded to vary from 0 to 1, except for years of schooling and years of age.

The religiosity measure requires some discussion. Whether a person belongs to a secular, traditional, orthodox or ultra-orthodox social network was measured by the question: 'How would you define yourself?' (0 = secular, 0.33 = traditional, 0.66 = orthodox, 1 = ultra-orthodox [Haredi]; mean = 0.26, std. deviation = 0.33). Religious self-definition was shown to be highly correlated with adherence to religious norms and rules.[49]

Results

Maximum likelihood estimation

The estimates for the model in which the full DPE scale serves as a dependent variable are presented in the left column of Table 1. Concerning the mean component of the equation, our key hypothesis was that as the level of religiosity increases, the evaluation of the democratic performance of Israel would decrease. This negative relationship is indeed observed: all else being equal, by moving from being a secular to being ultra-orthodox, DPE decreases 0.081 on a 0–1 scale, that is, by about one-twelfth of the range.[50]

Since democratic performance evaluations are generally under-explored, it is interesting to dwell on the effect of several control variables as well. Influential predictors in the mean equation in addition to religiosity are endorsement of democratic polity for Israel and economic status, both showing a positive relationship with DPE; holding all other variables constant in their mean values, moving from strongly resisting to democracy in Israel to strongly supporting it, generates a 0.064 increase in DPE (almost one-sixteenth of the range), and moving from the lowest to the highest economic status has similar positive effect (0.060). These influences usually reappear in the partial models, where components of DPE were explored separately.

Education and age were also found to be influential for DPE; their effect may seem negligible when judged by the tiny coefficients, but this is due to their large scales. In fact, by moving from the minimal to the maximum level of education (0 to 30 years), the DPE drops in about 0.101 – even larger than the effect of religiosity – and by moving from high school education to, say, a PhD (20 years), DPE drops 0.067.[51] It seems that while education increases democratic norms and values,[52]

Table 1. Religiosity as explaining Democratic Performance Evaluation of Israel.

	DPE	Rights	Institutions	Satisfaction
Mean equation				
Religiosity	**−0.081 (0.019)**	**−0.124 (0.026)**	−0.031 (0.023)	**−0.063 (0.031)**
Democracy desirable for Israel	**0.064 (0.018)**	**0.066 (0.023)**	0.026 (0.021)	**0.117 (0.029)**
Political left	0.021 (0.020)	0.015 (0.026)	0.026 (0.024)	0.017 (0.032)
Political knowledge	**0.034 (0.017)**	**0.049 (0.022)**	0.005 (0.020)	0.042 (0.027)
Economic status	**0.060 (0.018)**	0.028 (0.023)	**0.068 (0.022)**	**0.109 (0.029)**
Education	**−0.003 (0.002)**	*−0.004 (0.002)*	−0.002 (0.002)	−0.002 (0.002)
Age	**0.001 (0.000)**	**0.001 (0.000)**	0.000 (0.000)	*.001 (0.001)*
Immigrant from former USSR	**−0.039 (0.016)**	−0.016 (0.020)	−0.028 (0.019)	**−0.105 (0.024)**
Male	0.012 (0.010)	−0.000 (0.013)	**0.029 (0.013)**	−0.016 (0.016)
Constant	**0.437 (0.032)**	**0.529 (0.042)**	**0.357 (0.039)**	**0.377 (0.052)**
Variance equation				
Religiosity	**0.175 (0.083)**	**0.233 (0.079)**	−0.002	**0.171 (0.082)**
Young	−0.086	*−0.118*	(0.084)	0.000 (0.068)
Political knowledge	(0.070)	*(0.070)*	−0.111	*−0.150*
Education	*−0.151*	−0.072	(0.068)	*(0.081)*
Immigrant from former	*(0.087)*	(0.082)	−0.023	*−0.014*
USSR	−0.005	−0.007	(0.083)	*(0.008)*
Constant	(0.008)	(0.008)	−0.001	048 (0.068)
	0.053 (0.073)	0.018 (0.069)	(0.008)	**−1.264**
	−1.874	**−1.601**	−0.001	**(0.123)**
	(0.123)	**(0.119)**	(0.067)	
			−1.715	
			(0.125)	
Log likelihood	436.368	220.869	280.020	40.679

Notes: Table entries are maximum likelihood coefficients, std. errors in parenthesis; significance in two-tail 95% confidence level in **bold**, one-tail 95% confidence level in *italic*.

it also encourages scepticism, as it makes citizens more knowledgeable about underprovided democratic liberties and more aware of discrimination, deficiencies of governing institutions, and lack of implementation of democratic principles.

Additionally, moving from the minimum to the maximum value of age (18–88) increases the DPE by 0.052, so it seems to be the case that older individuals have a less flattering reference point for Israel's democracy; it may arguably be the case that Israel's democracy has notably improved throughout the years. Political knowledge was found to have a positive effect as well, such that wider knowledge correlated to higher evaluation. As expected, being an immigrant from the former USSR decreases the DPE. Interestingly, political ideology does not exhibit a coefficient at least twice in size of its standard error in any of the models explored. The overall regression model is significant according to the Wald test.

In addition to the hypothesis that religiosity would decrease DPE, we suggested a hypothesis concerning variance, stating that, as religious belief becomes more salient, the constructed evaluations of DP will be more ambivalent due to conflicting experiences. Indeed, the significant positive coefficient for religiosity in the stochastic component of the primary model implies that ambivalence increases with increasing religiosity, as hypothesized. In contrast, political knowledge decreases variance error in DPE, as was expected (coefficient -1.73 times the standard error for a one tailed hypothesis). None of the other controls was found to be influential.

Several alternative explanations were controlled for in the variance model, including political knowledge, age, education, and immigration from the former Soviet Union. Still, one may argue that the effect of religiosity on heterogeneity in democratic evaluations is conditioned. For instance, it could be the case that the effect of religiosity on instability in DPE only occurs for those scoring low in political knowledge, or only among young or relatively uneducated people. Thus, interactions were specified among each of the independent variables in the variance equation and religiosity, and added to the model one at a time. None of these interactive terms approached statistical significance, indicating that the effect of religiosity on instability is not conditioned.

Although the hypothesis about religiosity as contributing to ambivalence in DPE was strengthened, it is worthwhile to test the hypothesis that the variance in the model should in fact be constant. Since the homoskedastic model is a reduced form of the heteroskedastic model, we used the likelihood ratio to compute this test. The log likelihood of the reduced model was 431.84, compared to 436.37 in the heteroskedastic model. χ^2 test statistics from this likelihood ratio give a p value of 0.107, which permits rejecting the null of homoskedasticity at the 5% significance level. This further confirms our claim concerning the influence of religiosity on the variance of DPE.

Next, the possibility that the religiosity scale is not interval was examined by specifying dummy variables for religiosity, and submitting the model to Wald tests. First, the hypothesis that all three intervals simultaneously equal each other ($\beta 4 - \beta 3 = \beta 3 - \beta 2 = \beta 2$) cannot be rejected in the 95% level ($\chi^2(df = 2) = 4.92$). Next, two Wald tests examined the equality of each pair of intervals, and the null can not be rejected for any of them (($p(\chi^2) = 0.613$ for the test that secular – traditional = traditional – orthodox, and $p(\chi^2) = 0.163$ for the test that traditional – religious = religious). Accordingly, the interval measure of level of religiosity was retained.

Whereas ML estimation is sensitive to definitions of the dependent variable and error term functions, OLS is much more robust under different distributional assumptions and does not rely on the normal error assumption when large samples are involved. Thus, we ran OLS on the mean equation as well as estimating the stochastic component of the MLE model by obtaining the squared residuals from the OLS regression and regressed them on the variables from the variance equation.[53]

The results of the homoskedastic OLS model reveal the expected effect of religiosity on the mean equation for DPE. The OLS shows a negative association between level of religiosity and DPE; moving from non-religious to ultra-orthodox decreases 0.089 from the DPE (on a scale of 0–1; compared to −0.081 in the heteroskedastic model), with all other variables held constant in their mean values. This coefficient was again more than twice its standard error (t = −4.68).

In estimating the stochastic components (variance equation) of the MLE model via an OLS regression of squared residuals, religiosity retained its sign and was more than twice its standard error (a positive coefficient of 0.007, with a standard error of 0.003 and t = 2.06). Overall, OLS replicated the findings for religiosity and young age, as well as the non-significant effect of the rest of the predictors.

This is an important validation of the ML estimation, since OLS is more robust in different distributions, and does not rely on the assumption of normality of the errors. In regressions using OLS, violation of the assumption of normality of the errors does not disturb the BLUE properties of the estimators, and for inference, the central limit theorem can be relied upon for consistency since the sample employed here is fairly large.

The full measure of DPE employed in the MLE model, presented in the left column of Table 1, is aggregated over different dimensions. Such aggregation not only assigns arbitrary weights to the different components, but also may conceal different effects of religiosity across the various dimensions. To further explore the effect of religiosity on DPE, we deconstructed DPE to its three components and explored them separately. The estimates for these models are presented in the next three columns of Table 1.

Overall, the results concerning the two hypotheses on the effect of religiosity on DPE are replicated for the rights component and the satisfaction component, but not replicated for the institutions separately, where no effect due to religiosity is revealed. Thus, by moving from being secular to being ultra-orthodox, evaluation of the implementation of rights in Israel decreases 0.124 on a 0–1 scale, that is, by about one-eighth of the range, and the overall satisfaction from democratic quality in Israel decreases by 0.063. Furthermore, a significant positive coefficient emerges for religiosity in both variance equations, indicating increasing ambivalence in the rights evaluation and overall satisfaction.

Why are the hypotheses confirmed for the full DPE scale as well as for the rights and satisfaction components separately but not for the institutional dimension? We argued that the religious should be more critical and more ambivalent when evaluating the implementation of democratic principles because they experience one environment where non-democratic characteristics are present, and yet another environment in which democracy prevails. When evaluating the implementation of rights, for instance, the religious take into consideration their personal experience from both environments. But characteristics such as representativeness, accountability and governmental integrity can be evaluated mostly in one environment at the country level, and mainly in the Knesset (at least in the wording of our measures), such that experiences from religious everyday life are less relevant to this evaluation. Thus, as observed, conflicted experiences should not be expected in this dimension, at least as measured here.

Alternative proxies for the variance equation

While these findings hint that the heterogeneity observed in democratic evaluation is due to the clash between religious and democratic values, the statistical models do not directly measure a conflict of value, but rather specify religiosity as a proxy for it. Whereas the database includes no explicit measures for value conflict and ambivalence, it does measure two additional proxies. First, respondents answer whether democratic principles or the rule of Halacha should be favoured in case of a contradiction.[54]

Secondly, the survey measures individual priorities in case of a clash between the four most prevalent social values in Israel,[55] by asking: 'If we think of potential directions for development in Israel, there are four important values that clash with one another to some extent, which are important to different people in different degrees: a state with a Jewish majority, the Greater Land of Israel, a democratic state (equal political rights for all), and peace (low probability of war). Of these four values, which is the most important to you? And the second? Third? Fourth?' We coded the preference for the value of democracy compared to the other three social values to a 4-point scale, such that 1 indicates preferring democracy above all other values, and 0 indicates placing it fourth in the order of priorities.

Table 2 compares the models integrating these two proxies for a clash of value between religiosity and democracy to the baseline model from Table 1. If a clash between religious and democratic values were responsible for the instability in DPE, we would expect these two alternative proxies to reveal a significant effect, such that a preference for the law of Halacha over democracy will increase the variance in DPE, while higher priority for democracy will decrease the heterogeneity.

Indeed, the alternative proxies function as hypothesized. A significant positive coefficient[56] for preference of the rule of Halacha in the stochastic component indicates that instability in DPE increases with increasing preference of the dictates of the Jewish law. In a similar vein, the significant negative coefficient for preferring democracy over competing values suggests that instability in DPE decreases with increasing preference for democracy. These results strengthen our argument that the instability in DPE is due to conflict between democratic and religious values.

Inter attitudinal correlations

The analysis so far strengthens the hypotheses that increasing religiosity is associated with a more critical and more ambivalent DPE, but is silent on our third hypothesis, that reliance on DPE when forming other political attitudes will be weaker among the religious, to avoid a weak inter-attitudinal structure that may force frequent changes in their belief system.

To test this hypothesis, the DPE index, religiosity and their interactions were submitted to a series of regression analyses as independent variables explaining various political attitudes. If indeed the value conflict among the religious leads to decreased reliance on DPE as a consideration when forming relevant

Table 2. Religiosity and alternative measures for value conflict as explaining Democratic Performance Evaluation of Israel.

	DPE	DPE	DPE
Mean equation			
Religiosity	**−0.081 (0.019)**	**−0.063 (0.021)**	**−0.081 (0.020)**
Prefer Halacha over democracy	–	*−0.028 (0.015)*	
Democracy most important value	–	–	−0.010 (0.014)
Democracy desirable for Israel	**0.064 (0.018)**	**0.059 (0.018)**	**0.063 (0.018)**
Political left	0.021 (0.020)	0.014 (0.020)	*.033 (0.020)*
Political knowledge	**0.034 (0.017)**	**0.037 (0.017)**	*.032 (0.017)*
Economic status	**0.060 (0.018)**	**0.059 (0.018)**	**0.058 (0.018)**
Education	**−0.003 (0.002)**	**−0.004 (0.002)**	*−0.003 (0.002)*
Age	**0.001 (0.000)**	**0.001 (0.000)**	**0.001 (0.000)**
Immigrant from former USSR	**−0.039 (0.016)**	**−0.040 (0.016)**	**−0.040 (0.016)**
Male	0.012 (0.010)	0.011 (0.010)	0.010 (0.010)
Constant	**0.437 (0.032)**	**0.456 (0.034)**	**0.440 (0.033)**
Variance equation			
Religiosity	**0.175 (0.083)**	0.072 (0.101)	**0.179 (0.085)**
Prefer Halacha over democracy	–	*.126 (0.075)*	–
Democracy most important value	–	–	*−0.113 (0.068)*
Young	−0.086 (0.070)	−0.101 (0.073)	−0.073 (0.071)
Political knowledge	*−0.151 (0.087)*	*−0.169 (0.087)*	−0.129 (0.089)
Education	−0.005 (0.008)	−0.003 (0.008)	−0.006 (0.008)
Immigrant from former USSR	053 (0.073)	0.054 (0.073)	0.036 (0.073)
Constant	**− 1.874 (0.123)**	**− 1.919 (0.124)**	**− 1.827 (0.128)**
Log likelihood	436.368	435.734	429.081

Notes: Table entries are maximum likelihood coefficients, std. errors in parenthesis; significance in two-tail 95% confidence level in **bold**, one-tail 95% confidence level in *italic*.

political attitudes, then we should expect the coefficient for DPE to decrease as religiosity increases.

The overall effect of DPE on the political attitudes chosen is theoretically straightforward. Thus, it is generally expected that a person appraising the democratic regime as highly functioning will trust the democratic institutions to a greater extent, score higher on patriotism, feel increased political self-efficacy, and evaluate the overall condition of the country as more satisfying.

However, the interaction among religiosity and DPE does not reach standard statistical significance in most cases (with the exception of political self efficacy, $p = 0.048$). A closer examination revealed that while reliance on DPE indeed decreases as religiosity increases, the difference was primarily salient between the ultra orthodox and the rest of the groups, suggesting that more often than not, there is some critical level of value conflict that hinders reliance on DPE in political attitude formation. Table 3 presents the regression coefficients for the interactions among ultra orthodox (the baseline being other three groups) and DPE, when controlling for political ideology, democracy desirable for Israel,

Table 3. The interactive effect of religiosity and the reliance on DPE in political attitudes.

	Political self efficacy	Trust in institutions	Pride in being Israeli	Israel's condition in general
DPE	**0.120 (0.045)**	**0.301 (0.029)**	**0.085 (0.036)**	**0.669 (0.063)**
Ultra Orthodox	0.025 (0.069)	−*0.075 (0.043)*	−**0.230 (0.079)**	0.074 (0.086)
DPE* Ultra Orthodox	−**0.263 (0.132)**	−**0.168 (0.082)**	*.336 (0.181)*	−0.196 (0.195)
Democracy desirable for Israel	−0.005 (0.035)	0.017 (0.022)	**0.064 (0.029)**	*.058 (0.030)*
Political left	0.025 (0.036)	**0.098 (0.023)**	−**0.137 (0.030)**	0.014 (0.031)
Political knowledge	0.010 (0.033)	−*0.038 (0.021)*	−0.009 (0.028)	**0.080 (0.029)**
Economic status	0.009 (0.036)	0.029 (0.023)	0.037 (0.031)	−0.002 (0.003)
Education	**0.009 (0.003)**	−*0.004 (0.002)*	−**0.010 (0.003)**	0.000 (0.001)
Age	0.000 (0.001)	**0.001 (0.000)**	*.001 (0.000)*	−0.014 (0.025)
Immigrant from former USSR	−**0.125 (0.029)**	−0.010 (0.020)	−**0.109 (0.024)**	**0.050 (0.018)**
Male	−0.007 (0.020)	**0.027 (0.013)**	−0.021 (0.017)	0.001 (0.055)
Constant	**0.152 (0.060)**	**0.279 (0.038)**	**0.941 (0.049)**	**0.669 (0.063)**

Notes: Table entries are OLS coefficients, std. errors in parenthesis; significance in two-tail 95% confidence level in **bold**, one-tail 95% confidence level in *italic*.

political knowledge, economic status, education, age, immigration from former USSR and gender.

Generally speaking, results for trust in institutions, patriotism, and political efficacy overall show the expected two-way interaction between being ultra-orthodox and reliance on DPE, such that DPE is less relied upon among the ultra Orthodox, holding all else constant.

First, a significant interaction emerged between DPE and being ultra orthodox in explaining political self-efficacy (b = −0.263, p = 0.047, see first column, Table 3). Results show the expected relationship between DPE and efficacy among non-ultra orthodox, such that efficacy increases with DPE (b = 0.120, p = 0.007). However, there is no significant relationship between DPE and efficacy among the ultra orthodox, and in fact, the coefficient shows the opposite sign (b = −0.143, p = 0.252).

Secondly, a significant interaction emerged between DPE and being ultra orthodox in explaining trust in institutions (b = −0.168, p = 0.041, see second column). The expected relationship between DPE and trust in institutions among non-ultra orthodox emerges, such that trust increases with DPE (b = 0.301, p = 0.000). However, the relationship between DPE and trust is much milder and only marginally significant among the ultra orthodox (b = 0.132, p = 0.087).

Thirdly, a marginally significant interaction emerged between DPE and being ultra orthodox in explaining patriotism (b = 0.336, p = 0.063, see 3rd column). While pride in being Israeli increases with DPE among non-Ultra Orthodox (b = 0.085, p = 0.018), there is no relationship between DPE and patriotism amongst the Ultra Orthodox (b = 0.027, p = 0.536).

This two-way interaction is also insignificant in explaining evaluation of Israel's functioning in general (b = −0.196, p = 0.314). The evaluation of Israel's condition in general significantly increases with DPE for both publics, even though the relationship is stronger among non-ultra orthodox, t (b = 0.669, p = 0.000) relative to ultra orthodox (b = 0.472, p = 0.011). This suggests that even the ultra orthodox view the country's democratic functioning as a key consideration in evaluating its condition in general.

Conclusions

The mere process of democratization could foster a return of religion to the public sphere, by allowing for religious freedom and encouraging political organization and participation.[57] Yet, many scholars have argued that religion might have the effect of challenging democratic values and could pose an obstacle to political socialization shaping democratic values.[58] Is allowing for religious freedom a double edge sword, in which democratic regimes encourage anti-democratic values?

We show that religiosity indeed affects ambivalence in democratic performance evaluations, in addition to a more critical view, and that the religious are less likely to build on democratic evaluations when constructing a variety of political attitudes. These findings uncover a fuller picture of the influence of religious socialization and experiences on the establishment of democratic and political attitudes and judgements.

Further, this paper contributes to the literature on ambivalence as well, by generalizing attitudinal ambivalence to democratic evaluations, and by corroborating previous arguments[59] regarding the effects of ambivalence on individuals' inter-attitudinal − rather than intra-attitudinal − structure. We believe the present focus on policy attitudes to be the result of a narrow definition of ambivalence, which unnecessarily restricts the study of ambivalence in political attitudes. Viewing ambivalence as a result of conflicting experiences opens the door to the study of ambivalence and its consequences in a variety of political evaluations, judgements, and political knowledge.

How does this ambivalence affect the political behaviour of the Israeli religious public? On the one hand, a value conflict between democratic and religious values may result in lower adherence to the democratic culture. Extreme ambivalence may also be dangerous for the democratic system by increasing distrust and political apathy. However, destabilization in regime evaluations may allow for true critical thinking and questioning of the system, rather than indoctrination in support of government. Such an attentive and responsive public is an important engine of democratization and political reform.

This two-sided conclusion is in line with current views of the relationship between religiosity and democratization as dynamic and multifaceted.[60] Empirical findings report that religiosity is connected to prejudice, political intolerance, and non-democratic norms,[61] but at the same time there is evidence for a positive association between church attendance and electoral turnout, party membership, protest activism, philanthropy, and involvement in other civic organizations.[62] This study contributes to the literature by finding evidence for these contrasting effects of religiosity in the mass-level belief system, indicating that the religious public exhibits higher instability in democratic attitudes.

The question then becomes, what determines the extent to which religious ambivalence is translated into either constructive or destructive political behaviour? We suggest that the religious elites serve a potentially critical role in channeling the value conflict experienced by their constituency. In their influential 1995 article, Michael Alvarez and John Brehm suggest two possible patterns in which elites react to their public's ambivalence: 'to influence mass opinion on a certain policy choice, elites will either try to intensify the conflict between the principles, or...they may try to eliminate the conflict for many individuals'.[63] In the Israeli case, there seems to be evidence for both patterns.

On the one hand, it seems that, similar to their constituency, the Jewish religious elites are quite ambivalent about democracy as well, with different rabbis advocating vastly different approaches to the system and its institutions.[64] In effect, such a reaction to democracy means that the religious public and elites do not completely negate democracy, at least not in the short term, despite some possible aspirations for a theocracy in the long run. This ambivalent approach explains the paradox of religious parties in Israel, which deprive women of political roles, challenge the current democratic nature of the country, and rely on the decisions of non-elected rabbis, but at the same time encourage their constituency to partake in politics, vigorously participate in the government and Knesset, and forge coalitions with secular and even overtly anti-religious parties (for example Shas and Meretz in the 13th Knesset, Shinui and Mafdal in the 16th Knesset), thereby also strengthening Israeli democracy. If the alternative is a complete negation of democracy, as predicted by authoritarian personality theory and subsequent literature, an ambivalent stance on democratization, accompanied by active participation in civil society and democratic institutions, is not a bad choice, and is certainly a more democratic one.

But on the other hand, the religious elites often convey loud and clear preferences when the two sets of values are in direct contradiction. Just recently, dozens of rabbis across the country signed a petition expressing their support for a religiously motivated refusal to evict and dismantle settlements, declaring that 'loyalty to God is above all other loyalties, be it to the military or the government'.[65] This statement does not sound ambivalent or democratic. But one should keep in mind that more often than not, even the most undemocratic statements of religious elites are justified by democratic arguments about freedom of speech and civil rights, and are expressed in democratic conduct, such as petitions, open public discourse, and formal meetings with elected officials. Without further research, it is difficult to determine whether the employment of democratic tools in the service of undemocratic messages is the result of true ambivalence, or is a cynical exploitation of democratic jargon, institutions and processes.

Thus, while the normative consequences of our findings do not necessarily align with the critical tone of authoritarian personality theory, we would expect that given an explicit value conflict on hot button issues, religious elites may adopt a harsh tone, to compensate for their constituency's – and perhaps their own – ambivalence toward the democratic process.

Next, our assumption that the perception of democracy is subordinate to religiosity and not the other way around is based on a developmental line of research indicating that attitudes towards politics and democracy develop at a much older age than religious beliefs. When exposed to religion, children readily adopt to it at a young age, whereas political opinions are shaped only later.[66] Studies show that contrary to the ease with which religious belief is adopted, the understanding of abstract concepts required to comprehend certain core political concepts such as war, state, and nationality develops in adolescence.[67] Other studies indicate that it is not until the end of puberty that adolescents can refer to the abstract concepts of society, institutions, norms and laws.[68] Hence, we cautiously assume that the religious environment creates ambivalence in democratic attitudes, and not the other way around. In addition, while democratic performance evaluations are constructed on the spot from a variety of available considerations, religious belief is enduring and chronic.

While we build on developmental precedence to suggest that religiosity should mostly affect the attitude structure toward democracy, religiosity is affected by democratization as well. In their study of 65 countries, Inglehart and Baker associate modernization with a move toward secular–rational and self-expressive values.[69] It may be the case that tension between religious and democratic practices decreases as democratization and modernization in the country increase, and with the change of generations. One may expect decreasing ambivalence in DPE for younger cohorts in developing democratic nations. This is yet to be explored.

We expect our theoretical argument and empirical results to hold across monotheistic religions and democracies due to a universality of the tension between religious belief and democracy. While religious beliefs are typically associated with values such as security, tradition, and conformity, and suppress values such as stimulation and self-direction,[70] democratization encourages the latter group of values and suppresses the former.[71] Additionally, empirical comparative studies demonstrate that the effects associated with strength of religious self-identification among Jews[72] and Roman Catholics[73] show overall common political patterns above and beyond geographical settings on issues such as gender equality for the latter and civil versus religious laws in Israel for the former. Nonetheless, this hypothesis has yet to be empirically tested.

Further exploration of the differences in evaluations of democratic quality carries implications for many public opinion inquiries and for the measurement of democratization, as well as for applied fields such as education and political advertising. Being ambivalent, DPE among the religious may be more susceptible to persuasion appeals,[74] with implications for election campaigns as well as democratic socialization and education in democratic norms and citizenship.

But most interestingly, our study raises new research questions. For instance, what consequences for religious belief systems ensue from reducing the ambivalence religious people have towards democratic attitudes, what impact on their practice of democratic citizenship, and their evaluation of other aspects of the political system? What portion of the criticism the religious minority expresses toward democratic performance is due to religious practices, and what part is due to unsatisfying democratic practices? What is the relationship between low democratic performance evaluation and low democratic commitments among the religious? Answering these and other new research questions raised by this study will further our comprehension of democratic culture and citizenship.

Acknowledgments

This paper is in the memory of Asher Arian, founder of modern political science in Israel, a thoroughly influential scholar of public opinion and political psychology, a mentor to generations of scholars, and a precious friend, who passed away in July 2010. Working with him on this and other projects was both educating and sheer fun. He is sorely missed.

The authors would like to thank Stanley Feldman for his helpful comments on a previous version of this manuscript. The data analysed in this study were made possible by the Israel Democracy Institute, Jerusalem, Israel.

Notes

1. Almond and Verba, *The Civic Culture*; Putnam, *Making Democracy Work*.
2. Inglehart, *Culture Shift*.
3. Schwartz and Huismans, 'Value Priorities and Religiosity'; Roccas and Schwartz, 'Church-State Relations'; Saroglou, Delpierre, and Dernelle, 'Values and Religiosity'.
4. For example, Schwartz and Sagie, 'Value Consensus and Importance'.
5. Adorno et al., *The Authoritarian Personality*; also see Altemeyer, *The Authoritarian Specter*.
6. For Judaism, see Liebman, 'Religion and Democracy in Israel'; Beit Hallahmi and Argyle, *The Psychology of Religious Behavior*; Barnea and Schwartz, 'Values and Voting'.
7. Canetti-Nisim, 'The Effect of Religiosity'; Eisenstein, 'Rethinking the Relationship'.
8. For example, Jamal, 'Democratizing State-religion Relations'.
9. Converse, 'The Nature of Belief Systems'.
10. See Cacioppo and Berntson, 'Relationship between Attitudes'.
11. Barsalou, 'The Instability of Graded Structure'; Zaller, *The Nature and Origins*; Zaller and Feldman, 'A Simple Theory'.
12. Feldman, 'Answering Survey Questions'.
13. Lavine, 'The Electoral Consequences of Ambivalence'; Steenbergen and Brewer, 'The Not-So-Ambivalent Public'.
14. Zaller and Feldman, 'A Simple Theory'; Alvarez and Brehm, *Hard Choices, Easy Answers*.
15. Alvarez and Brehm, *Hard Choices, Easy Answers*; Franklin, 'Eschewing Obfuscation'.
16. Alvarez and Brehm, *Hard Choices, Easy Answers*.
17. Feldman and Zaller, 'The Political Culture of Ambivalence'; Alvarez and Brehm, 'American Ambivalence toward Abortion Policy'; Alvarez and Brehm, *Hard Choices, Easy Answers*; Lavine, 'The Electoral Consequences of Ambivalence'.
18. Alvarez and Brehm, 'American Ambivalence toward Abortion Policy'; Alvarez and Brehm, 'Are Americans Ambivalent'; Feldman and Zaller, 'The Political Culture of Ambivalence'; Rudolph, 'Group Attachment'; but see Steenbergen and Brewer, 'The Not-So-Ambivalent Public'.

19. Lavine, 'The Electoral Consequences of Ambivalence'; Basinger and Lavine, 'Ambivalence, Information'; McGraw, Hasecke, and Conger, 'Ambivalence, Uncertainty'.
20. Eagly and Chaiken, *The Psychology of Attitudes*; Cacioppo and Berntson, 'Relationship between Attitudes'.
21. See Lavine, 'The Electoral Consequences of Ambivalence'.
22. For Orthodox Judaism in Israel see for example Liebman and Don-Yehiya, *Civil Religion in Israel*; Liebman, 'Religion and Democracy in Israel'; Peres and Yuchtman-Yaar, *Trends in Israeli Democracy*.
23. Stated more formally, since one's response on a survey question is constructed based on recently activated considerations from the top of the respondent's head (Zaller, *The Nature and Origins*), increases in the variance of relevant beliefs on which the person bases their evaluation increases the possibility they will change their evaluation in repeated sampling as a result of sampling from different experiences in the distribution. In contrast, when most relevant experiences a person holds point in a similar direction, his or her considerations' distribution has a narrower variance, and the overall evaluation is expected to be more stable in repeated questioning.
24. For example Zaller and Feldman, 'A Simple Theory'; Lavine, 'The Electoral Consequences of Ambivalence'.
25. Meffert, Guge, and Lodge, 'Good, Bad, and Ambivalent'.
26. Bargh et al., 'The Generality of the Automatic Attitude'.
27. Eagly and Chaiken, *The Psychology of Attitudes*.
28. Basinger and Lavine, 'Ambivalence, Information'.
29. Evans and Whitefield, 'The Politics and Economics of Democratic Commitment'; Rose, Mishler, and Haerpfer, *Democracy and Its Alternatives*; Wells and Krieckhaus, 'Does National Context Influence'.
30. Foweraker and Krznaric, 'How to Construct a Database', 2.
31. For example, Gibson, Duch, and Tedin, 'Democratic Values'.
32. Foweraker and Krznaric, 'Measuring Liberal Democratic Performance'.
33. Arian, Barnea, and Ben-Nun, *The 2004 Israeli Democracy Index*; Arian et al., *The 2005 Israeli Democracy Index*; Arian, Atmor, and Hadar, *Auditing Israeli Democracy – 2006*.
34. Kedem, 'Dimensions of Jewish Religiosity'.
35. Keren and Barzilai, *The Integration of Peripheral Groups*.
36. Kedem, 'Dimensions of Jewish Religiosity'.
37. Peres and Yuchtman-Yaar, *Trends in Israeli Democracy*.
38. Liebman, 'Religion and Democracy in Israel'.
39. Peres, 'Religious Adherence'; Peres and Yuchtman-Yaar, *Trends in Israeli Democracy*; Shamir and Shamir, *The Anatomy of Public Opinion*; but see Eisenstein, 'Rethinking the Relationship'; Canetti-Nisim, 'The Effect of Religiosity'.
40. Peres, 'Religious Adherence'.
41. Peres and Yuchtman-Yaar, *Trends in Israeli Democracy*.
42. Liebman, 'Religion and Democracy in Israel'.
43. Geiger, *Judaism and Democracy*; Liebman and Don-Yehiya, *Civil Religion in Israel*.
44. Arian, Atmor, and Hadar, *Auditing Israeli Democracy – 2006*.
45. Zaller and Feldman, 'A Simple Theory'; Lavine, 'The Electoral Consequences of Ambivalence'.
46. Franklin, 'Eschewing Obfuscation'; Alvarez and Brehm, 'American Ambivalence toward Abortion Policy'; Alvarez and Brehm, *Hard Choices, Easy Answers*.
47. Arian, Philippov, and Knafelman, *Auditing Israeli Democracy – 2009*.
48. Note that the hypothesis concerning age predicts a certain threshold, rather than a continuous progress, which would imply that cognitive capacity and contextual

knowledge are improved with age. The threshold was set at 25, such that 18–24 year-olds are 'young'.

49. Ben-Meir and Kedem, 'Index of Religiosity'.
50. An alternative explanation for the effect of religiosity on DPE may be incumbency, that is that the criticism pointed at the democracy is merely the voice of a deprived minority. Yet, this argument does not account for the ambivalence revealed. In addition, the extremely high representativeness characterizing the Israeli political system assures that the religious minority enjoys some political power. Indeed, it was shown that the difference in democratic satisfaction between incumbents and electoral losers was reduced in consensual political systems (Wells and Krieckhaus, 'Does National Context Influence').
51. Following a comment by an anonymous reviewer, we were curious to test whether education has a different effect for religious and secular Israelis. However, this interaction is insignificant for all dimensions of DPE as well as for the joint scale (with p levels of .7–.9).
52. To strengthen this prevalent view, we ran a regression using the same control variables as in Table 1, with the dependent variable being a scale of eight democratic norms and values (supports freedom of speech for all; supports fully equal rights between Jews and Arabs; democracy is the best type of government; believes that every couple in Israel should be allowed to marry in any way they wish; men are more successful political leaders (reversed); supports economic rights; supports violence in achieving political goals (reversed); supports strong leaders (reversed)). In this model, education had a positive and significant effect ($b = .003$, $t = 2.30$) on support for democratic values, while religiosity had the expected negative and significant effect ($b = -.094$, $t = -5.73$). Again, there was no significant interactive effect between religiosity and education, suggesting that education increases support for democratic values, regardless of the type of schooling, religious or not.
53. Franklin, 'Eschewing Obfuscation'.
54. 'In some situations, democracy contradicts the rule of Halacha. In case of a contradiction, should we prefer the principles of democracy or the dictates of the Halacha?'
55. For example, Shamir, and Shamir, *The Anatomy of Public Opinion*.
56. Note that the hypotheses in this section are directional, thus a one-tail 95% confidence level would be the appropriate choice.
57. Jamal, 'Democratizing State-religion Relations'.
58. Lipset, *Political Man*; Stark, 'Reconceptualizing Religion'.
59. Lavine, 'The Electoral Consequences of Ambivalence'.
60. Künkler and Leininger, 'The Multi-faceted Role of Religious Actors'; Jamal, 'Democratizing State-religion Relations'.
61. Altemeyer, *The Authoritarian Specter*; Gibson, 'The Political Consequences of Intolerance'; Hunsberger, 'Religion and Prejudice'.
62. For example, Norris and Inglehart, *Sacred and Secular*.
63. Alvarez and Brehm, 'American Ambivalence toward Abortion Policy', 1077.
64. See Geiger, *Judaism and Democracy*; Liebman and Don-Yehiya, *Civil Religion in Israel*.
65. Nahshoni, 'Rabbis Sign Hesder Yeshiva Support Petition'.
66. Beit-Hallahmi and Argyle, *The Psychology of Religious Behavior*, 147.
67. Piaget and Weil, 'The Development in Children'; Sigel and Cocking, *Cognitive Development*.
68. Torney-Purta, 'Youth in Relation to Social Institutes'.
69. Inglehart and Baker, 'Modernization, Cultural Change'.
70. Schwartz and Huismans, 'Value Priorities and Religiosity'; Roccas and Schwartz, 'Church-State Relations'; Saroglou, Delpierre, and Dernelle, 'Values and Religiosity'.
71. Schwartz and Sagie, 'Value Consensus and Importance'.

72. Wald and Martinez, 'Jewish Religiosity and Political Attitudes'.
73. Wilcox and Jelen, 'Catholicism and Opposition to Gender Equality'; Jelen and Wilcox, 'Attitudes toward Abortion'.
74. Bassili, 'Meta-Judgmental versus Operational Indexes'.

Notes on contributors

Pazit Ben-Nun Bloom is a Post-Doctoral fellow at Tel Aviv University, Tel Aviv, Israel.

Mina Zemach is a Psychologist and the Head of 'Dahaf' Public Opinion Survey Institute, Tel Aviv, Israel.

Asher Arian is a Distinguished Professor of Political Science at the City University of New York Graduate Center, New York, USA, University of Haifa, Haifa, Israel, and Senior Fellow at the Israel Democracy Institute, Jerusalem, Israel.

Bibliography

Adorno, T.W., E. Frenkel-Brunswik, D.J. Levinson, and R.N. Sanford. *The Authoritarian Personality*. New York: Harper and Row, 1950.
Almond, G.A., and S. Verba. *The Civic Culture*. Princeton, NJ: Princeton University Press, 1963.
Altemeyer, B. *The Authoritarian Specter*. Cambridge, MA: Harvard University Press, 1996.
Alvarez, R.M., and J. Brehm. 'American Ambivalence toward Abortion Policy: Development of a Heteroskedastic Probit Model of Competing Values'. *American Journal of Political Science* 39 (1995): 1055–82.
Alvarez, R.M., and J. Brehm. 'Are Americans Ambivalent towards Racial Policies?'. *American Journal of Political Science* 41 (1997): 345–74.
Alvarez, R.M., and J. Brehm. *Hard Choices, Easy Answers*. Princeton, NJ: Princeton University Press, 2002.
Arian, A., N. Atmor, and Y. Hadar. *Auditing Israeli Democracy – 2006*. Jerusalem: The Israeli Democracy Institute, 2006.
Arian, A., S. Barnea, and P. Ben-Nun. *The 2004 Israeli Democracy Index*. Jerusalem: The Israeli Democracy Institute, 2004.
Arian, A., S. Barnea, P. Ben-Nun, R. Ventura, and M. Shamir. *The 2005 Israeli Democracy Index*. Jerusalem: The Israeli Democracy Institute, 2005.
Arian, A., M. Philippov, and A. Knafelman. *Auditing Israeli Democracy—2009*. Jerusalem: The Israeli Democracy Institute, 2009.
Bargh, J.A, S. Chaiken, R. Govender, and F. Pratto. 'The Generality of the Automatic Attitude Activation Effect'. *Journal of Personality and Social Psychology* 62 (1992): 893–912.
Barnea, M.F., and S.H. Schwartz. 'Values and Voting'. *Political Psychology* 19 (1998): 17–40.
Barsalou, L.W. 'The Instability of Graded Structure: Implications for the Nature of Concepts', in *Concepts and Conceptual Development: Ecological and Intellectual Factors in Categorization*, ed. U. Neisser, 101–40. New York: Cambridge University Press, 1987.
Basinger, S., and H. Lavine. 'Ambivalence, Information, and Electoral Choice'. *American Political Science Review* 99 (2005): 169–84.
Bassili, J.N. 'Meta-Judgmental versus Operational Indexes of Psychological Attributes: The Case of Measures of Attitude Strength'. *Journal of Personality and Social Psychology* 71 (1996): 637–53.

Beit-Hallahmi, B., and M. Argyle, *The Psychology of Religious Behavior, Belief, and Experience.* London and New York: Routledge, 1997.

Ben-Meir, Y., and P. Kedem. 'Index of Religiosity of the Jewish Population of Israel'. *Megamot* 24 (1979): 353–62 (in Hebrew).

Cacioppo, J.T., and G. Berntson, 'Relationship between Attitudes and Evaluative Space: A Critical Review, with Emphasis on Separability of Positive and Negative Sub-strates'. *Psychological Bulletin* 115 (1994): 401–23.

Canetti-Nisim, D. 'The Effect of Religiosity on Endorsement of Democratic Values: The Mediating Influence of Authoritarianism'. *Political Behavior* 26 (2004): 377–98.

Converse, P.E. 'The Nature of Belief Systems in Mass Publics', in *Ideology and Discontent*, ed. David E. Apter, 206–61. New York: Free Press, 1964.

Eagly, A.H., and S. Chaiken. *The Psychology of Attitudes.* New York: Harcourt Brace Jovanovich, 1993.

Eisenstein, M.A. 'Rethinking the Relationship between Religion and Political Tolerance in the US'. *Political Behavior* 28 (2006): 327–48.

Evans, G., and S. Whitefield. 'The Politics and Economics of Democratic Commitment: Support for Democracy in Transition Societies'. *British Journal of Political Science* 25, no. 4 (1995): 485–514.

Feldman, S. 'Answering Survey Questions: The Measurement and Meaning of Public Opinion', in *Political Judgment: Structure and Process*, ed. Milton Lodge and Kathleen M. McGraw, 249–270. Ann Arbor, MI: University of Michigan Press, 1995.

Feldman, S., and J.R. Zaller. 'The Political Culture of Ambivalence: Ideological Responses to the Welfare State'. *American Journal of Political Science* 36 (1992): 268–307.

Foweraker, J., and R. Krznaric. 'Measuring Liberal Democratic Performance: An Empirical and Conceptual Critique'. *Political Studies* 48 (2000): 759–87.

Foweraker, J., and R. Krznaric. 'How to Construct a Database of Liberal Democratic Performance'. *Democratization* 8, no. 3 (2001): 1–25.

Franklin, C. 'Eschewing Obfuscation? Campaigns and the Perception of US Senate Candidates'. *American Political Science Review* 85, no. 4 (1991): 1193–214.

Geiger, Y. *Judaism and Democracy.* Israel: Ministry of Education and Culture, Bar-Ilan University, 1999. [Hebrew].

Gibson, J.L. 'The Political Consequences of Intolerance: Cultural Conformity and Political Freedom'. *American Political Science Review* 86, no. 2 (1992): 338–56.

Gibson. J.L., R.M. Duch, and K.L. Tedin. 'Democratic Values and the Transformation of the Soviet Union'. *The Journal of Politics* 54, no. 2 (1992): 329–71.

Hunsberger, B. 'Religion and Prejudice: The Role of Religious Fundamentalism, Quest and Right-Wing Authoritarianism'. *Journal of Social Issues* 51, no. 2 (1995): 113–29.

Inglehart, R. *Culture Shift in Advanced Industrial Society.* Princeton, NJ: Princeton University Press, 1990.

Inglehart, R., and W.E. Baker. 'Modernization, Cultural Change, and the Persistence of Traditional Values'. *American Sociological Review* 65 (2000): 19–51.

Jamal, A. 'Democratizing State-religion Relations: A Comparative Study of Turkey, Egypt and Israel'. *Democratization* 16, no. 6 (2009): 1143–71.

Jelen, T.G., and C. Wilcox. 'Attitudes toward Abortion in Poland and the United States'. *Social Science Quarterly* 78 (1997): 97–114.

Kedem, P. 'Dimensions of Jewish Religiosity', in *Israeli Judaism: The Sociology of Religion in Israel*, ed. S. Deshen, C.S. Liebman, and M. Shokeid, 33–62. New Brunswick, NJ and London: Transaction Publishers, 1995.

Keren, M., and G. Barzilai. *The Integration of Peripheral Groups into Society and Politics in the Peace Era.* Jerusalem: Israel Institute for Democracy, 1998. [Hebrew].

Künkler. M., and J. Leininger. 'The Multi-faceted Role of Religious Actors in Democratization Processes: Empirical Evidence from Five Young Democracies'. *Democratization* 16, no. 6 (2009): 1058–92.

Lavine, H. 'The Electoral Consequences of Ambivalence toward Presidential Candidates'. *American Journal of Political Science* 45 (2001): 915–29.

Liebman, C.S. 'Religion and Democracy in Israel', in *Israeli Judaism: The Sociology of Religion in Israel*, ed. S. Deshen, C.S. Liebman, and M. Shokeid, 347–366. New Brunswick, NJ and London: Transaction Publishers, 1995.

Liebman, C.S., and E. Don-Yehiya. *Civil Religion in Israel: Traditional Judaism and Political Culture in the Jewish State*. California, USA: University of California Press, 1983.

Lipset, S.M. *Political Man: The Social Basis of Politics*. Baltimore, MD: The Johns Hopkins University Press, 1981.

McGraw, K.M., E. Hasecke, and K. Conger. 'Ambivalence, Uncertainty, and Processes of Candidate Evaluation'. *Political Psychology* 24 (2003): 21–448.

Meffert, M.F., M. Guge, and M. Lodge. 'Good, Bad, and Ambivalent: The Consequences of Multidimensional Political Attitudes', in *Studies in Public Opinion: Attitudes, Nonattitudes, Measurement Error, and Change*, W.E. Saris and P.M. Sniderman, 63–92. Princeton, NJ: Princeton University Press, 2004.

Nahshoni. 'Rabbis Sign Hesder Yeshiva Support Petition'. *Ynet news.com*, December 18, 2009 (In Hebrew).

Norris, P., and R. Inglehart. *Sacred and Secular: Religion and Politics Worldwide*. Cambridge and New York: Cambridge University Press, 2004.

Peres, Y. 'Religious Adherence and Political Attitudes', in *Israeli Judaism: The Sociology of Religion in Israel*, ed. S. Deshen, C.S. Liebman, and M. Shokeid, 87–106. New Brunswick, NJ and London: Transaction Publishers, 1995.

Peres, Y., and E. Yuchtman-Yaar. *Trends in Israeli Democracy: The Public's View*. Boulder, CO: Lynne Rienner, 1992.

Piaget, J., and A.N. Weil. 'The Development in Children of the Idea of Homeland and Relations with Other Countries'. *International Social Science Bulletin* 3 (1951): 561–78.

Putnam, R.D. *Making Democracy Work: Civic Traditions in Modern Italy*. Princeton, NJ: Princeton University Press, 1993.

Roccas, S., and S.H. Schwartz. 'Church-State Relations and the Associations of Religiosity with Values: A Study of Catholics in Six Countries'. *Cross-Cultural Research* 31 (1997): 356–75.

Rose, R., W. Mishler, and C. Haerpfer. *Democracy and Its Alternatives*. Baltimore, MD: Johns Hopkins University Press, 1998.

Rudolph, T.J. 'Group Attachment and the Reduction of Value-Driven Ambivalence'. *Political Psychology* 26, no. 6 (2005): 905–28.

Saroglou, V., V. Delpierre, and R. Dernelle. 'Values and Religiosity: A Meta-Analysis of Studies Using Schwartz's Model'. *Personality and Individual Differences* 37 (2004): 721–34.

Schwartz, S. H., and S. Huismans. 'Value Priorities and Religiosity in Four Western Religions'. *Social Psychology Quarterly* 58 (1995): 88–107.

Schwartz, S.H., and G. Sagie. 'Value Consensus and Importance: A Cross-National Study'. *Journal of Cross-Cultural Psychology* 31 (2000): 465–97.

Shamir, J., and M. Shamir. *The Anatomy of Public Opinion*. Ann Arbor: The University of Michigan Press, 2000.

Sigel, I.E., and R.R. Cocking. *Cognitive Development from Childhood to Adolescence: A Constructivist Perspective*. New York: Holt, Rinehart and Winston, 1977.

Stark, R. 'Reconceptualizing Religion, Magic, and Science'. *Review of Religious Research* 43, no. 2 (2001): 101–20.

Steenbergen, M.R., and P.R. Brewer. 'The Not-So-Ambivalent Public: Policy Attitudes in the Political Culture of Ambivalence', in *Studies in Public Opinion: Attitudes, Nonattitudes, Measurement Error, and Change*, ed. W.E. Saris and P.M. Sniderman, 93–129. Princeton, NJ: Princeton University Press, 2004.

Torney-Purta, J. 'Youth in Relation to Social Institutes', in *At the Threshold: The Developing Adolescent*, ed. S. Feldman and G.R. Elliott, 457–478. Cambridge, MA: Harvard University Press, 1990.

Wald, K.D., and M.D. Martinez, 'Jewish Religiosity and Political Attitudes in the United States and Israel'. *Political Behavior* 23, no. 4 (2001): 377–97.

Wells, J.M., and J. Krieckhaus. 'Does National Context Influence Democratic Satisfaction? A Multi-Level Analysis'. *Political Research Quarterly* 59, no. 4 (2006): 569–78.

Wilcox, C., and T.G. Jelen. 'Catholicism and Opposition to Gender Equality in Western Europe'. *International Journal of Public Opinion Research* 5 (1993): 40–59.

Zaller, J.R. *The Nature and Origins of Mass Opinion*. New York: Cambridge University Press, 1992.

Zaller, J.R., and S. Feldman, 'A Simple Theory of the Survey Response: Answering Questions versus Revealing Preferences'. *American Journal of Political Science* 36 (1992): 579–616.

Appendix

Table A1.　Measures.

Democratic Performance Evaluation

The institutional aspect	*Representativeness*: 'To what extent does the balance of powers in the Knesset express, in your opinion, the distribution of views in the larger public?' ($\bar{y} = 0.55$, s $= 0.30$); *Accountability*: 'The politicians we elect try to keep their campaign promises' ($\bar{y} = 0.36$, s $= 0.34$); *Governmental integrity*: 'To what extent do you think corruption exists in Israel?' ($\bar{y} = 0.13$, s $= 0.21$); *Israel's stability*: 'In your opinion and compared to other democratic countries, is the political system in Israel stable or unstable?' ($\bar{y} = 0.56$, s $= 0.34$).
The legal aspect (rights)	*Equal rights*: 'In your opinion, to what extent do equal rights exist or do not exist in Israel?' ($\bar{y} = 0.45$, s $= 0.28$); *The rule of law*: 'the rule of law?' ($\bar{y} = 0.53$, s $= 0.28$); *Equality before the law*: 'equality before the law?' ($\bar{y} = 0.47$, s $= 0.29$); *Freedom of speech*: 'freedom of speech?' ($\bar{y} = 0.70$, s $= 0.30$); *Religious freedom*: 'religious freedom?' ($\bar{y} = 0.69$, s $= 0.31$).
Overall satisfaction	'In your opinion, is the state of Israel presently democratic to a suitable degree, too democratic or not democratic enough?' ($\bar{y} = 0.63$, s $= 0.33$); 'In general, to what extent are you satisfied or dissatisfied with the way in which Israel's democracy functions?' ($\bar{y} = 0.45$, s $= 0.25$).

Independent Variables

Religiosity	'How would you define yourself?' (secular, traditional, orthodox, ultra-orthodox) ($\bar{y} = 0.26$, s $= 0.33$).
Democracy desirable for Israel	'Democracy is a desirable regime for Israel' ($\bar{y} = 0.82$, s $= 0.29$).
Political identification	'We hear a lot of talk these days about right and left in politics. Which of the following best describes your own political views on the left-right scale, when 1 is the right pole and 7 is the left pole?' ($\bar{y} = 0.39$, s $= 0.29$).
Political knowledge	A scale composed of adding correct responses to 3 questions (for example, 'what is the threshold required to win a seat in Knesset elections?') ($\bar{y} = 0.44$, s $= 0.32$; $\alpha = 0.48$).
Economic status	'The monthly income for an average family of four came to about 9300 NIS last month. Considering your family's expenses, do you spend. . .below average, average, above average?' ($\bar{y} = 0.46$, s $= 0.30$).
Education	Years of schooling ($\bar{y} = 13.8$, s $= 3.3$).
Age	Years of age; to test the hypothesis about the effect on the variance, age was also composed as a dummy variable, wherein young participants (ages 18 to 24) were coded as 1, and participants 25 and up were the baseline ($\bar{y} = 45.2$, s $= 17.9$).
Russian	Immigrated to Israel from former USSR in 1988 or later $= 1$, $0 = $ else ($\bar{y} = 0.19$, s $= 0.39$).
Gender	$1 = $ male ($\bar{y} = 0.48$, s $= 0.50$).

Political issues for inter-attitudinal relations

Trust in institutions	'To what degree do you have trust in the following people or institutions? Political Parties/Prime Minister/The media/State Attorney/Supreme Court/The police/President of Israel/Chief Rabbinate/The Knesset/The Israel Defense Forces/The Histadrut (Israel's workers organization)/Government ministers' ($\bar{y} = 0.48$, $s = 0.20$; $\alpha = 0.81$).
Pride in being Israeli	'To what degree are you proud to be an Israeli?' ($\bar{y} = 0.84$, $s = 0.25$).
Political self-efficacy	'To what extent can you and your friends have an impact on government policy?' ($\bar{y} = 0.32$, $s = 0.30$).

Index

The Islamic Law of
Personal Status

ARAB AND ISLAMIC LAWS SERIES

Volume 23

Series General Editor
Dr. Mark S.W. Hoyle

The titles published in this series are listed at the end of this volume.